THE SCHOOL OF LOVE

THE EVOLUTION OF THE STUART
LOVE LYRIC

I goe th' exact'st professor of
Desire, in its diviner sence,
That ever in the Scoole of Love
Did yet commence.

CHARLES COTTON

THE SCHOOL
OF LOVE

THE EVOLUTION OF THE
STUART LOVE LYRIC

BY H. M. RICHMOND

PRINCETON, NEW JERSEY
PRINCETON UNIVERSITY PRESS
1964

Publication of this book has been aided by
the Ford Foundation Program to support
publication through university presses, of
works in the humanities and social sciences.

❖

Printed in the United States of America
by Princeton University Press, Princeton, New Jersey

Pro Europa

····ᘒ P R E F A C E ᘖ····

T H E present essay originated during two years at Wadham College, in the reading required for a doctoral thesis presented at the University of Oxford in 1957. The intention of that thesis was chiefly to coordinate meaningfully the sources of some of the more prominent lyric conventions of the Stuart love poets. In the course of this survey of a cross section of Stuart lyrics and their prototypes it became increasingly clear that there were certain comparatively little recognized insights shared by many Stuart poets which distinguished them from most of their predecessors. Since 1957 I have discussed this matter in a series of short articles devoted to various aspects of lyric composition—theme, attitude, imagery, syntax and so forth (see the bibliography at the end of this work). However, what was involved demanded a more sustained argument and exposition than these specific issues permitted. This present, longer work makes use of classical, medieval, and Renaissance European sources as a foil to Stuart poets' achievements. The advantages of this comparison are primarily aesthetic, but the essay aspires to a sense of what I can only call "historical psychology." This in turn assumes in the critic and the poet a sense of the cumulative force of literary tradition, which is used as a means of critical analysis. Such "syncretic criticism" is the core of the essay, which ventures to advocate that only by such an historical perspective can a critical evaluation of particular works be objectively justified.

It would be difficult to identify all the numerous debts which this study owes to various individuals and institutions for material, ideas, and practical resources. My studies at Emmanuel College, Cambridge, exposed me to the wise scholarship of Mr. H. S. Bennett to whom I am deeply in-

PREFACE

debted in endless ways, as well as to the fascinating puritan severity of Dr. Leavis' university lectures. At Oxford and ever since I have owed most of my extending awareness of the European literary tradition to the catholic and profoundly alert scholarship of Mr. J. B. Leishman, whose advice has governed the evolution of this study and inspired most of its more convincing insights. I am also very grateful to Miss Helen Gardner for her kind attention and meticulous counsel. Since I have taught at the University of California I have also profited from the suggestions and comments of Professors Willard Farnham, Wayne Shumaker, and Josephine Miles. There are numerous other debts of gratitude I owe, not the least to my wife whose encouragement and help was essential to overcoming the inevitable if often unexpected problems involved in such a study as this. I must add my thanks to such institutions as the Bodleian Library, the University of California (which graciously gave me the time and funds to complete this work), the Goldsmiths' Company of London, and Princeton University Press; all in various ways made this work possible. If I could only fuse in this study even some of the excellencies of those fostering it, I would have satisfaction indeed.

H.M.R.

Berkeley, April 1962

᪲ CONTENTS ᪲

THE SCHOOL OF LOVE

THE EVOLUTION OF THE STUART
LOVE LYRIC

···⟡ CHAPTER I ⟡···

THE EVOLUTION OF
SENSIBILITY

IN 1933 J. W. N. Sullivan, a mathematician, completed a book entitled *The Limitations of Science*. Though he was both a philosopher and a musician of repute, he felt able to observe that, by contrast with the mental barriers broken by men of science, "in the refinement and subtilizing of his emotions and bodily sensation it is doubtful if man has made much of an advance. It is doubtful whether, in these matters, we have advanced much beyond the Greeks or Romans, or whether we know more about these matters than was known to the great civilizations of India and China."[1] In the ranks of the major literary critics of the previous century he found many who would have agreed with him. A hundred years before, Shelley had written indignantly in his *Defence of Poetry* that "the cultivation of those sciences, which have enlarged the limits of the empire of man over the external world, has, for want of the poetical faculty, proportionally circumscribed those of the internal world; and man, having enslaved the elements, remains himself a slave."[2] And in the next generation another young poet, Matthew Arnold, prefaced his first book of poems with a denunciation of his age as one "of spiritual discomfort" which was "wanting in moral grandeur."[3] He went on firmly to say "that in the sincere endeavour to learn and practise, amid the bewildering confu-

---

[1] J. W. N. Sullivan, *The Limitations of Science* (New York, 1949), p. 48.

[2] *English Critical Essays* (*Nineteenth Century*), ed. Edmund D. Jones (Oxford, 1947), p. 131.

[3] Matthew Arnold, *Poetical Works*, ed. A. T. Quiller-Couch (Oxford, 1942), p. 14.

sion of our times, what is sound and true in poetical art, I seemed to myself to find the only sure guidance, the only solid footing, among the ancients."[4] In *Culture and Anarchy* this assertion became a systematic panegyric of Greek excellence, in which Arnold passed judgment on the contemporary decline of sensibility. This conservative pessimism about man's spiritual evolution was shared by a later critic, and contemporary of Sullivan, T. S. Eliot. His ingenious summary of the impoverishment of the mind of modern man, under the heading of "dissociation of sensibility," has been accepted by many critics and literary historians of post-Renaissance literature, at least until very recently. Speaking of the whole development of Western culture Eliot gloomily remarks that, "this development, refinement perhaps, complication certainly, is not, from the point of view of the artist, any improvement. Perhaps not even an improvement from the point of view of the psychologist or not to the extent which we imagine; perhaps only in the end based upon a complication in economics and machinery."[5]

In literature, any argument questioning perhaps the central tenet of most such humanistic studies—that the classical authors remain necessarily the supreme models for later writers—may well appear unconventional. Such an inquiry, reminiscent of the old and inconclusive Battle of the Books, may only be properly justified now if it can be proved that literature uses a variety of fairly stable forms and motifs in which an evolution can be detected. To show this on the scale of the works of, say, the major tragedians would demand a mechanism of argument beyond our present scope. It will be possible to qualify the superiority of the ancients only if some compact form of literature provides these firm norms from which any departure is self-evident. Should this

---

[4] *Ibid.*, p. 15.
[5] T. S. Eliot, *Selected Essays* (London, 1934), p. 16.

literary evidence exist, there will be a little less difficulty in judging the case presented by Sullivan and the other critics; and in this process some useful refinements of critical method should emerge also.

The description of the ideal literary form for such analysis —compact, complex, standardized—is highly appropriate to one conventional pattern of writing—the sonnet. Unfortunately, but from our point of view significantly, sonnets were not written in classical times—their origin dates from the time of the troubadours and is sometimes associated with Piero della Vigna at the brilliant thirteenth-century court of Emperor Frederick II of Sicily.[6] However, there are other patterns in lyric verse in which considerable standardization also occurs. These patterns persist in lyric verse from the earliest surviving fragments of European poetry, through the works of all the major poets of the West, down to the lyrics of the latest American musical. The qualities of each composition involved in one of these sequences may, therefore, be accurately determined by the close and legitimate comparison of it with the others in the same sequence. But, while the continuity of these sequences is illustrated by most lyric traditions, their diversity and number would defeat any clarity of impression if a general survey of them were made as they appear in all forms of lyricism.

Of the major types of lyricism, among which may be numbered the religious, political, comic, and amatory, the one which would best serve to challenge Sullivan's assertion that man has failed to develop his "emotions and bodily sensation" is perhaps love poetry. Sexual passion would seem to reveal man at his most complex and passionate. The virtue of the love lyric as the basis for our argument is not confined to this highly emotional character, nor even to its role as a kind of elaborate historical document incidentally revealing the poets'

6 Ernst Kantorowicz, *Frederick the Second* (New York, 1957), p. 333.

actual relationships and conduct. The poet also undergoes the discipline of considering how best to communicate his sentiments, this obligation to be publicly intelligible being the distinctive virtue of artistic expression. No true poet simply pours out his feelings, since at the very least the discipline of versification objectifies them to some extent, as Wordsworth pointed out in his Preface to the *Lyrical Ballads*. When a poet is too directly under the influence of private emotion, the effect is inartistic because the poem is incoherent and exclamatory. This is perhaps true of Keats' hectic sonnet to Fanny Brawne, "I cry your mercy—pity—love!—aye, love! . . . ,"[7] which is more a symptom of sexual desire than a communication of it. The fully effective lyric necessarily combines the ritual resonance and poise provided by accumulated artistic tradition with the unique personal accent that rises from the poet's own experience either as a lover or a craftsman or both. All important love poems are also likely to display the most distinctive characteristics of contemporary literary sensibility and, in so doing, to give significance to chronological comparisons of the kind we have anticipated.

This shared inheritance which normally distinguishes the best lyrics appears even in highly autobiographical authors for whose poems few "sources" have been discovered. A good example of this is Shakespeare's famous Sonnet 130, "My mistress' eyes are nothing like the sun," which will also serve as the occasion for a preliminary demonstration of our method in the rest of this book. The poem shows the emergence of some interesting new capacities but it is also founded on a deep-rooted and once popular tradition. The rather perverse denigration of a mistress with which it begins was a familiar motif in sixteenth-century satirical love poetry. Berni and Tasso had both ridiculed their mistresses in such

[7] John Keats, *Poetical Works*, ed. H. Buxton Forman (Oxford, 1908), p. 440.

stylized parodies of conventional praise.[8] The licentious
Pietro Aretino had characteristically suggested that a lover
might have written to his girl in these terms:

> Per tutto l'or del mondo,
> donna, in lodarvi non direi menzogna,
> perché a me e a voi farei vergogna;
> per Dio che non direi
> che in bocca abbiate odor d'Indi o Sabei;
> né che i vostri capelli
> de l'oro sien piú belli.
> Né che ne gli occhi vostri alberghi amore,
> né che da quelli il Sol toglie il splendore,
> né che le labbra e i denti
> sien bianche perle e bei rubini ardenti:
> né che i vostri costumi
> faccino nel bordello andare i fiume.
> Io dirò ben che buona robba sete,
> piú che donna che sia.
> E che tal grazia avete,
> che a farvelo un Romito scapparia.
> Ma non vo' dir che voi siate divina
> non piscando acqua lanfa per orina.[9]

(I would not lie in praising you, lady, for all the gold in the
world, because it would shame both of us. By God, I would
not say that you have the perfumes of India or Sheba in your
mouth; nor that your hair is finer than gold; nor that Love
dwells in your eyes; nor that from these the sun takes his
splendor; nor that your methods make rivers flow in the
brothel. I say fairly that you are a demimondaine rather
than that you may be a lady, and that you have as much

---

[8] See F. Berni, *Opere*, ed. G. Daelli (Milan, 1864), I, 154; T. Tasso,
Le Rime, ed. A. Solerti (Bologna, 1898-1899), III, 190.
[9] P. Aretino, *Piacevoli e Capricciosi Ragionamenti*, ed. A. P. Stella
(Milan, 1944), p. 142.

grace as would make a hermit throw off his monkish cowl. But I don't want to say that you are a goddess: you don't piss orange-flower-water for urine.)

The poem modulates dexterously from bluntness to obscenity in this summary of unpraised attributes. By contrast Shakespeare's sonnet, having caught the incantatory rhythm of earlier "honest" rejections of easy fancies, twists even more dexterously away from Aretino's obscenities into a gracious tribute of affection:

> My mistress' eyes are nothing like the sun;
> Coral is far more red than her lips' red;
> If snow be white, why then her breasts are dun;
> If hairs be wires, black wires grow on her head.
> I have seen roses damask'd, red and white,
> But no such roses see I in her cheeks;
> And in some perfumes is there more delight
> Than in the breath that from my mistress reeks.
> I love to hear her speak, yet well I know
> That music hath a far more pleasing sound;
> I grant I never saw a goddess go;
> My mistress, when she walks, treads on the ground.
> And yet, by heaven, I think my love as rare
> As any she belied with false compare.[10]

This loving conclusion more than offsets the poem's preceding bluntness. Shakespeare's poem is intimately linked to Aretino's, whether directly or indirectly hardly matters. The occasion and treatment are almost identical with the significant exception, from our point of view, of the conclusion, whose importance is emphasized by the juxtaposition of two poems otherwise so similar. The willful bluntness of Aretino, literary rather than social in its motives, here contrasts with

[10] W. Shakespeare, *Complete Works*, ed. Hardin Craig (New York, 1951), p. 492.

Shakespeare's characteristically gracious reconciliation of "literary" frankness with a more humane mode of expression, through the ultimate abandonment of the insolence to the supposed mistress. In neither poem is there necessarily a real mistress involved, but in Shakespeare's sonnet the literary verve of Aretino now fits the actual requirements of a social situation better. Hence Sonnet 130 is an important and popular poem, Aretino's only a curious and historically interesting piece of virtuosity. It would seem quite likely, should several more prominent examples confirm these tendencies in literary modes, that the cinquecento Italian poets and their audiences were clever but removed from the practical issues which still dynamically concerned the more healthily practical and vigorous culture of England. The more fully such analogies are investigated the more distinct become the nature and skill of each of the poets (with which critics are primarily concerned) and the values and manners of the societies for which they write (which take us into the wider world of historical sociology and psychology). Even Shakespeare's originality in his sonnet's forthright conclusion is a little offset by typical remarks in Sidney's *Astrophel and Stella* which already approve of such "unsophisticated" love. The fifty-fifth sonnet in Sidney's cycle decries "sugaring" and favors "true but naked show" in love poetry,[11] and his fifteenth sonnet had censured, as did Shakespeare implicitly in Sonnet 130:

> You that do search for every purling spring
> Which from the ribs of old Parnassus flows,[12]

on the grounds that, unlike Shakespeare's sonnet,

> those far-fet hopes be such
> As do bewray a want of inward touch.

[11] *Silver Poets of the Sixteenth Century*, ed. Gerald Bullett (London, 1947), p. 193.
[12] *Ibid.*, p. 178.

Such detailed exploration of the literary context of a lyric helps to define its uniqueness and permits thereby a confident vindication of our critical approval of it.

It may seem inaccurate to insist on the customary conformity of both the lover and the poet to such rigid social patterns of behavior and thought, but anthropology gives some authority to the idea. Ruth Benedict has written in *Patterns of Culture*, "The cultural pattern of any civilization makes use of a certain segment of the great arc of potential human purposes and motivations . . . . The great arc along which all the possible human behaviours are distributed is far too immense and too full of contradictions for any one culture to utilize even any considerable portion of it. Selection is the first requirement. Without selection no culture could ever achieve intelligibility."[13] Thereafter, according to Dr. Benedict, "Even given the freest scope by their institutions, men are never inventive enough to make more than minute changes. From the point of view of an outsider the most radical innovations in any culture amount to no more than a minor revision."[14] This view implies that human institutions, patterns of behavior, and the literature that reflects them will all show considerable homogeneity even within the same major cultural tradition, such as western Europe's, and even if drawn from sources farther apart in time and space than Aretino and Shakespeare. Nevertheless, in the course of centuries, significant changes on a larger scale than those envisaged by Dr. Benedict do appear, no matter how gradually, and the continuity of the culture makes these dramatically evident when patterns from different epochs are abruptly juxtaposed. Thus, for example, an Alexandrine poet and Herrick both indulge in a playful ritual tallying of their varied mistresses, but the Greek lyricist simply juggles with

[13] Ruth Benedict, *Patterns of Culture* (New York, 1948), p. 219.
[14] *Ibid.,* p. 76.

undifferentiated urban statistics ("thirty-five loves in Athens
. . . "), while Herrick evokes a series of individuals.[15] "Personality," in the modern sense of individuality, not type, has
emerged in the interim.

If we grant Dr. Benedict her assertion of the immense
possibilities of human existence as a whole, it is nevertheless
clear that, in the particular matter of the fulfillment of sexual
desire, there is a finite number of basic issues and crises available to both the lover and the poet before the final consummation or repudiation is reached. Briefly one might summarize the possibilities by saying that either the poet has or
has not a mistress, is pleased with her or not if he has one,
and is loved by her or not in return. This rigid Aristotelian
substructure for analysis would permit a correlation of love
poetry of even radically different cultures—such as the
Oriental and European; but a more detailed account of themes
is required for a rewarding literary comparison.

Fortunately each of the major permutations of the lover's
triad of alternatives finds numerous detailed but still conventional occasions for its exposition in lyric verse, and it is here
perhaps that Dr. Benedict's assertion of the selective expression of behavior is best vindicated. Within the European
tradition the occasions through which the lover's condition
is revealed in lyric verse are highly standardized, reflecting
probably a similar specialization in real life. For example,
poets' love for their mistresses finds a conventional reflection
in the envy they express for the lot of something close to
these mistresses, wishing to become a ring, a bird, a mirror,
or a dress. Hundreds of poems have conformed to this choice
of subject from classical Greek times onwards. Again, in trying to praise their mistresses European poets have almost

[15] *Greek Elegy and Iambus*, ed. J. M. Edmonds (London, 1931), II,
Anacreontea, p. 34; Robert Herrick, *Poetical Works*, ed. L. C. Martin
(Oxford, 1956), p. 15.

always either listed equations of her physical attributes with precious substances in the way repudiated by Aretino and Shakespeare or celebrated her charms in a few customary poses only—singing, dancing, sitting before her mirror, or, unexpectedly, sick in bed. Both these modes are normally ways of expressing an appreciative but often unreturned love. There are a number of other suitable themes for this attitude and a series of quite different ones for others. If this is generally the case then a specific theme or situation will recur frequently in the lyric tradition, and such a theme once detected readily extends the kind of comparison sketched out in our examination of the poems by Aretino and Shakespeare. While founded on the observations of the sociologist, the recognition of such analogies is clearly of prime critical interest. For example, we find that a poem such as that of Sappho describing the symptoms of her love proves to be very similar in content to an account by Theocritus, another of Catullus, one by Dante, and others by Ronsard, Sidney and Spenser.[16] Some of these poems may be directly linked to each other by literary tradition, some reflect persistent attitudes in many complex societies, and others relate to basic human instincts—but the material of all is closely related in some way, and their differences express the change in taste from one society to another. If we wish to illustrate a development in sensibility over a long period, the study of such a sustained pattern is a useful beginning. Here, for example, the classical poets are concerned chiefly with the instinctive, physical reactions of lovers, while the Renaissance poets discuss the social and psychological causes of these reactions. A single sequence such as this is no more reliable as a guide to an age's outlook or even to an individual's capacities than the comparison between Aretino

[16] See pp. 37-49 of this text.

and Shakespeare made earlier. A poet's performance is obviously variable. But if the best work of the most noted poets of each age does fit into a number of such sequences, then a reasonable generalization may well be made. Equally the individual poet's capacities will be clarified by a series of such comparisons.

It will be urged that the conventional situations are the least important part of such poems and that to stress them is an irritating intrusion of sociology on something which is completely unrelated to the nominal situation. T. S. Eliot suggests of the episode of Paolo and Francesca in the *Inferno* that "the intensity of the poetry is something quite different from whatever intensity in the supposed experience it may give the impression of."[17] This divorce of content and treatment, of literal or explicit meaning and the artist's technical resources, seems rather ominous. Paolo Veronese's painting, "The Marriage at Cana," and his other religious feast scenes illustrate the dangers of permitting such a divorce. These paintings' bustling crowds came under severe theological censure as incompatible with the nature of their nominal subjects; and in fact the work in them *is* inferior, not because of any incompetent workmanship in detail, but simply because of its lack of focus. "The Marriage at Cana," in its lack of theological sense, of any profound awareness of the historical nature of its raw material, produces an aesthetic disunity in turn which is a symptom of the divorce between its theme and the arts of expression. But it is the failure to understand the situation which determines the artistic failure. A great work of art or literature is not simply a masterpiece of craft, or even a personal impression, but normally a coherent and dependent extension of that objective and systematic knowledge, reli-

[17] *Selected Essays*, p. 19.

gious, philosophic, social, political, or whatever else it may be, on which it draws for its subject.

What each lyricist accomplishes in a successful love poem is, therefore, not simply to individualize or dramatize a conventional topic but to express more fully the necessary facts and logical outcome of that kind of situation. Marvell's popular ode "To his Coy Mistress" serves as a surprisingly good illustration. The poem's elaborate texture is fascinating, while it seems obvious that the full dramatic realization of the personalities involved (particularly that of the lady) is scarcely attempted and that the social situation, a plea for sexual indulgence, is uninspiringly and rigidly explicit, and of the most traditional form. However, what makes the poem most memorable is not the humor and the brilliant surface with its ingenious deployment of traditional tropes. Rather, the poem is distinguished by the fact that its argument consciously subjects all these diverse details to the requirements of its basic situation. The argument is thus conducted logically and yet urbanely, without pedantry and without embarrassment. If these are aesthetic virtues, they are also social and moral ones. "To his Coy Mistress" handles sexual love with the kind of intellectual discipline that the Middle Ages chose usually to devote only to religion. Little of this sustained logic unifies Catullus' comparable "Vivamus mea Lesbia atque amemus," though the texture of the two poems is very similar. The Latin poem is slighter, but while its brevity affords less opportunity to develop the basic situation its purpose is also less important. It seeks only to assemble three related but not necessarily consecutive admonitions, which are finely expressed indeed but not syllogistically interdependent like the contents of Marvell's longer and more diversified poem. The importance of Marvell's plea is directly related to the author's understanding of his raw material. Even though the imagery of his poem is more brilliant than that of Catullus it is Marvell's insight into the necessary demands of the situation which raises the later poem decisively above the earlier one. A development in relation to the situation and theme thus makes a vital contribution to the success of a love lyric.

While the situations on which love lyrics are based seem commonly to be conventional, even if given impetus by some personal experience of the author, it might be assumed that the choice of his mode of communication would be entirely within the poet's own creative power. However, once the poet has committed himself to some well-defined traditional pattern this does not prove to be the case. The inescapable logic of that situation at once constrains the author to adopt certain methods of communicating the relationship. He finds certain methods carefully adapted to the theme by traditional practice and experiment, be it in the use of description, narrative, dialogue, or soliloquy. Thus in the two poems of Marvell and Catullus, in which the poets are seeking the release of sexual desire, despite the millennia separating them both poets adopt the posture of a lover speaking directly to his mistress. But once past this major decision of format each poet finds that more detailed prescriptions begin to operate. Both use the imperative form of verb in an emphatic manner; each heaps up verb forms, usually words of great energy and drama. The relentless logic of the situation leads the two poets to the same images and preoccupations—death, the sun, secrecy. Less predictably, both poets seek to achieve a hypnotic effect on the woman by juggling with a dizzying progression of numerals—one remembers the use of the same entrancing effect as a technique in the mystical cult of mathematics adopted by Pythagoras and Plato. Marvell and Catullus, separated by several cycles of cultural change, share words, ideas, posture, and theme. Only Marvell's ratiocinative power and his greater elaboration and control of detail show the accumulation of resources acquired during the intervening period and demonstrate the meaning of the passage of time. It must be noted incidentally that, despite the analogies to the Catullian lyric, Marvell's poem is no self-conscious imitation of it (unlike Jonson's "Come my Celia," which is much closer to the Latin text). The number of "original" poems like Marvell's involving love with numbers is, in fact, considerable. It includes Paschasius' poem "Ad Sabinam,"[18] which first suggests Marvell's physiological arithmetic, Donne's "The Computation," and Cowley's copy of it, "My Diet"—all pleas for love. Long before Catullus, the Anacreontic poet had intoxicated himself with the dizzy mathematics of his love affairs.[19] In the regular recurrence of this unpredictable "numbers" motif there is some little evidence that "men are never inventive enough to make more than minute changes," though I hope to show that these minute changes are nevertheless ultimately more significant than Dr. Benedict recognizes.

The consistency of the love poet's themes and style has now been tentatively illustrated, and we have seen some proof of the utility of this consistency as an instrument of critical analysis. The possibility of using it as a starting point in the study of evolving sensibility is also clear. There remains a third important factor in addition to theme and style which might impair the stability of a tradition—the poet's attitude to the whole process. One poem will closely follow the same patterns as another equally successful, yet differ totally in impact. Donne's "The Flea," for example, follows closely the pattern of admonitory poems like Waller's "Go, lovely rose," or its model, Martial's "I felix rosa." The argument for indulgence in sensual pleasure is maintained in each case by a carefully elaborated analogy. The same imperatives are used to quicken the movement. Yet Donne's poem is humorously

---

[18] *Delitiae cc. Poetarum Gallorum*, ed. R. Gherus (Frankfurt, 1609), II, 1,000.
[19] See Note 15 to this chapter.

improbable if it is considered simply as a plea for love, while Martial's and Waller's are graceful, and even convincing. The difference is chiefly one of mood and attitude, resulting in this illustration from the importation of material from a popular comic tradition—the adventures of a flea. The change of mood is analogous, though in reverse, to that achieved by Shakespeare in Sonnet 130. However, these apparent changes of attitude in both Donne's and Shakespeare's poems merely give further proof of the difficulty of evading tradition, for such negating and reversing of conventional propositions and effects were standard modes of evoking an apparently novel attitude in the Renaissance. Raleigh accomplishes the same effect in his presentation of the nymph's answer to Marlowe's "Passionate Shepherd." The nymph replaces the melodious rivers of the shepherd's plea with raging ones, mutes his nightingale, and wholly reverses the effect of each succeeding image while generally otherwise maintaining the allusions and syntactical patterns of Marlowe's lines. Any convention of thought or expression in lyric verse may thus be linked to hostile versions of the same patterns, which in fact form a convention themselves.

There are many more of these apparent evasions of conventions beyond simple negations of set terms. Catullus is much more deeply committed to the situation in his poem to Lesbia than Marvell is to that in "To his Coy Mistress" because Lesbia is a person of greater immediacy to him than the supposed coy young woman, whoever she may have been, is to Marvell. Catullus desperately wanted to charm Lesbia, and his poem has the brief, intimate, melodious quality likely to win her attention. Marvell hardly evokes a sense of an historical mistress in the reader's mind, and is much more concerned to explore the lover's arguments demanded by his theme, conforming in this to "metaphysical" practice. Many of the poems of Herbert and Donne deal not with urgent, historical events in their own lives, but win curious insights into the human mind by analyzing attitudes that were perhaps merely drawn to their attention by their own experiences. "Aire and Angels," with its analytic tone, is a good example. The result of such a difference is that while we are fascinated by Catullus as a man and delighted by his poems, we are challenged and even instructed by the lyrics of the later poets. Yet while such unmistakable differences of intention and tone do distinguish otherwise similar poems, even in these shades of mood there are conventions and mannerisms which may be inherited by poets. The reproduction of the convincing details of such elusive attitudes has been studied and accurately defined by the careful experiments of generations of poets. This is how even Catullus' apparent frankness came to be assimilated—by the seventeenth century, poets can sound deeply and authentically moved without actually being so at cost to their poetical skill or analytic intelligence. Perhaps the most persuasive testimony for the decisiveness of convention even in such shades of expression as distinguish affectation from passion is in fact that of the poets themselves. A particular example of such an artificial "mood," and one appropriate to our argument, is that of critical renunciation of convention by the poet.

To find this affectation of independence we must examine a group of artists who were terrified of suffocation by an atmosphere of excessive devotion to the past, such as is found in humanist Europe of the later Renaissance. At this time Ronsard had spurred on Du Bellay to write his denunciation of medieval forms of verse and to vindicate vernacular poetry based on classical models in his *Défense et Illustration de la Langue Française*; but neither poet probably realized that its author would thereafter write, not merely, "Contre les Petrarquistes":

J'ay oublié l'art de Petrarquizer,
Je veulx d'Amour franchement deviser.[20]

(I have forgotten the art of imitating Petrarch and I wish to talk unaffectedly of love.)

but, more dramatically still:

Je ne veulx fueilleter les exemplaires Grecs,
Je ne veulx retracer les beaux traicts d'un Horace,
Et moins veulx-je imiter d'un Petrarque la grace,
Ou la voix d'un Ronsard, pour chanter mes Regrets, . . .
Je me contenteray de simplement escrire
Ce que la passion seulement me fait dire,
Sans rechercher ailleurs plus graues argumens.[21]

(*Regrets*, iv)

(I don't want to flip through Greek texts, I don't want to recapitulate the fine effects of a Horace, and I want even less to imitate the grace of a Petrarch or the voice of a Ronsard, in order to sing my laments, . . . I shall content myself by writing simply what passion alone makes me say, without searching weightier themes elsewhere.)

Here we seem to see at least the appearance of a revolution against all models, not simply the substitution of classical for medieval French ones; but such a "revolution" would in fact merely restore French verse to the pattern implied by protestations and attitudes current even before the activities of the Pléiade. For Clement Marot is supposed to have written an elegy "A une mal contente d'avoir esté sobrement louée, et se plaignant non sobrement." He here protests his good will to the offended lady but thanks heaven that he does not need to seek her favors at the price of lies and flattery. He lists the fatuous comparisons to her charms which weaker men make, their allusions to the sun, to coral, to classical goddesses—the

---

[20] Joachim Du Bellay, *Poësies*, ed. M. Hervier (Paris, 1954), iii, 74.
[21] *Ibid.*, ii, 289.

list that Shakespeare later ridicules in Sonnet 130. Then, in approaching his conclusion, he observes:

> Or quant à moy, je ne sçaurois avoir
> Sens ne loysir d'aprendre ce sçavoir,
> Ne mon esprit est d'assez bonne marque
> Pour suivre ainsi Jean de Meun ou Petrarque.[22]

(Now as for me, I would not have the skill or leisure to learn this knowledge, nor is my wit fine enough to follow Jean de Meun or Petrarch like that.)

And he adds finally and discreetly that despite his refusal to praise her extravagantly the lady would have more to show off "between the sheets" than many who were prouder! Thus we find that Marot anticipated some of Shakespeare's effects in Sonnet 130 and matched those of his contemporary Aretino. But he also takes the same line of "purists" such as Du Bellay and Sidney—that of ridiculing slavish debts to literary tradition. None of the later poets was really liberating himself from tradition by claiming to do so, since in fact the repudiation of Petrarchan effects is a convention not only used by Marot but started by Petrarch himself when he decided that he had overindulged an unsympathetic Laura:

> Mai non vo' piú cantar com'io soleva . . . [23](cv)
> (I do not ever wish to sing again as I used to . . .)

The sixteenth-century poems protesting independence of tradition form a compact, closely related group. There may be interesting departures from the norm in this body of work, but its general character is well defined. Shakespeare's triumph in his poem lies in getting into the brief sonnet structure all the significant effects of the genre which the earlier poets

[22] Clement Marot, Œuvres Complètes, ed. P. Jannet (Paris, n.d.), II, 59.
[23] Francesco Petrarca, Le Rime, ed. G. Carducci et al. (Florence, 1957), p. 150.

only partially caught in theirs (or which in Marot's case took sixty-six lines to accumulate). Shakespeare also avoids such failures as Marot's verbosity and Aretino's crudeness.

Even so strictly defined a tradition does not, however, prevent a distinct evolution from taking place within it in later poets, which it is my purpose to discuss. In this case the evolution fostered by seventeenth-century lyricists appears in an anonymous poem (probably Carew's):

> I will not Saint my Cœlia, for shee
> More glorious is in her Humanity,
> Nor in a heat of Fancy pluck a Starr,
> And rob the needy World to fixe Her there.
>   These are the subtle raptures of the times,
> Wherewith the wanton Poet makes his Rhymes
> Run high, as doth his Blood; whiles some proud Shee
> Pamperd with such new-cookd diuinity
> Surfets belieuing in a pride of Soule
> Those Fictions True; so Sinns without controule.
>   Besides, admitt I could; I might conferr
> Praise on my selfe, but not aduantage Her.
> Wee prize not Gold made by the Chymic Stone
> As Gold, but for the Transmutation.
> Can Angels boast Habituall Purity?
> Noe: Tis in Them Impeccability;
> And therefore not Praise-worthy; they have nor Will
> Nor Power, to Think, much lesse to Practise Ill.
>   With Her tis otherwise; for Shee may sinn
> Beyond hope of Repentance; and therin
> Appeares the odds, that, maugre flesh and blood,
> Beauty, Temptation, Deuil, Shee is Good.[24]

The general rhythm of thought is similar to that of the other poems—"I reject conventional praise of beauty in favor of

[24] Thomas Carew, *Poems*, ed. Rhodes Dunlap (Oxford, 1957), p. 193.

honest realism, but I show that I honor my mistress the more by doing so." This poet's "consolation" to his "unsanctified" mistress is as gracious as Shakespeare's but the elegant precision of the argument which vindicates the poet's love marks a further assimilation of contemporary experience by the poet that is as distinctive as Shakespeare's reconciliation of a literary pose with a potentially actual relationship. As with Marvell's "To his Coy Mistress," we find Carew revising a familiar amatory convention under the discipline of controlled analysis. It is to the exposition of the implications of such discreet yet important changes in standard patterns that this study is dedicated.

It may seem fatal to the appreciation of poetry to classify lyrical writing in this way. However, my intention is not to impair enjoyment of individual achievements but to illustrate general trends by identifying these achievements with precision and finality. The methods used will be less applicable to comparisons between the works of individual authors only because the range of material covered in their writing will be much less extensive than when the work of an era or a whole society is involved. All that is perhaps necessary for effective criticism of individual authors is to reduce the historical range of comparison to closely related authors of a particular period —the individual poet's characteristics then emerge very plainly. We may find a good illustration of this in the study later in the book of the attempt at pastoral seduction proffered in its most popular form by Marlowe's "Passionate Shepherd."[25] This was too elegant and picturesque a poem not to be eagerly imitated or revised by the most diverse poets—Raleigh, Donne, Herrick, Cotton, and many others. Any attempt to identify the attractions of any one of these poets might well begin by distinguishing the ways in which the particular poet gave his own distinctive variants to this pattern.

[25] See pp. 155-161.

In the following chapters, therefore, the reader is not merely invited to recapitulate the obsolete concerns of the Battle of the Books, nor even simply to assist at an exposition of the slow but unmistakable flowering of human awareness as illustrated in European love poetry, but also to consider a method of critical analysis which may perhaps serve to bridge the apparent gap between literary research and practical criticism. It may be of particular usefulness in harmonizing the critical alertness of the New Critics with the traditional scholarship of their opponents. For, while fostering accuracy of identification, it should also provide subtler and more objective means for the vindication of personal approval than are available to any contemporary critics who depend on the comparatively clumsy tools of conventional anthropology, Freudian or Jungian dogma, or such assumptions as the primacy of "complexity" or "irony."

···ᡰᢓ CHAPTER II ᡛᢔ····

THE CLASSIC THEMES

[i]

T H E earliest practical issue for a lover is that of undirected desire, of love without an object. This concern finds expression in at least two standard situations. In the role of a woman the poet may soliloquize about the terrors of spinsterhood and display the pathos of charms as yet unappreciated and soon to fade. This is a familiar theme in many western folk songs and oriental lyrics, but these are chiefly in a minor key and hardly form a prominent tradition. Much more popular, inevitably, is the soliloquy in which the poet himself defines to his own satisfaction the mistress (or boy) who will incarnate his ideals. The classical versions of this theme tend to a kind of practical sensuality about the physique of one's whore, along the lines of Rufinus' epigram in *The Greek Anthology*:

Μήτ᾽ ἰσχνὴν λίην περιλάμβανε, μήτε παχεῖαν·
τούτων δ᾽ ἀμφοτέρων τὴν μεσότητα θέλε.
τῇ μὲν γὰρ λείπει σαρκῶν χύσις, ἡ δὲ περισσὴν
κέκτηται· λεῖπον μὴ θέλε, μηδὲ πλέον.   (v, 37)

(Take not to your arms a woman who is too slender nor one too stout, but choose the mean between the two. The first has not enough abundance of flesh, and the second has too much. Choose neither deficiency nor excess.)[1]

The approximation to an Aristotelian mean in this specification does little to refine the poet's awareness of the nature of love, which is scarcely subtler than that of Nicarchus:

[1] *Greek Anthology*, Loeb edn., trans. W. R. Paton (London, 1916), I, 146-147.

Εὐμεγέθης πείθει με καλὴ γυνή, ἄν τε καὶ ἀκμῆς
ἅπτητ', ἄν τε καὶ ᾖ, Σιμύλε, πρεσβυτέρη. . . . (v, 38)
(A fine and largely built woman attracts me, Similus,
whether she be in her prime, or elderly. . . .)[2]

The trouble with this kind of speculation is partly the primi-
tiveness of the criteria considered necessary for happy love.
While Martial frequently makes the same kind of narrow
judgment,[3] he at least occasionally registers awareness of the
broader ranges of attributes which his intended love is likely
to possess. His ideal boy friend, for example, has a much more
distinct personality than most classical anticipations of future
loves:

Si quis forte mihi possit praestare roganti,
    audi, quem puerum, Flacce, rogare velim.
Niliacis primum puer hic nascatur in oris:
    nequitias tellus scit dare nulla magis.
sit nive candidior: namque in Mareotide fusca
    pulchrior est quanto rarior iste color.
lumina sideribus certent mollesque flagellent
    colla comae: tortas non amo, Flacce, comas.
frons brevis atque modus leviter sit naribus uncis,
    Paestanis rubeant aemula labra rosis.
saepe et nolentem cogat nolitque volentem,
    liberior domino saepe sit ille suo; . . . (iv, xlii)

(If any could by chance guarantee me the boon at my
asking, hear, Flaccus, what kind of boy I would wish to
ask for. First of all, let this boy be born on the shores of the
Nile; no country knows better how to beget roguish ways.
Let him be fairer than snow; for in swarthy Mareotis that
hue is more beautiful by its rarity. Let his eyes vie with
stars, and his soft locks tumble over his neck; I like not,

[2] *Ibid.*
[3] See *Epigrams* i, lvii, and iii, xxxiii, for examples.

Flaccus, braided locks. Let his brow be low and his nose slightly aquiline, let his lips rival the red of Paestan roses. And let him oft compel endearments when I am loath, and refuse them when I am fain; may he oft be more free than his lord! . . .)[4]

Our sense of the unusual vividness of these details in comparison with other accounts of future loves is vindicated by the conclusion of the poem, in which Martial admits that he is hoping for a new love as fair as one already possessed by his friend in the past.

Martial's desires are more sophisticated than the Greek epigrammatists', but paradoxically are much less likely to be realized. The more elaborate the anticipations the more certain is the falsification of at least some of them by an actual relationship. This defect is shared by the yet more charming but no less ominously elaborate fancies in Crashaw's "Wishes to his Supposed Mistress" and in the twentieth century by the unabashed sentimentality of "The Girl that I Marry" in that interestingly feminist American musical *Annie Get Your Gun*. All these lyrics illustrate the feeble self-delusions of the daydream, doomed almost necessarily to frustration by actual experience, as Milton grimly points out in *Paradise Lost* (x, 898ff.). Only very occasionally does an early poet sympathetically recognize the inappropriateness of such standards to the fulfillment of a future relationship. One may praise another *Anthology* lyricist, Marcus Argentarius, for unusual insight in a classical poet when he writes:

Οὐκ ἔσθ᾽ οὗτος ἔρως, εἴ τις καλὸν εἶδος ἔχουσαν
βούλετ᾽ ἔχειν, φρονίμοις ὄμμασι πειθόμενος·
ἀλλ᾽ ὅστις κακόμορφον ἰδών, τετορημένος ἰοῖς
στέργει, μαινομένης ἐκ φρενὸς αἰθόμενος,

[4] Martial, *Epigrams*, Loeb edn., trans. W. C. Ker (London, 1950), I, 258-259.

οὗτος ἔρως, πῦρ τοῦτο· τὰ γὰρ καλὰ πάντας ὁμοίως
τέρπει τοὺς κρίνειν εἶδος ἐπισταμένους. (v, 89)

(That is not love if one, trusting his judicious eyes, wishes to possess a beauty. But he who seeing a homely face is pierced by arrows and loves, set alight by fury of the heart—that is love, that is fire; for beauty delights equally all who are good judges of form.)[5]

For the most part classical love poets do not recognize this potentiality that their desire may elude conventional expression.

More modern poets, like Crashaw, are frequently defective in this respect, and while the sequence from Martial to the "Wishes to his Supposed Mistress" clearly indicates a steady progression, like Plato's ladder, from the crudely physical desires of many pagan classical poets to the more romantic ideas of the post-Renaissance era, such wishful or wistful thinking lacks decisive patterns of thought, expression, and action. Typically the great lyric poets of later periods have for the most part bypassed the theme in its most obvious classical form in favor of an ingenious and picturesque variant of it. The variant is one of those negative patterns mentioned earlier, and this gives it a situation, movement of thought, and syntactical rhythm lacking in orthodox versions of the theme. It gains these by striking an attitude against the views of those poets, either of an earlier age or inferior sensibility, who have limited themselves to guessed sensory attributes in anticipating their mistresses' characters. By contrast, the more imaginative poets conceive of something less arbitrary but more bizarre—an actual attachment to a mistress at once unknown and unidentifiable, the intangible woman postulated by the strength of their desire. The theme has exactly the virtues of all important

[5] Loeb edn., trans. W. R. Paton, i, 170-171.

lyric traditions. It presupposes an actual, even a desperate relationship between the poet and his elusive love, whose nature his attachment alone defines, and because of its strangeness it gives full scope to the psychological and technical resources of each poet and era.

Just where in the complex pattern of lyric tradition this subtle phantom first emerged is hard to say. Hints appear in the version of the rape of Helen favored by Euripides, which asserts that Helen's virtue was preserved by concealment in Egypt, while Paris' desire left him enamored of an insubstantial wraith provided by Juno, goddess of marriage. The story calls to mind the fate of Ixion, who deceived himself into thinking he was making love to Juno herself when a mere cloud was involved. A more precise and intimate account of such an experience appears in Petronius Arbiter, always a poet interested by quaint amatory activity:

> Pulchra comis annisque decens et candida vultu
> dulce quiescenti basia blanda dabas.
> si te iam vigilans non unquam cernere possum,
> somne, precor, iugitur lumina nostra tene.[6]

(With your lovely hair, winning youth and fair face, sweetly you gave me caressing kisses while I slept. If I cannot ever see you again waking, I pray, O Sleep, that you keep our lives united as before.)

This is outwardly a conventional dream poem, but usually sensual dream poems involve the enjoyment of the form of a familiar, if often unkind mistress, who can be recognized by the poet when he wakes. Here, despite faint hints of her physical characteristics, the girl has no tangible form, and the poet clearly doubts the possibility of her incarnation.

None of these potential sources is very decisive, and it is

[6] *Medieval Latin Lyrics,* ed. H. Waddell (London, 1929), p. 20.

symptomatic of the modes of evolution of European lyric tradition that a reference complicating the direct line between classical and Renaissance love poetry does much to illustrate whence this particular theme and many others may have taken vital impetus. This most helpful key to the theme's later development lies in the third chapter of a prose treatise on love by one of the most famous Hispano-Arabic writers of the eleventh century, Ibn Hazm. A. R. Nykl summarizes the chapter as follows:

"Every love must have a *cause* which is the *origin* of it. The most unbelievable of these is the one I was told by a friend who saw a *ğāriya* in a dream and became passionately enamoured of that vision. I remonstrated with him saying: 'It is a great sin for you to trouble yourself about something unreal, something non-existent. Do you know who she is?' He said: 'No, by God!' And I said: 'You are weak of judgment if you love someone you have never seen, and if you had fallen in love with an image one sees in the bath-houses I could have more excuse for you.'

"And on this subject I composed a poem, from which I quote:

"1.   Would that I knew who she was and how she
         traveled at night!
      Was she the sunrise or was she the full moon?

"2.   Was she an *idea* of the *mind,* created by its *power of
         imagination,*
      Or an *image* of the spirit, created in me by *thoughts?*

"3.   Or an image shaped in the *soul* by my hope
      And my eye had the illusion of having perceived it?

"4.   Or all this has not happened, and it was an occurrence,
      By which God's decree has brought to me the cause
         of my death?"[7]

[7] A. R. Nykl, *Hispano-Arabic Poetry and Its Relations with the Old Provençal Troubadours* (Baltimore, 1946), p. 83.

The passage shows affinities with a classical poet like Petronius Arbiter, but there is something present which is wholly alien to classical love poets—a spirit of objective, intellectual analysis of the experience, appropriate to the author, who was *"vir immensae doctrinae . . .* more famous as a philosopher of religion than as a poet.["]8 Here indeed, in such a man's treatise on love, is a prototype for the theologically oriented love poet of the Middle Ages.

How the whole Arabic tradition subtly modified the European love lyric is part of an elaborate pattern that will not concern us at this point. But whether there is any direct debt or not, it is clear that it is from such non-classical formulation as Ibn Hazm's that we can probably expect to derive a curious madrigal by Ronsard, which may well have drawn on even more varied sources to condense this firm pattern:

L'homme est bien sot qui aime sans cognoistre.
J'aime et jamais je ne vy ce que j'aime;
D'un faux penser je me deçoy moy-mesme,
Je suis esclave et ne cognois mon maistre.
L'imaginer seulement me fait estre
Comme je suis en une peine extresme.
L'œil peut faillir, l'aureille fait de mesme,
Mais nul des sens mon amour n'a fait naistre.
Je n'ay ny veu, ny ouï, ny touché,
Ce qui m'offense à mes yeux est caché,
La playe au cœur à credit m'est venue.
Ou nos esprits se cognoissent aux Cieux
Ains que d'avoir nostre terre vestue,
Qui vont gardant la mesme affection
Dedans les corps qu'au Ciel ils avoyent euë;
Ou je suis fol; encore vaut-il mieux
Aimer en l'air une chose incognuë

8 *Ibid.*, p. 73.

Que n'aimer rien, imitant Ixion,
Qui pour Junon embrassoit une nuë.[9]

(That man is very foolish who loves what he does not
know. I love and never see what I love; I dupe myself
with a deluding thought; I am a slave who does not know
his master. Mere imagination makes me feel as if I suffer
greatly. The eye can fail and the ear the same, but none
of the senses brought about my love. I have neither seen,
heard, nor touched; what provokes me is hidden from my
eyes; the wound in my heart arrived without an account.
Either our minds met in the heavens before having assumed flesh and keep still the same condition in bodies as
they had in heaven; or I am mad. Yet it is better to love
something unknown in the air than not to love anything,
imitating Ixion who embraced a cloud thinking it was
Juno.)

One senses the deliberate virtuosity of the poem's analytic
and realistic texture, in comparison with the more conventional dream frame and evasive brevity of Petronius Arbiter's
lyric. Only a faint hint of Platonic mysticism "explains" the
situation at all in the familiar terms of Ronsard's time, and
the orthodox appreciation of an ideally endowed mistress is
specifically omitted. The poem nevertheless does explore
the same theme as lyrics describing a future mistress, though
with the abstractness of Ibn Hazm, and with a sense of the
complexity of human awareness which is only latent in the
tentative classical prototypes which we have found for it.
Ronsard's stress on the two apparently incompatible attributes of his experience, its frustrating elusiveness and its
unmistakable actuality, show in comparison with the classical
poems a surprising extension of self-awareness, from the

[9] Ronsard, *Œuvres Complètes*, ed. G. Cohen (Paris, 1958), i, 206.

sensory to the psychological. As is half suggested by the Arab philosopher, he is describing the mental pressure of unlocalized sexual desire, and doing so with great precision. Love is seen as something divorced from specific sensuous prescription. No longer are a future mistress' physical attributes a primary, even a unique issue for her hopeful lover. What will link the lovers together is something already active in the poet's mind. The disturbing pressure of this expectation has an actuality in Ronsard's poem which the hypothetical and unlikely ideals of other poets never had. These luxurious objects are now replaced by a form which, while unmistakably substantial, has correctly as yet none of the customary attributes. The historical circumstances of a real encounter, not prophecy, can alone associate it with these attributes sometime in the future.

It is interesting to see how readily one turns to the terminology of metaphysics, the science of mental entities, to give an objective account of Ronsard's poem. It therefore comes as no surprise to find that the condition of Ronsard's lover is duplicated in the circumstances described at the start of Donne's "Aire and Angels":

> Twice or thrice had I loved thee,
> Before I knew thy face or name,
> So in a voice, so in a shapelesse flame,
> *Angells* affect us oft, and worship'd bee;
>   Still when, to where thou wert, I came,
>   Some lovely glorious nothing I did see.[10]

In this poem the lover is so conditioned to his wholly introverted awareness of his mistress that even after meeting the woman he cannot focus his desire on her objective attributes, which bear little relation to what he required of her in his imagination. He finds her beauty merely confusing and is

---

[10] John Donne, *Poems*, ed. H. J. C. Grierson (Oxford, 1933), p. 21.

only satisfied when he recognizes in her love for him the sole and essential attribute of that elusive form which she has hitherto been for him. Still closer in line with Ronsard's poem is Donne's "Negative Love," which confines itself to the lover before he meets his ideal mistress:

> I never stoop'd so low, as they
> Which on an eye, cheeke, lip, can prey,
>   Seldome to them, which soare no higher
>   Than vertue or the mind to'admire,
> For sense, and understanding may
>   Know, what gives fuell to their fire:
> My love, though silly, is more brave,
> For may I misse, when ere I crave,
> If I know yet, what I would have.[11]

The firm repudiation of conventional appreciations of beauty gives some rhetorical style to the piece, reminiscent of the pattern in Shakespeare's Sonnet 130. However, there is more to Donne's repudiation of conventional desires than a piquant mannerism. Like Ronsard, Donne is substituting for the casual, airy fancies of a lover contemplating his ideal the precise illustration of the mind of a man consciously seeking a significant relation with a woman. The prediction by the lover of any detailed physical or even moral qualities for this woman is misleading since the sole certain attributes she will have are the intangible ones of arousing love and returning it. She cannot be guaranteed to be either a brunette, or a girl with a good figure, or even a Roman Catholic, since these facts may not in practice prove to be the bases of the relationship which develops. To love someone exclusively because of her state of mind, not for her mental and physical endowments, is something so unusual for the lovers of the sixteenth century that Donne and Ronsard may well feel

[11] *Ibid.*, p. 59.

diffident about their anticipations of future loves. However, Donne reaffirms his view of the situation boldly in his second stanza:

> If that be simply perfectest
> Which can by no way be exprest
> But *Negatives,* my love is so.
> To All, which all love, I say no.
> If any who deciphers best,
> What we know not, our selves, can know,
> Let him teach mee that nothing; This
> As yet my ease, and comfort is,
> Though I speed not, I cannot misse.

Donne's open mind about the attributes of his future mistress at least does not impair the chances of a potential love affair as naïve prescriptions might. His attitude gives his poem both a distinctive movement and psychological accuracy, not to say wisdom—for both of which he may be partially indebted to the precursors we have noted, but which emerge in his poem with unique clarity. The scholastic description of God as "perfect negatives" to all finite experience happens logically to fit the character of an anticipated but unseen mistress. She even shares with God the quality of being definable only in terms of attitude toward her lover. It is characteristic of Donne as a Stuart poet that he generally uses metaphysics as he does here, less to startle than to define attitudes with philosophical precision, unlike those vapid false prophecies which many hopeful lovers indulge in.

Such an analysis as Donne's, with its deflation of a whole conventional pattern, could only come after the refinement of scholastic discriminations about states of being and consciousness, and the beginning of the penetration of nontheological attitudes by them. Any poet who, after reading "Negative Love," postulates detailed characteristics for his future love is guilty at best of a charming anachronism—which is the case with Crashaw's diffuse and disordered "Wishes to his Supposed Mistress." Jonson was subtler than Crashaw and a better poet. Without the bewildering precision of Donne he yet makes the same point in "The Dreame" which returns to the classical precedent, here the poem of Petronius Arbiter, in a way typical of Jonson:

> Or Scorne, or pittie on me take,
> I must a true Relation make,
> I am undone to night.
> Love in a subtile Dreame disguis'd,
> Hath both my heart and me surpriz'd,
> Whom never yet he durst attempt awake;
> Nor will he tell me for whose sake
> > He did me the Delight,
> > > Or Spight,
> But leaves me to inquire,
> In all my wild desire,
> Of sleepe againe, who was his Aid;
> And sleepe so guiltie and afraid,
> As since he dares not come within my sight.[12]

Though the occasion of this poem approximates to those of Petronius and Ibn Hazm, its interpretation is fully in harmony with Donne's. Desire anticipates a future mistress; but with the same accuracy which distinguishes Donne's poem, if not so certainly that of the Latin poet, it does not attempt to create a detailed image in the lover's mind. Thus Donne and Jonson show themselves alert to an evolution in man's psychological self-awareness, of which Crashaw lacks knowledge.

To see how this awareness was carried yet further, by a

[12] *Ben Jonson*, ed. C. H. Herford and P. Simpson (Oxford, 1947), VIII, 150.

contemporary of Crashaw, we must turn to a lyric of Suckling's which fits this evolution fully into the orthodox pattern of melodious lyricism hardly cultivated by Donne, just as the art of ratiocination about amatory problems which his virtuosity aggressively flaunted in "The Flea" was suavely assimilated to the sonorous phrases of the orthodox "carpe diem" poem by Marvell's "To his Coy Mistress." Suckling, like Marvell, abandons Donne's scholastic machinery, and also the quaint particularity of Jonson, leaving only an urbane statement of the operation of desire. The poet observes to Cupid, as the deity of impending loves:

> Of thee, kind boy, I ask no red and white,
>   To make up my delight;
>   No odd becoming graces,
> Black eyes, or little know-not-whats in faces;
> Make me but mad enough, give me good store
> Of love for her I court:
>   I ask no more,
> 'Tis love in love that makes the sport.[13]

Suckling is not so sure as Donne in "Aire and Angels" of the means by which this "madness" is fostered, but he does share the insights of "Negative Love" and rejects naïve particularities much more lucidly than Donne. In such a poem we see that, just as a heaven of precious stones and anthropomorphic images proved trivial and inadequate for sophisticated religious thought, so the wonderfully subtle mechanism of analysis developed by the scholastic theologians to supplement such finite visions provided ultimately the means of supplanting the idea that profane love dwells in a flashing eye, a delicate complexion, and other more intimate sensuous specifications. Sexual love no less than that

---

[13] *Minor Poets of the Seventeenth Century*, ed. R. G. Howarth (London, 1953), p. 192.

of God proves to be, not an aspiration after tangible ends, but an orientation of feelings, a mental tension which will lend itself to exposition without metaphor by metaphysics.

It seems that, with the analysis of the poetic treatment of the very first situation in the phases of love, the argument against a postclassical evolution of sensibility collapses because there is an unmistakable progression from almost all classical prescriptions for a mistress to the poems of Ronsard, Donne, and Suckling—and one which significantly enlarges the range of human emotion. Since Suckling was very popular in the Restoration as numerous references show, it may not be too fanciful to wonder if Restoration promiscuity was not fostered by such perceptive attitudes as these which certainly facilitate the effective maturing of love affairs.

[ii]

One of the major reasons for the avoidance of conventional prescriptions for a future mistress by competent poets is the poverty of the theme in dramatic or verbal potentialities. Only with Ronsard and Donne does a rhetorical flourish become possible, through the apparent folly of the poet's attitude and his resolute rejection of more orthodox patterns. Even their lyrics seem unlocalized and abstract. Mere exposition, without the picturesque details of a focusing episode, ensures that none of these poems is either long or superficially memorable, however important as evidence for the evolution of sensibility. By contrast drama, immediacy, and vivifying concrete detail are essential to the first truly social situation love's appearance affords the poet—the lover's first encounters with his mistress. The situation provokes distinctive reactions and provides the poet with an interesting audience to hear about them in the person of the lady. The reactions conventionally assumed to take place in the lover in fact demand that the poet communicate at leisure, and in writing, with her. For, while the conjunction of two practiced lovers in a Restoration comedy may occur amidst a fashionably witty and vivacious repartee, this is only because of a then very recent change of attitudes toward new love. To those for whom love was truly an initiation, tradition had prescribed a standard reaction of a most dislocating kind when they encountered the person by whom they were attracted. No one has recorded these symptoms more vividly than Sappho:

Φαίνεταί μοι κῆνος ἴσος θέοισιν
ἔμμεν ὤνηρ ὄττις ἐνάντιός τοι
ἰζάνει καὶ πλάσιον ἆδυ φονεί-
σας ὑπακούει

καὶ γελαίσας ἰμμέροεν, τό μ’ἦ μὰν
κάρζαν ἐν στήθεσσιν ἐπεπτόασεν·
ὡς γὰρ ἔς τ’ἴδω βροχέ, ὥς με φώνας
οὖδεν ἔτ’ ἴκει,

ἀλλὰ κὰμ μὲν γλῶσσα ϝέαγε, λέπτον
δ’αὔτικα χρῷ πῦρ ὑπαδεδρόμακεν,
ὀππάτεσσι δ’οὖδεν ὄρημ’, ἐπιρρόμ-
βεισι δ’ ἄκουαι,

ἀ δέ μ’ἴδρως κακχέεται, τρόμος δὲ
παῖσαν ἀγρη, χλωροτέρα δὲ ποίας
ἔμμι, τεθνάκην δ’ὀλίγω ’πιδεύϝην
φαίνομαι· . . .

(It is to be a god, methinks, to sit before you and listen close by to the sweet accents and winning laughter which have made the heart in my breast beat fast, I warrant you. When I look on you for a moment my speech comes short or fails me quite, I am tongue-tied; in a moment a delicate fire has overrun my flesh; my eyes grow dim and my ears sing, the sweat runs down me, a trembling takes me altogether, till I am as green and pale as grass, and death itself seems not far away; . . .)[14]

The truth (or resonance) of Sappho's observations is confirmed by the reappearance of these symptoms in "Aire and Angels," with the confusion which Donne felt at his first overpowering encounters with his mistress' physical presence. Typically Donne's poem compresses the two classic themes we have now encountered into one composite structure, and a much more explicit analogy for Sappho's poem is found in Theocritus' close conformity to Sappho's motifs:

> . . . ἐγὼ δέ νιν ὡς ἐνόησα
> ἄρτι θύρας ὑπὲρ οὐδὸν ἀμειβόμενον ποδὶ κούφῳ-
> φράζεό μευ τὸν ἔρωθ' ὅθεν ἵκετο, πότνα Σελάνα-
> πᾶσα μὲν ἐψύχθην κιόνος πλέον, ἐκ δὲ μετώπω
> ἱδρώς μευ κοχύδεσκεν ἴσον νοτίαισιν ἔρσαις,
> οὐδέ τι φωνῆσαι δυνάμαν, οὐδ' ὅσσον ἐν ὕπνῳ
> κνυζεῦντα φωνεῦντα φίλαν ποτὶ ματέρα τέκνα·
> ἀλλ' ἐπάγην δαγῦδι καλὸν χρόα πάντοθεν ἴσα. (II, 103-110)

(. . . and I no sooner was aware of him stepping light-foot across the threshold of my door (mark, Lady Moon, whence came my love) than chiller I turned than snow from head to foot, and from my brow, like the damp dews, started the sweat, nor could I speak a word, nay, not so much as babes that whimper in their sleep calling to their mother dear, but all my fair body grew stiff as it were a doll's.)[15]

This is obviously inferior stuff compared to Sappho's poem. It scarcely achieves lyric status, being buried in a lengthy and

[14] *Lyra Graeca*, ed. and trans. J. M. Edmonds (London, 1928), I, 186-187. Line 7 is corrected to the reading of D. Page, in *Sappho and Alcaeus* (Oxford, 1955), p. 19.

[15] Theocritus, *Idylls*, ed. and trans. A. S. F. Gow (Oxford, 1952), I, 22-23.

frigid apostrophe to the moon, and is not at all a succinct and poignant address to the loved one like the earlier poem. The elaboration of the imagery is not dynamically helpful—rather it diffuses the precise notation of physical sensation in Sappho. However, the basic data of both poems is very similar, even though one poem talks of ice and the other of fire, a paradox in the description of the same sensation which later poets would weaken to a conventional allusion.

Much more precise and authentic than Theocritus' lines is Catullus' conscious version of Sappho's poem:

> Ille mi par esse deo videtur,
> Ille, si fas est, superare divos,
> qui sedens adversus identidem te
>   Spectat et audit
> dulce ridentem, misero quod omnis
> eripit sensus mihi; nam simul te,
> Lesbia, aspexi, nihil est super mi
>   vocis in ore,
> lingua sed torpet, tenuis sub artus
> flamma demanat, sonitu suopte
> tintinant aures, gemina teguntur
>   lumina nocte.
> otium, Catulle, tibi molestum est;
> otio exultas nimiumque gestis.
> otium et reges prius et beatas
>   perdidit urbes. (LI)

(He seems to me to be equal to a god, he, if it may be, seems to surpass the gods who, sitting opposite you again and again gazes at you and hears you sweetly laughing. Such a thing takes away all my senses, alas! for whenever I see you, Lesbia, at once no sound of voice remains within my mouth, but my tongue falters, a subtle flame steals through my limbs, my ears tingle with inward humming, and my eyes are drowned in twofold night. Idleness, Catullus, does you harm, you riot in your idleness and wanton too much. Idleness ere now has ruined both kings and wealthy cities.)[16]

Superficially the poem might seem to be simply a translation. However, the effects are by no means identical. The brisk movement of the last four lines has worried scholars, but, though some have doubted it, the poem is surely correct as it stands, for Catullus here introduces something missing in the Greek poems, a sense of dramatic interchange and dialogue. Either Lesbia replies sharply to what she considers sentimentality in speaking to her, or Catullus' own spirit checks him in the act of penning such emotions for her perusal. The latter interpretation is preferable, though less dramatic, because it does not involve the poet in fluent speech with Lesbia, an effect in conflict with his statement "lingua sed torpet." Either way Catullus confirms the tradition by translating it into Latin and maintaining its great simplicity and naturalness while adding a more dramatic conclusion.

Some of the effects of these pagan lyrics are clearly present in a sonnet of Dante's in the *Vita Nuova*, written over a thousand years later; but one might not recognize the common theme so considerably has it been modified to suit the new tastes and values which have evolved in the interim. The juxtaposition of the poems epitomizes the evolution of a whole new civilization on the ruins of the classical world:

> Tanto gentile et tanto onesta pare
>   La donna mia, quand'ella altrui saluta,
>   Ch'ogni lingua devien tremando muta,
>   E gli occhi no l'ardiscon di guardare.
> Ella si va, sentendosi laudare,
>   Benignamente d'umiltà vestuta;

[16] *Catullus,* Loeb edn., trans. F. W. Cornish (London, 1950), pp. 58-59.

E par che sia una cosa venuta
Da cielo in terra a miracol mostrare.
Mostrasi si piacente a chi la mira,
   Che dà per gli occhi una dolcezza al core,
   Che intender non la può chi no la prova.
E par che della sua labbia si muova
   Un spirito soave pien d'amore,
   Che va dicendo all'anima: sospira.[17] (xv)

(So sweet and virtuous my lady seems when she greets others that every tongue becomes tremulously silent and eyes do not dare to look. She goes on, aware that she is praised, yet clothed in generous humility and she seems to be something come from heaven to show a miracle on earth. She shows herself so gracious to those who admire her that through the eyes she gives a peace to the heart which cannot be understood until it is experienced. And it seems that from her lips flows a gentle spirit full of love which goes to the soul saying: sigh.)

The first four lines describe the same symptoms of love we found in Catullus and Sappho but more casually and succinctly. The main weight of the poem has been moved elsewhere. Instead of the various distinct symptoms in an individual, which the pagan lovers noted with such self-conscious care, what happens in this poem is that all hearers quaver into silence at Beatrice's greeting and lower their eyes. The reasons for the reactions have been transformed proportionately. It is not the effect of the woman's physical beauty or sexual attraction working on the excited sensibility of a particular lover which achieves these results, but her kindness and a virtue clear to all observers. By Dante's time a thousand years of Christianity have deeply saturated amatory sentiment so that ethical rather than sensory considerations govern the

[17] Dante, *Opere*, ed. E. Moore (Oxford, 1924), p. 224.

power and fascination of a woman. The physical effects of such moral beauty are necessarily peripheral, and something more positive is called for in the observer than a deathly trance. There is a more appealing quality in the warmth and life-giving virtue of Beatrice's glance than the Gorgon-like power of the classical beauties. However, the loss of physical immediacy in the poem is a loss to its vividness and energy. Dante is not addressing his lady directly or recalling a single intense moment of experience, but for the most part describing her impact on others in general terms. Of course this very withdrawal from drama is meaningful and contributes to the delicate, cool charm of Dante's sexual fascination with Beatrice but one may well question whether this is a reasonable basis for most lovers to found a relationship on. It amounts to a highly sophisticated and disciplined attitude to sexual relations as a whole rather than a simple and logical extension of the situation first defined by Sappho. However, despite the retrenchments on the plane of physical awareness there is no doubt about the compensating extension of sensibility shown in Dante's concern with the moral character of his lady, a quality whose absence in Lesbia cost Catullus dearly. It is ironic that the celestial allusions in these two poets carry such different implications, while at the same time conserving a characteristic motif of the theme.

That Dante's view of the effect of a woman's beauty on susceptible admirers marked an extreme in one direction is confirmed by the suaver tendencies of later versions such as Petrarch's. Petrarch seems to be among the less dynamic of the great love poets. His works afford at best a magnificent quarry for more selective sculptors than he was. Wyatt, Sidney, and Milton built lyric reputations with a fraction of their Italian master's materials. His sense of lyric relationships is limited. One might well feel that his handling of the theme of new lovers' mutual responses is a debasement of its best qualities, though like Dante he compensates us for the losses:

> Quando giugne per gli occhi al cor profondo
>   L'imagin donna, ogni altra indi si parte,
>   E le vertú che l'anima comparte
>   Lascian le membra quasi immobil pondo.
> E del primo miracolo il secondo
>   Nasce talor: che la scacciata parte,
>   Da sé stessa fuggendo, arriva in parte
>   Che fa vendetta e 'l suo essilio giocondo.
> Quinci in duo volti un color morte appare,
>   Perché 'l vigor che vivi gli mostrava
>   Da nessun lato è piú là dove stava.
> E di questo in quel dí me ricordava
>   Ch' i' vidi duo amanti trasformare
>   E far qual io mi soglio in vista fare.[18] (XCIV)

(When the mistress image arrives through the eyes to the bottom of the heart, every other departs thence, and the power which makes up the soul leaves every limb set almost lifeless. And from this first miracle is then born a second: that the expelled soul, fleeing voluntarily, arrives in the place [the beloved's body], which it makes its amends and its happy exile. Whence it comes that a deathly pallor appears in two faces, because the vigor shown by live people is no longer in any place where it had been. And of this I bethought me on that day when I saw two lovers transformed in face as I used to be.)

No wonder one of Petrarch's editors observed that this exposition was more ingenious than reasonable. If Dante's poem lacked drama, this one is almost wholly lacking in the vividness and actuality necessary to recapture any feeling.

[18] Carducci, p. 137.

Only the last two lines hint at an actual situation animating Petrarch's elaborately erroneous theory about the trance imposed by love on new lovers. Nevertheless it is just the presence of this theory which makes Petrarch's sonnet of interest. The pagan poets gave us precise physical data, Dante gives moral dimension, and Petrarch adds logical analysis, even an attempt at scientific diagnosis, however wrongheaded. The flatness of this early rationalization may be forgotten in the face of the new configurations which such analytic powers will foster in lyric verse.

It can hardly be claimed that such resources were effectively exploited by the earlier imitators of Petrarch. Ronsard merely falls back on the physiological data of the pagans,[19] spun out in greater detail still, while Spenser, if neater and more literary, is even less inventive:

> but looking still on her I stand amazed,
> at wondrous sight of so celestiall hew.
> So when my toung would speak her praises dew,
> it stopped is with thoughts astonishment:
> and when my pen would write her titles true,
> it rauisht is with fancies wonderment:[20] (iii)

Such competent copywork is no answer to Sullivan's arguments. When we turn to Spenser's contemporary, Sir Philip Sidney, we at length find something worthy of comparison with Catullus:

> Because I breathe not love to every one,
> Nor do not use set colours for to wear,
> Nor nourish special locks of vowèd hair,
> Nor give each speech a full point of a groan,
> The courtly nymphs, acquainted with the moan
> Of them which in their lips Love's standard bear,

---

[19] "Quand je vous voy, ou quand je pense en vous," Cohen, I, 42.
[20] E. Spenser, *Works*, ed. J. C. Smith and E. De Selincourt (Oxford, 1912), p. 563.

'What, he!' say they of me, 'now I dear swear
He cannot love! No, no, let him alone.'
And think so still, so Stella know my mind;
Profess indeed I do not Cupid's art;
But you, fair maids, at length this truth shall find,
That his right badge is but worn in the heart.
Dumb swans, not chattering pies, do lovers prove:
They love indeed who quake to say they love.[21] (LIV)

The basic argument is that of Sappho and Catullus—a lover is tongue-tied and ill at ease if he is truly in love, not poised and eloquent. However, on this observation Sidney has constructed a poem which is vivid and intimate because it is energetically argumentative and the lover is anxious to vindicate his own character. There is a movement and point lacking in Petrarch's sonnet. The four accumulated negatives of the first quatrain, the irony and mimicry of the second one, all throw into relief the earnestness of the sestet. The excellence of the poem is marked by the implied sense of consecutive thought which the reader is bound to detect in the first explosive word— "because," and by the eager, vehement flow of the sentences. In this sonnet we see a standard theme in love poetry adjusted to the personality of an individualized speaker and given pace and conviction thereby in a way which we have only previously seen in Sappho and Catullus. However, Sidney has shown as marked an independence of the classical tradition as did Dante—only the reference to dumbness and the sonnet's last line, "They love indeed who quake to say they love," echo the old data. But Petrarch's analytic powers are also missing.

These reappear finally in a revision of Petrarch's rather flat sonnet that is, with Sappho's poem, among the most famous in this series—Donne's "The Extasie." There is perhaps some-

[21] *Silver Poets*, p. 193.

thing improbable to modern tastes about the posture of
Donne's lovers:

> And whil'st our souls negotiate there,
>   Wee like sepulchrall statues lay;
> All day, the same our postures were,
>   And wee said nothing, all the day.[22]

until the entrancement of Sappho and her imitators is recalled
—"death itself seems not very far away" she says; "all my body
grew stiff as a doll's" says Theocritus' heroine; the flight of
the soul "leaves every limb almost lifeless" and "a deathly
pallor appears" according to Petrarch. To the latter source
Donne probably owes some of the details of the theory for the
optical elements of their relation, but Donne's resolute efforts
to break the trance is his own dramatic contribution to the
pattern. It duplicates dynamically what was accomplished
analytically in "Aire and Angels." The identification of the
basic theme of "The Extasie" as the breaking out of this initial trance of love is a fact of assistance in repudiating the already dubious idea that the poem is primarily a plea for the
complete sexual consummation of the relationship. "Sex" is in
fact explicitly repudiated as a feature of the relationship.
What is sought by Donne is rather the enhancement of the
lovers' mutual understanding by such means as their traditional entranced wonder has at first denied them. By the use of
their faculties, speech, and gesture, they will be able through
the speaker's initiative to do something to turn aside the reproach of neurotic lethargy with which Catullus spurred himself to more effective activity at the end of his poem.

In Donne's poem is seen again how the working out of the
logic of the situation gives a poem major interest to its readers. Earlier poets had simply sat down to vindicate in verse
their awkwardness in action, an effort accomplished with the

[22] Grierson, p. 46.

fullest self-awareness by Sidney. It is left for Donne to insist that, normal as this entrancement may be, lovers must break it in each other's presence if their relationship is to become fully articulated. If it be heartily assumed that this is an elementary discovery, it need only be pointed out that recent literature is studded with examples of lovers who failed to strive for this effective communication and suffered for it. This is the subject of Browning's "The Statue and the Bust," of Tennyson's "The Lady of Shallot," and the misfortune of Marcel and Albertine in Proust's novel. In real life the pathetically abortive romance of Balzac and his Polish countess illustrates dramatically that the inhibitions of the sensitive persist in modern love affairs.

As before, it is Suckling who gives the most explicit expression to the warning implicit in Donne's scene, with a brisk reproach to a tongue-tied young man. The poem's fame shows that the salutariness of the sentiment was recognized:

> Why so pale and wan, fond lover?
>   Prithee, why so pale?
> Will, when looking well can't move her,
>   Looking ill prevail?
>   Prithee, why so pale?
>
> Why so dull and mute, young sinner?
>   Prithee, why so mute?
> Will, when speaking well can't win her
>   Saying nothing do't?
>   Prithee, why so mute?
>
> Quit, quit for shame; this will not move,
>   This cannot take her;
> If of herself she will not love,
>   Nothing can make her:
>   The devil take her![23]

[23] Howarth, p. 190.

This is a useful corrective to Sappho and the rest, who risk glorying in their sensations. Catullus' abrupt twist to his conclusion proves that he at least realizes the dangers of servility to a headstrong woman. He also vindicates, by the sharp tone of his self-reproach, the propriety of Suckling's common sense brusqueness. In Sidney, Donne, and Suckling we find therefore a more complete and authoritative exposition of the nature and possibilities of the situation than any related group of poets (or psychologists) had before devised.

[i i i]

The effect of these last two poems is to assist in the breakup of lover's inhibitions, though there is no trace of any psychoanalytical technique or theory behind this tendency. It is hardly surprising that the pursuit of a fully realized sexual relationship should put a considerable strain on the mind of the male, who is conventionally regarded (even if he is not always actually) as the positive agent of the two lovers. This strain in turn leads naturally to the compensatory, or exploratory, outlet offered by dreams, as Freud so dramatically emphasized. It is, unfortunately, hardly possible to survey here the vast importance of the dream frame for all kinds of artistic expression, since it flourishes throughout literary history. In lyric verse, however, the theme is used with comparative simplicity and brevity, despite its considerable popularity.

Dream fantasies may explore potential experiences, in this case sexual intimacy most typically; but the positive role of these dreams is much more likely to be lost in the lover's desire to compensate for such ineffectiveness as we have just examined, or to avoid the painful demands on one's feelings involved in the successful consummation of a complex relationship. Love poets have rarely failed to favor the escapist value of dreams. Typical of such an approach is a little poem in the *Anacreontea*[24] in which the poet wakes regretfully from a fantasy in which he has gaily sported with a group of girls. His one desire is to sleep and dream again. A more cynical classical poet[25] dreams that he has spent a whole night with the most expensive whore in town and complacently decides, "No longer shall I implore the cruel beauty, nor mourn for myself, now I have Sleep to grant me what he granted." Though it is more graciously written, one remembers Petronius' brief lyric, copied by Jonson, with its conclusion that if he is not to find the young beauty of his dream, "never let me wake."

These classical evasions of the external world are perhaps less immediately serious in that they are not an escape from some actual and urgent problem of individual relationships. It is curious to have to recognize in Renaissance poets both a greater subtlety and a greater danger of mental disorder in their use of the theme than in the classical writers. Boiardo writes to his dream image,

> Non mi lassar, o sogno fugitivo;
>   Ché io me contento de inganar me stesso
>   Godendomi quel ben che io son privo.[26]

(Do not leave me evanescent dream, for I am happy to deceive myself, delighting myself with the good fortune that I lack.)

Here the dangers of self-delusion are clearly invited, with the intention of falsifying the lover's real relationship with his beloved. Ronsard also invites self-deception to conceal his real situation from himself, in a sonnet which begins picturesquely:

[24] *Greek Elegy and Iambus*, ed. and trans. J. M. Edmonds, Volume II, *Anacreontea*, pp. 68-69.
[25] *Greek Anthology*, v, 2; Loeb edn., trans. W. R. Paton, I, 128-129.
[26] Boiardo, *Poesie* (Bologna, 1894), p. 233.

Ces longues nuicts d'hyver, où la Lune ocieuse
Tourne si lentement son char tout à l'entour,
Où le coq si tardif nous annonce le jour,
Où la nuit semble un an à l'ame soucieuse,
 Je fusse mort d'ennuy sans ta forme douteuse . . .[27]

(These long winter nights, when the indolent moon moves her chariot so slowly quite round; when the cock is so slow to announce the day to us; when the night seems like a year to the uneasy soul: I would have been dead with weariness without your deceptive image. . . .)

This image of Hélène behaves as sensually as the real one does coldly:

Rien ne m'est refusé. Le bon sommeil ainsi
Abuse par le faux mon amoureux souci.
S'abuser en amour n'est pas mauvaise chose.

(Nothing is refused me. Kind sleep thus deceives my loving care with fiction. To deceive oneself in love is not a bad thing.)

One can hardly avoid taking exception to the willfulness of the last line. Ronsard's view may be expedient but it is hardly wise. The medieval devils who took the form of succubi clearly figure in this kind of experience, and the haunting and fatal quality such fantasies acquire are the theme of countless works, including the paintings of the temptations of St. Anthony by Breughel, Bosch and others; the deception of the Red Cross Knight in Book I, Canto i, 44 ff. of Spenser's *Faerie Queene;* "Lamia" and "La Belle Dame sans Merci" by Keats; and the eerie story by Oliver Onions, "The Beckoning Fair One," a modern tale showing that such experiences are not alien to our own times. Drummond shows, in a poem slightly

[27] Cohen, I, 259.

indebted to Sannazaro, the insidious transfer of such dreams as Ronsard's to the full hallucinations implicit in the other works:

> The Iuorie, Corrall, Gold,
> Of Brest, of Lips, of Haire,
> So liuely *Sleepe* doth show to inward Sight,
> That wake I thinke I hold
> No Shadow, but my Faire:
> My selfe so to deceaue
> With long-shut Eyes I shunne the irkesome Light.
> Such Pleasure thus I haue
> Delighting in false Gleames
> If *Death* Sleepes Brother bee?
> > And Soules relieu'd of Sense haue so sweete Dreames?
> > That I would wish mee thus to dreame and die.[28]

The same schizophrenic tendencies threaten Stanley also:

> That I might ever dream thus! that some power
> To my eternal sleep would join this hour!
> So willingly deceiv'd, I might possess
> In seeming joys a real happiness.[29]

These poems all show a greatly sophisticated awareness of the possibilities of human introversion in the face of hostile circumstances by comparison with their classical models, but they are not wholly characteristic of their age and serve best as foils to Wyatt's views on the matter, which anticipate the psychological distinction of Donne's tenth elegy, "The Dream." Wyatt ruefully contemplates the ruin of a love affair in one of his lyrics. In his misery he reflects:

[28] William Drummond, *Works*, ed. L. E. Kastner (Manchester, 1913), I, 46 (see note).
[29] *Minor Poets of the Caroline Period*, ed. G. Saintsbury (Oxford, 1905), III, 102.

> Yett some wolde say assueredly
>   Thou mayst appele for thy relesse
>   To fantasy.
>
> To fantasy pertaynys to chose:
>   All thys I knowe, for fantasy
> Ffurst vnto love dyd me induse;
>   But yet I knowe as stedefastly
> That yff love haue no faster knott,
>   So nyce a choyce slyppes sodenly:
>   Yt lastyth nott.[30]

Here there are hints of a searching awareness of the dangers of the imagination, but they are parenthetic rather than central to the lyric. Donne's elegy conforms to the major pattern of dream poem nominally, but on a different moral plane, closer to Wyatt's, from all the earlier examples. The elegy is much subtler and more illuminating than his own more lyrical version with the same title, which reads merely like a clever version of Muretus' "Somnium." Donne's elegy deserves consideration in full:

> Image of her whom I love, more than she,
>   Whose faire impression in my faithfull heart,
> Makes mee her *Medall*, and makes her love mee,
>   As Kings do coynes, to which their stamps impart
> The value: goe, and take my heart from hence,
>   Which now is growne too great and good for me:
> *Honours* oppresse weake spirits, and our sense
>   Strong objects dull; the more, the lesse wee see.
> When you are gone, and *Reason* gone with you,
>   Then *Fantasie* is Queene and Soule, and all;
> She can present joyes meaner than you do;
>   Convenient, and more proportionall.

[30] Sir Thomas Wyatt, *Collected Poems*, ed. Kenneth Muir (Cambridge, Mass., 1950), p. 112.

So, if I dreame I have you, I have you,
　　For, all our joyes are but fantasticall.
And so I scape the paine, for paine is true;
　　And sleepe which locks up sense, doth lock out all.
After such fruition I shall wake,
　　And, but the waking, nothing shall repent;
And shall to love more thankfull Sonnets make,
　　Then if more *honour, teares,* and *paines* were spent.
But dearest heart, and dearer image, stay;
　　Alas, true joyes at best are *dreame* enough;
Though you stay here you passe too fast away:
　　For even at first lifes *Taper* is a snuffe.
Fill'd with her love, may I be rather grown
Mad with much *heart,* than *ideott* with none.[31]

The excellence of the poem lies, like the interest of Petrarch's sonnet discussed earlier, primarily on the analytic level, not in any dramatic or verbal felicities beyond those of precise communication with the reader. The stilted form of an apostrophe (to a "picture" of his mistress) is merely a device for avoiding simple monologue. The "image" is surely not a real picture but his inner sense of his mistress' actuality both physical and spiritual. There is a hint of irony in saying she loves him for conforming to this image, but the real point is that he seeks to share her virtue. This effort explains why his awareness of her is so challenging an experience. If he could only forget this disturbing reality by recasting her nature in his imagination as he would prefer it to be, everything would be much more agreeable. He would thus find all the sensual relief and sentimental satisfaction permitted by earlier poets' dreams of their mistresses. Thus far Donne agrees with Boiardo, Ronsard, and Drummond in preferring convenient self-deception to harsh reality. But unlike them his stiffer moral

[31] Grierson, p. 84.

fiber prevents him from relaxing into hallucination. Like Wyatt, he finally rejects fantasy in favor of truth, because truth itself is so fleeting that unless every effort is made all substantial achievement in life will be lost. A lover is better facing the rigor of his lady's ideals than going mad agreeably with a false image of her. In all the dream poems we have so far examined, only Donne's evokes the fascination of dreams for the struggling lover and then resolutely defines and revokes their dangers to his mental stability.

Perhaps it is necessary at this point to clarify the distinction between these comparatively realistic poems both analytic and escapist in which the situation is primary, and the markedly different, essentially "literary," dream poems. These belong to a category of verse carefully excluded from this chapter, because their topics have been sophisticated for more superficial aesthetic purposes. Typical of such verse is a *Greek Anthology* epigram:

Τὴν φιλοπουλυγέλωτα κόρην ἐπὶ νυκτὸς ὀνείρου
    εἶχον, ἐπισφίγξας πήχεσιν ἡμετέροις.
πείθετό μα ξύμπαντα, καὶ οὐκ ἀλέγιζεν, ἐμεῖο
    κύπριδι παντοίῃ σώματος ἁπτομένου·
ἀλλὰ βαρύζηλός τις Ἔρως καὶ νύκτα λοχήσας
    ἐξέχεεν φιλίην, ὕπνον ἀποσκεδάσας.
ὧδέ μοι οὐδ' αὐτοῖσιν ἐν ὑπναλέοισιν ὀνείροις
    ἄφθονός ἐστιν Ἔρως κέρδεος ἡδυγάμου.   (v, 243)

(I held the laughter-loving girl clasped in my arms in a dream. She yielded herself entirely to me and offered no protest to any of my caprices. But some jealous Love lay in ambush for me even at night, and frightening sleep away spilt my cup of bliss. So even in the dreams of my sleep Love envies me the sweet attainment of my desire.)[32]

[32] Loeb edn., trans. W. R. Paton, i, 250-253.

The point of the poem, apart from the incidental vicarious sexual thrill for the reader, lies in the neat generalization with which the epigram concludes. Jonson's dream poem really belongs also in this tradition, but the witty pattern is perfected by Sherburne in the seventeenth century, based on a sonnet of Marino which ends:

> Allor la bacio, ella ribacia e sugge;
> lasso! ma'l bacio in nulla ecco si scoglie,
> e con la gioia insieme il sonno fugge.
>
> Or qual, perfido amor, frà tante doglie
> deggio attender mercé da chi mi strugge,
> se i mentiti diletti anco mi toglie?[33]

(Then I kiss her, she kisses me back and encourages me, but alas see the kiss fades away, and with my delight the dream takes flight. Now how, perfidious Love, among so many pains can I expect kindness from her who destroys me, if even the false delights are taken from me?)

Sherburne's version surpasses this in virtuosity in every way:

> Fair shadow! faithless as my Sun!
>   Of peace she robs my mind,
> And to my sense, which rest doth shun,
>   Thou art no less unkind.
>
> She my address disdainfull flies,
>   And thou like her art fleet;
> The real beauty she denies,
>   And thou the counterfeit.
>
> To cross my innocent desires,
>   And make my Griefs extreme
> A cruel mistress thus conspires
>   With a delusive dream.[34]

[33] G. Marino, *Poesie Varie*, ed. B. Croce (Bari, 1913), p. 104.
[34] *The Works of the English Poets*, ed. A. Chalmers (London, 1810), VI, 628.

Here the neat generalization of *The Greek Anthology* is articulated through three stanzas without effort or clumsiness, instead of being confined to a single stroke of wit. The effect could hardly be developed beyond this triple diversification. But it is obvious also that here the poet's ingenuity, not his contribution to the understanding of the situation or his titillating evocative powers, is the crucial characteristic of his poem. For the most part our study of such virtuosity and its more positive results will be confined to the next chapter, though all the themes of the present one lend themselves to such diverting developments.

[iv]

According to popular convention the pivotal exchange in most love affairs is the proposal of marriage rather than the physical consummation which follows the formal contract. Ironically the proposal of marriage is an insignificant theme for lyricism. One reason is perhaps that love and marriage have not necessarily been linked at various points in European social history, and certainly not in the class of patrons for whom lyric poets usually wrote. Dynastic, diplomatic, social, or economic motives have often superseded sexual attraction as a basis for marriage. The proposal of marriage is therefore better displayed in a genre where such more elaborate issues could be adequately discussed, like the drama, or better still the novel, as Ian Watt has shown so well in his recent study, *The Rise of the Novel.*

In lyric verse the theme of sexual consummation could be better handled in the narrower terms of the art of seduction. For pagan times the practice of this art was apparently a primary activity of the lyric poet. Poems inviting, cajoling, or coercing young women into their lovers' beds were among the most popular and numerous of all amatory poems. But when the impact of Christianity on social mores began to have a radical effect, it became more difficult for the fashionable lyric poet to do justice to the full complexity of the issue as it now appeared. Frank invitations to sensual indulgence decline in popularity from the time of Petronius, despite the veiled delight in adultery which characterizes courtly love. Only in the "vulgar" art of Villon and the wandering scholars does pagan sensuality openly flourish in lyric form. No major poet from the time of Dante can easily reconcile sensual satisfaction with the beliefs of his more serious moments (witness Chaucer's "Retraction"). This is not to say that conventional pleas for extramarital love do not survive at least until about 1660, but they have usually an archaic flavor of quaint paganism, rather than the dynamic actuality which they clearly had for Catullus or Ovid. When the high Renaissance attempts literary seduction it does so with tongue in cheek, rarely in the bitter earnest of sexual desire. Its best pleas are not so much convincing or even moving arguments that really might tempt a girl from virtue as they are virtuoso performances that will flatter or amuse her, at best perhaps ingratiating the poet into the circle of her intimates. By the early 1700's the power of Puritanism was such that in England even these invitations were quite unfashionable. The role of Lovelace in *Clarissa* is founded on the horror of such sentiments, carefully fostered by writers like Addison and Steele.

It is necessary to stress this fact in order to clarify the apparent failure in the sequence of serious arguments for sexual indulgence, of the kind epitomized by Catullus' "Vivamus mea Lesbia," during the course of the seventeenth century. Marvell's "To his Coy Mistress" does nothing to qualify this statement, for while the sentiments offered by Catullus about the definitiveness of death were his literal belief and that of his age, those of Marvell's lover can in no way be reconciled either with the beliefs of the age or with the author's own religious poems and status as a devoted servant of the Puritan Commonwealth (which would scarcely have employed a free thinker). It is significant that while Lesbia was recognizably a real person, Clodia, wife of Quintus Metellus Celer, no scholar has felt that the identity of Marvell's coy mistress was a matter worth research or controversy. Equally no one cares to imagine a young woman seducible by Donne's "The Flea." Even Jonson's "Come my Celia" is spoken in a play by a diabolic grandee to a horrified young wife. What remains to the Renaissance love lyricist who is planning to compose an apparently sincere invitation to dalliance, is frequently only an interesting series of evasions of reality. Both the acceptance and the avoidance of these deceptions reveal explicitly the change of outlook from classical times.

One of the more gracious and long-lived of the pagan arguments for indulgence which might be advanced by a classical poet to his reluctant lady depends on analogies showing how fleeting an opportunity is given to women to make any choice at all. The most elegant and famous is Ausonius' "De Rosis Nascentibus," which is sufficiently impressive for some scholars to have ascribed it to Virgil. The poet describes his walk, one fine spring morning, through a rose garden. He admires the flowers, some budding, others full blown. He observes the various stages of their blossoming to the last stage of dropping petals:

> haec modo, quae toto rutilaverat igne comarum
>   pallida conlapsis deseritur foliis.
> mirabar celerem fugitava aetate rapinam
>   et, dum nascuntur, consenuisse rosas . . .
> Conquerimur, Natura, brevis quod gratia talis:
>   ostentata oculis illico dona rapis.
> quam longa una dies, aetas tam longa rosarum: . . .
>   cum pubescenti iuncta senecta brevis. . . .

collige, virgo, rosas, dum flos novus et nova pubes,
et memor esto aevum sic properare tuum. (33ff.)

(Another, which but late had glowed with all the fires of
her bloom, now fades, abandoned by her falling petals. I
marveled at the swift ruin wrought by the fleeting season,
to see the roses all withered even while they bloom. . . .
Nature, we grieve that such beauty is short-lived: once displayed to our eyes forthwith you snatch away your gifts. As
long as is one day, so long is the life of the rose; . . . her
brief youth and age go hand in hand. . . . Then, maidens,
gather roses, while blooms are fresh and youth is fresh, and
be mindful that so your life-time hastes away.)[35]

The poem is as much an account of the garden as an admonition, and its modest conclusion makes it a suitable model for
Christian poets, partly perhaps because it is more elegant than
dramatic. Poets like Ronsard recaptured Ausonius' effects with
no less elegance but much greater brevity. Ronsard's famous
"Mignonne, allons voir si la rose" is as picturesque as Ausonius
and conserves his main points, but it conveys them in a fraction of his length and gives the sentiments direction by clearly
focusing the poem on a single listener:

> Mignonne, allons voir si la rose
> Qui ce matin avoit desclose
> Sa robe de pourpre au Soleil,
> A point perdu cette vesprée
> Les plis de sa robe pourprée,
> Et son teint au vostre pareil.
>
> Las! voyez comme en peu d'espace,
> Mignonne, elle a dessus la place
> Las! las! ses beautez laissé cheoir!

[35] *Ausonius,* Loeb edn., trans. H. G. Evelyn White (London, 1919),
II, 276ff.

O vraiment marastre Nature,
Puisqu'une telle fleur ne dure
Que du matin jusques au soir!
Donc, si vous me croyez, mignonne,
Tandis que vostre âge fleuronne
En sa plus verte nouveauté,
Cueillez, cueillez vostre jeunesse:
Comme à ceste fleur la vieillesse
Fera ternir vostre beauté.[36]

(Darling, let us go to see if the rose which this morning had exposed its purple dress to the sun has not quite lost this evening the folds of its purple dress, and its complexion equal to yours. Alas! you see how in a little time, darling, it has on the spot, alas, alas, let fall its beauties! O truly hard-hearted mother Nature, since such a flower only lasts from morning until evening. Then, if you believe me, darling, while your age blossoms in its greenest freshness, pick, pick your youth: age will cause your beauty to tarnish as it did this flower's.)

Despite the recurring picturesque detail of Ausonius there is little doubt that Ronsard has substantially advanced the presentation of the topic. Not only is his audience personalized by the repeated "mignonne," but the poet's own involvement is dramatically communicated by the carefully spaced repetitions "Las, las," "cueillez, cueillez," and the exclamations of the central paragraph. By comparison Ausonius is sententious and aloof. Though his carefully modulated style is never verbose, it lacks the economy and energy of much great art.

Herrick's no less famous "To the Virgins, to make much of Time" marks another kind of advance on earlier models. The opening indeed declares its debt to the traditional allusion:

[36] Cohen, I, 419.

> Gather ye Rose-buds while ye may,
>   Old Time is still a flying:
> And this same flower that smiles today,
>   Tomorrow will be dying.[37]

But the poem no longer depends primarily on the Ausonius motif. The second stanza develops a different but roughly analogous pattern drawn obviously from Catullus, though with his pagan sense of death's finality discreetly erased as we might expect from an Anglican divine:

> The glorious Lamp of Heaven, the Sun,
>   The higher he's a getting;
> The sooner will his Race be run,
>   And nearer he's to Setting.

The sense of personality and situation is conspicuously weaker than in Ronsard, though the naturalness of tone and energy is if anything superior to the French poet's rhetoric—as illustrated by the effective imperative opening "Gather" and the colloquialism and elision of "he's a getting." Perhaps only in its sense of argumentative continuity does the poem clearly surpass Ronsard's. The first and second stanzas are held together firmly by a logical connection generalized in the third stanza:

> That Age is best, which is the first,
>   When Youth and Blood are warmer;
> But being spent, the worse, and worst
>   Times still succeed the former.

Again there is nothing un-Christian in this sentiment—it is quite in harmony with most phases of Reformation thought about the condition of the world. The cumulative effect of the triply diversified argument gives emphasis to the final stanza:

[37] Robert Herrick, *Poetical Works*, ed. L. C. Martin (Oxford, 1956), p. 84.

> Then be not coy, but use your time;
>   And while ye may, goe marry:
> For having lost but once your prime,
>   You may for ever tarry.

The logical extension of these earlier arguments implicit in this stanza's opening: "Then be not coy, . . ." is much more decisive than Ronsard's more casual "Donc, si vous me croyez mignonne, . . . cueillez vostre jeunesse." Ronsard's concession, "si vous me croyez," is conversational, but it weakens the power and continuity of the argument. On the other hand, Herrick's unexpectedly detached, organizing mind slackens the pace of the poem.

It is Waller who manages to strike a pose sustaining almost all the potentialities of the theme in one of his poems. Its first stanza keeps the explicit setting of the garden from both Ausonius' and Ronsard's poems, and the immediacy and naturalness of the latter:

> Sees not my love how time resumes
> The glory which he lent these flowers?
> Though none should taste of their perfumes,
> Yet must they live but some few hours;
> Time what we forbear devours.[38]

However, Waller does not linger over these sonorous traditional images as does Herrick in his second stanza. The significant generalization comes at the end of Waller's first stanza. His second one directs the generalization to human nature in particular, with a subtle change of tone:

> Had Helen, or the Egyptian queen,
> Been ne'er so thrifty of their graces,
> Those beauties must at length have been

[38] Edmund Waller, *Poems*, ed. G. Thorn Drury (London, 1905), I, 113.

> The spoil of age, which finds out faces
> In the most retired places.

There is a delicate blend of rhetorical emphasis, through the alliteration of "Had Helen" and "finds out faces," with good-humored satire, which derives more from the quaint sound of the double rhymes, "graces," "faces," "places," than from the vocabulary, since only "thrifty" carries mocking overtones. The sentiment is weighted, however, by the sonorous allusions to antiquity. The third stanza is the least effective, as it merely clarifies the ideas of the first two by stressing that forbearance and sacrifice do not soften fate's effect:

> Should some malignant planet bring
> A barren drought, or ceaseless shower,
> Upon the autumn or the spring,
> And spare us neither fruit nor flower;
> Winter would not stay an hour.

The poem's approach to the topic of the mistress' severity is sharply heralded by the allusion to the "malignant planet" which is the counterpart of her hostility to the poet's fertile love. The last stanza firmly directs the argument at the lady herself:

> Could the resolve of love's neglect
> Preserve you from the violation
> Of coming years, then more respect
> Were due to so divine a fashion,
> Nor would I indulge my passion.

The analogies with Marvell's irony over the "rate" at which his mistress might be loved and the rhetorical conditional tense with which his poem opens, like the last three of Waller's stanzas, show that this poem did not go unnoted by contemporary poets. But there were numerous less poised rearrangements of the motif in the seventeenth century.

What is to be learned here from Ronsard, Herrick, and Waller is that an urbane encouragement to a woman to live to the full was possible to non-pagan poets without archaism. But only the absence of blunt sensuality in this form of the genre permitted its use by their discreet tastes without breaking the classical mold. There is also an unmistakable change in the treatment of the topic. While the classical manner of using it subordinated sensuality to prettiness, thus permitting its survival in the most modest society, the later poets develop the effectiveness of the argument at the expense of its picturesqueness. Thus even such pretty poems as Herrick's and Waller's have a certain residual moral tension and seriousness in their structure, which typifies their age, and is lacking in their classical models. Words like "dying," "worst," "devours," "malignant," "barren," "violation" import the seriousness of Catullus into this prettier style, giving the poems a greater immediacy and urgency than Ausonius had. The modern poets are careful to keep out any pagan allusion which would violate a Christian world picture. The precision of execution involved in this accomplishment is a virtue of the poems, but it renders them marginal to the serious love poetry of the time, which accepts a direct encounter with the complex moral issues of the day.

A more typical and explicit classical plea for sexual indulgence proved less fully adaptable to postclassical tastes. A passage offering such an alien precedent appears in Ovid's *Ars Amatoria:*

> Dum facit ingenium, petite hinc praecepta, puellae,
> Quas pudor et leges et sua iura sinunt.
> Venturae memores iam nunc estote senectae:
> Sic nullum vobis tempus abibit iners.
> Dum licet, et vernos etiamnum educitis annos,
> Ludite: eunt anni more fluentis aquae;

Nec quae praeteriit, iterum revocabitur unda,
  Nec quae praeteriit, hora redire potest.
Utendum est aetate: cito pede labitur aetas,
  Nec bona tam sequitur, quam bona prima fuit. . . .[39]

(III, 57-66)

(While [Cytherea] inspires me, seek here the precepts, O women, which propriety and the laws of your own rights allow. Now already be mindful of the old age which is to come; thus no hour will slip wasted from you. While you can, and still are in your spring-time, have your sport; for the years pass like flowing water; the wave that has gone by cannot be called back, the hour that has gone by cannot return. You must employ your time: time glides on with speedy foot, nor is that which follows so good as that which went before. . . .)

These lines have several points of importance. The qualification of the second line is crucial—here we have no "virgins" or a lady like Ronsard's or Waller's, but the class of demimondaines who enjoyed special liberties in Rome like the hetairai of classical Greece. Secondly, the terms throughout are wholly temporal and material. Neither in this passage nor the long development which follows it are transcendent or spiritual values given the least weight. Lastly, the passage may fairly be considered as a unit despite its place in the full elegy because it is unified by a stylistic device—the repetitions of "dum" and "nec." Set this passage against one written in a spirit of classical versifying during the sixteenth century like this written by Octavius:

Dum manet incolumis, dum florida, dum viget iuventus,
  Caretque rugis, dum cutis serena,

[39] Ovid, *The Art of Love*, Loeb edn., trans. J. H. Mozley (London, 1929), p. 122.

Vtere, diua, choris et cantibus, et chely sonora,
   Laetosque spernas neu fugax amores.
Semper adest, semper mors imminet, ominbusque; dicit
   Gaudete nunc, cras forte non licebit.[40]

(While youth remains whole, while it flowers, while it blooms, and lacks wrinkles, while you are smooth skinned, lady, enjoy yourself with dancing and singing and resonant lyre and do not reject happiness, fleeing love. Always death advances, always it is close, and to all people; it says, "Enjoy yourself now, tomorrow perhaps it will not be permitted.")

The rhetorical flow of Ovid is visibly emulated in the repetitions of "dum" and "semper." On the other hand the poet is addressing no woman of easy virtue, but a "diva" or lady, as his more modest, less flippant tone suggests. Her presence reveals that society's standards are no longer so arbitrary and schizophrenic as those of the era of Ovid (and Caesar's wife), but it also qualifies the poet's expectations. "Dancing and singing" sound more innocent than Ovid's "sports," though they may well be euphemisms, and love is mentioned only at the end of the list. As for spiritual values, the poet steers round the question dexterously in his ambiguous "cras forte non licebit." "Tomorrow perhaps it will not be permitted" neatly covers both the possibilities of old age and eternity. Marvell's "To his Coy Mistress" equally maintains this high social status of the poet's "lady" and the rhetorical pattern of Ovid, which survives in the repeated "now" of Marvell's last paragraph. However, as we have observed, the puritan poet finds no means of integrating spiritual values into his poem, and the failure to take into account the spiritual and theological issues raised by his pagan picture may well have been a serious limitation for fully aware contemporary readers, including the

[40] *Delitiae cc. Italorum Poetarum*, ed. R. Gherus (Frankfurt, 1608), II, 138.

"lady." It ensures a lack of authenticity and actuality which makes it—like the earlier Renaissance invitation to song and dance, music and love—more charming than challenging.

Marvell avoided the difficulty of adjusting the sensual demands of his poem to contemporary moral values by suppressing the latter. Jasper Mayne's stylish ode on the same theme produces a different impression. It starts briskly, indeed, on the familiar topic of material decay:

> Time is a feathered thing,
>   And whilst I praise
> The sparkling of thy looks and call them rays,
>   Takes wing,
>   Leaving behind him as he flies
> An unperceivëd dimness in thine eyes.[41]

This leads to the inevitable invitation to physical delights; but Mayne is less careful than Marvell to sustain the archaic pagan frame of reference, and he concludes with the Neo-Platonic ecstasy of a Vaughan returned to amatory verse:

> Let the heavens new motions feel
> And by our embraces wheel.
>   And whilst we try the way,
>   By which Love doth convey
>   Soul into soul,
>   And mingling so
>   Makes them such raptures know
>   As makes them entrancëd lie
>   In mutual ecstasy,
> Let the harmonious spheres in music roll.

The disconnection between this poem's preliminary sensual concerns and its almost mystical conclusion illustrates the obsolescence of the plea for sexual satisfaction as a suitable

---

[41] *Seventeenth Century Lyrics,* ed. N. Ault (New York, 1950), p. 229.

vehicle for postmedieval sensibility. None of Donne's best
poems show quite this ambiguity—either they have an underlying consistency of serious attitude, or the metaphorical bra-
vado of the allusions is evident throughout. But Mayne wants
to demand both the sensual satisfaction of a conventionally
frustrated lover and the spiritual communion of ecstatic sympathies, without making any serious effort to disentangle the
paradox that this involves in traditional thought. The spiritual
communion of the conclusion is wholly incompatible with
the naïve aims of the opening. Marvell was less contemporary
but more tactful.

Many poets who, by contrast to Mayne, were aware of the
difficulties of the traditional and now archaic plea for love
avoided attempting it seriously by such witty evasions as
Donne uses in "The Flea," where the intention is more to
achieve piquancy than realism. Less dazzling but equally dis-
tracting is Kynaston's opening to this lyric, obviously founded
on Catullus:

> Dear Cynthia, though thou bear'st the name
>   Of the pale Queen of Night,
> Who changing yet is still the same,
>   Renewing still her light:
> Who monthly doth herself conceal,
>   And her bright face doth hide,
> That she may to Endymion steal,
>   And kiss him unespied.
>
> Do not thou so, not being sure,
>   When this thy beauty's gone,
> Thou such another canst procure,
>   And wear it as thine own, . . .[42]

The witty exploitation of the lady's name and the Endymion
story masks skillfully the outmoded stereotype which governs

[42] Saintsbury, II, 171.

its movement. This concealment of archaic purpose by modern virtuosity is also the characteristic of one of Ronsard's subtler sonnets which argues:

> Si la beauté se perd, fais-en part de bonne heure,
> Tandis qu'en son printempts tu la vois fleuronner.
> Si elle ne se perd, ne crain point de donner
> A tes amis le bien qui tousjours to demeure. . . .[48]

(If beauty fades, use it soon while you see it flower in its springtime: if it does not fade, do not fear to give to your friends the good which will always remain with you. . . .)

This neat logic might well dazzle the victim into accepting what is in fact only a specious argument, to which even Ronsard fails to give full weight in the rest of the poem. It was left to Carew to recognize the hypnotic virtuosity of the argument and give it pride of place in his poem:

> If the quick spirits in your eye
> Now languish, and anon must dye;
> If every sweet, and every grace,
> Must fly from that forsaken face,
>   Then (*Celia*) let us reape our joyes,
>   E're time such goodly fruit destroyes.
>
> Or, if that golden fleece must grow
> For ever, free from aged snow;
> If those bright Suns must know no shade,
> Nor your fresh beauties ever fade:
> Then feare not (*Celia*) to bestow,
> What still being gather'd, still must grow.
>   Thus, either *Time* his Sickle brings
>   In vaine, or else in vaine his wings.[44]

The exquisite facility of this verse, coupled with the poise of the logic, makes this a distinguished poem. But it evokes a wholly false situation since the first conclusion clashes with contemporary religious thought and attempts no resolution of this conflict, while the second clashes with all conventional experience. The poetic virtuosity of such a poem thus isolates itself from a truly dramatic situation and approximates that "literary" quality detected in certain dream poems. What was once a practical issue is finally surrendered to a primarily aesthetic intention, a typical fate for many basic classical themes in the seventeenth century.

The problem in all the poems so far discussed in this section remains the same. A Renaissance poet writing a "carpe diem" admonition has to pretend he has no knowledge of the teachings of Christianity, if he is to maintain his models' predatory intentions. Logically, however, there is an alternative, though it changes the theme radically. It is to recognize the power of ethical or metaphysical arguments for chastity, but to vindicate a materialistic or sensual view of life by refuting them. Mere cynicism, such as supports Henry Bold and other libertine poetasters of the time, will not do if the poem is to have distinction. This solution involves, rather, the fullest expression of the author's powers as a thinker, as well as the most effective versifying. To see what resources such a poem must draw on it is only necessary to compare Carew's above-quoted "Persuasions to Enjoy" with the following poem by an obscure poet, Thomas Weaver, called "To Jean of Chipping Norton," a quaint but convincingly precise title in comparison with Carew's gracefully anonymous one:

> Tell me no more that Chastity
> 'mongst Vestals did reside,
> Or that in Cels or Cloysters shee
> doth chiefly now abide:

Where Vowes make chast, it may be sed
An Oath is rather kept, then Maiden-head.

They that with bolted doors and spies,
    from temptings are secur'd,
Or in their own deformities
    more safely are immur'd:
Such Virgins rather may be sed
Not to have lost, then kept their Maiden-head.

Give me a Girle whom Gold doth wooe,
    fit time and place allure,
That from her own warm temper too
    temptations doth endure;
If she stand firm, it may be sed,
That she hath truly kept her Maiden-head.

The praise (sweet *Jean*) to be thus chast
    hath long been due to thee,
But what was Vertue yet at last
    may prove necessity:
Resign it then e're it be sed
That thou hast too long kept thy Maiden-head.[45]

One sees that this poem works in quite different dimensions, not merely of ethical, but of psychological awareness from Ovid's advice, or even Marvell's. It shows a subtle sense of the poised, unconstricted nature of true virtue, reminiscent of Carew's praise of his "unsanctified mistress"; but its conclusion adds a very modern perception—that principle is dangerous if too exclusive in its operation. Weaver advocates a poised chastity which can recognize a proper occasion to surrender—though Weaver does not openly offer marriage. To see how truly contemporary Weaver's poem was, one has only to compare it with one of the most famous pieces of English prose,

[45] Thomas Weaver, *Songs and Poems* (London, 1654), p. 57.

which appeared ten years earlier. In *Areopagitica* Milton had written:

> As therefore the state of man now is, what wisdom can there be to choose, what continence to forbear without the knowledge of evil? He that can apprehend and consider vice with all her baits and seeming pleasures, and yet abstain, and yet distinguish, and yet prefer that which is truly better, he is the true warfaring Christian. I cannot praise a fugitive and cloistered virtue, unexercised and unbreathed, that never sallies out and sees her adversary, but slinks out of the race, where that immortal garland is to be run for, not without dust and heat.[46]

Ironically, behind Milton's puritan self-confidence lies a sly aside from Montaigne, who records that:

> A Queen of our time wittily said that "to repel these approaches was a testimony of weakness, and an accusation of her own facility; and that lady who had not been tempted could not vaunt her chastity."[47]

Montaigne goes on to claim that, as Weaver urges, honor "is quite able, without transgressing, to relax its severity, and give itself a freer rein."

Weaver is thus suavely absorbing some of the most sophisticated (if potentially dangerous) ideas of his own age and the major influences on it. Carew's "Persuasions" has no contact with thought on this level and it is the poorer for this, as is Marvell's ode. Weaver brings the plea for love fully up to date, and his redeployment of a Miltonic sentiment so neatly to serve an ancient and previously outmoded theme is at least as considerable an achievement as Carew's detection and ex-

[46] *Selected Prose of John Milton*, ed. Malcolm W. Wallace (Oxford, 1925), p. 290.
[47] *The Essays of Montaigne*, trans. E. J. Trechman (Oxford, n.d.), II, 320.

pansion of a brilliant stroke in a Ronsard sonnet, or Marvell's imposition of logical sequence on the conventional elements of Catullian invitations to dalliance.

Only such intellectual recognition of the real views of contemporary society could have redeemed the plea for love from the picturesque superficiality, or cynical crudeness, to which it seemed doomed in the high Renaissance. To expect an outright refutation of Christian ethics from a would-be seducer is more than our historical knowledge of the age, with its horror of heresy let alone atheism, would permit. In fact, however, Christian opinion about sex has always been more proscriptive than regulatory,[48] and few poems in the seventeenth century bother to attempt to challenge deeply seated dogmatic church beliefs. The spiritualizing of sexual love was much more the role of Neo-Platonic thought, which grafted a metaphysical structure on to troubadour sentiment. It was with the precise, regulated affections of Platonists like Lorenzo de' Medici and Pontus de Tyard rather than Christian conventions that most seducers had to cope as a traditional opposition to sensuality in love. And while it would be outrageous if not dangerous to attack Christian doctrine, no one could be offended if one attacked and refuted the pagan philosopher who inspired many of the attitudes of Petrarchan verse. Thus the form taken by serious vindications of the pagan "carpe diem" poem, or the more explicit plea for sexual indulgence, was frequently that of an "anti-Platonic" argument. This possibility, once recognized, allowed the poets to standardize a fully articulated scene between lovers, based on the tense and well-defined relationship of the eager but subtle male and his Platonic mistress. Of course there were many pseudophilosophic prose precedents for this situation, dating back perhaps to Alcibiades' speech in the *Symposium*, but in the sixteenth cen-

[48] See St. Paul, 1 Corinthians 7, which the New English Bible renders as "It is a good thing for a man to have nothing to do with women."

tury the balance in such arguments begins to swing in favor
of the more physical view of love, as we see in such typical
exchanges as those in Ebreo's *Dialoghi d'Amore*, where the
lover (Philo) has frequently the advantage of the lady
(Sophia). Ronsard characteristically attempts an early version
of the theme in one of his *Sonnets pour Hélène*:

> Bienque l'esprit humain s'enfle par la doctrine
> De Platon, qui vante influxion des Cieux,
> Si est-ce sans le corps qu'il seroit ocieux,
> Et auroit beau louer sa celeste origine.
>
> Par les sens l'ame voit, ell' oyt, ell' imagine,
> Ell' a ses actions du corps officieux;
> L'esprit incorporé devient ingenieux,
> La matiere le rend plus parfait et plus digne.
>
> Or' vous aimez l'esprit, et sans discretion
> Vous dites que des corps les amours sont pollues.
> Tel dire n'est sinon qu'imagination,
>
> Qui embrasse le faux pour les choses cognues,
> Et c'est renouveller la fable d'Ixion
> Qui se passoit de vent et n'aimoit que des nues.[49]

(Although the human spirit puffs itself up with the Platonic doctrine which boasts heavenly inspiration, such it is
that without the body it would be dormant and would
praise in vain its celestial origins. By the senses the soul
sees, it hears, it imagines, and receives its motions from the
serviceable body. The incarnate spirit becomes skilful, matter makes it more perfect and noble. Now you love the spirit,
and you say without discretion that loves are tainted by the
body. Such an observation is nothing but fantasy, which
seizes illusions as known objects; and it is to renew the fable
of Ixion who satisfied himself with the wind, and made love
only to clouds.)

[49] Cohen, I, 236.

Though the tone is that of a pedantic philosophic debate, lacking fire and urgency like Petrarch's sonnet in the previous section and concluded by a stale piece of mythology neatly but not wittily applied, the piece remains significant because it has shape and purpose of a kind which inspires better compositions by later poets. The evolution of the theme in the next century is vividly illustrated by Cartwright's vivacious "No Platonic Love":

> Tell me no more of minds embracing minds,
>   And hearts exchang'd for hearts;
> That spirits meet, as winds do winds,
>   And mix their subtlest parts;
> That two unbodi'd essences may kiss,
> And then, like angels, twist and feel one bliss.
>
> I was that silly thing that once was wrought
>   To practise this thin love;
> I climb'd from sex to soul, from soul to thought;
>   But thinking there to move,
> Headlong I rowl'd from thought to soul, and then
> From soul I lighted at the sex agen.
>
> As some strict down-look'd men pretend to fast,
>   Who yet in closets eat;
> So lovers who profess they spirits taste,
>   Feed yet on grosser meat;
> I know they boast they souls to souls convey,
> How e'r they meet, the body is the way.
>
> Come, I will undeceive thee, they that tread
>   Those vain aëriall waies,
> Are like young heyrs, and alchymists misled
>   To waste their wealth and days,

For searching thus to be for ever rich
They only find a med'cine for the itch.[50]

The tone here is brisk and personal. The point is made as efficiently as in Ronsard, without his elaborate explanations. The difference between the two poems is well illustrated by the subdued conditional clause with which Ronsard's opens and the aggressive, dramatic imperative which Cartwright's borrows from an English lyric convention.[51]

Cartwright's poem owes more to English models than just its first line. In one of Sidney's sonnets,[52] the lover had admitted that in Stella lay "all vice's overthrow," but still he ended desperately: "But ah, Desire still cries: 'Give me some food!'" Such authentic violence of feeling is one of the ways in which English poets typically endowed interesting foreign conventions with dramatic color. Poems like these are the only convincingly contemporary pleas for physical love in the Renaissance, even though they show a move, by their reasoned vindication of sensuality, away from the elementary material issues of pagan pleas for love. They show also an analytic power and a sense of dramatic tension which is more challenging to us than the pagan poets are, because the issues are more complex. To the familiar problems of coyness and propriety, a whole battery of philosophical and psychological concerns has been added, even though initially one might conclude such verses were merely pagan. It is the failure to understand the presence of this new vigorous dialectic in all lyric verse, but particularly in the new form of the plea for love, which has led to misestimates such as Sullivan's. One twentieth-century commentator observes typically, of such down-

[50] W. Cartwright, *Comedies, Tragi-Comedies, with Other Poems* (London, 1651), p. 246.
[51] See pp. 107ff.
[52] *Silver Poets*, p. 199.

to-earth challenges to Platonic affectation as Cartwright's—
"the claims of the[se] opponents [of Platonic love] are expressed in all the grossness of Restoration immorality."[53] On
the contrary, they mark an interesting and salutary reaction
to the sentimentality in the new range of subjective concerns
opening to lyric poets, but a reaction which yet retains the
logical finesse which had vindicated the extension of sensibility in these new directions. There are possibilities and dangers in such attitudes and poetry that were scarcely dreamed
of in classical times.

[v]

The approach toward physical consummation of love is the
most poetically productive part of all love affairs. The demands made by the various inevitable phases of a developing
relationship have crystallized the well-defined themes we have
so far examined. Obviously four such focal themes as thoughts
of future love, the character of a new sexual relationship,
dreams about love, and pleas for indulgence do not in any
sense exhaust the possibilities of an evolving love affair. They
are, however, basic expressions of sensual desire in its least
sublimated forms, and round them cluster a group of lesser
themes that are closely related. Each, for example, has a less
popular feminine approximation or corollary, whose popularity
significantly increases during the Renaissance as a symptom of
the enhanced status of women. The character of one's future
lover is freely canvassed by supposed or actual female poets.
The lover's compensatory dream finds its counterpart in the
poet's conception of how delights once either shared or, more
likely, missed are recalled by women. And, while the man is
at a loss for words in the presence of his mistress, she in-

[53] J. S. Harrison, *Platonism in English Poetry* (New York, 1903),
p. 162.

stinctively takes flight from the possibility of love whether attracted to the man or not. When the lover urges the need for indulgence, she explains (in the Renaissance at least) the social, ethical, or metaphysical reasons for not doing so. There are also many other more oblique ways to approach the basic topics of which these feminine themes are offshoots. The plea for love may take the form of an invitation to get up in the morning for a country walk, when the poet may draw interesting morals from nature, like those found in *aubades* such as Herrick's "Corinna's going a Maying." Or it may be the conscious attempt at arousing lust which characterizes Carew's "A Rapture." The discussion of all the earlier stages of a love affair is capable of similar diversification and extension. Further, the mode of exposition of these themes is very flexible. The same theme may be described or dramatized; it may be analyzed objectively, portrayed from the perspective of the man, the woman, or an observer; the poet may address his reader or readers, his beloved, the lover, himself, or even an inanimate object. It will be seen that with all these possibilities the number of standard permutations begins to approach the range of actual poetic performance in treating the most urgent aspects of love in an explicit manner.

With the negative aspects of love, however, the possibilities are much more limited. Hence the conspicuous conventionality of the form of the love lament. Here perhaps the merely compensatory function of the poetry minimizes the author's power of creative thought, as the frustrated lover customarily adopts a very standardized exclamatory style. This is a characteristic postclassical theme, for the positive role (for good or evil) of women is much advanced in most commemorations of a failed relationship, as we see in the heroines of poems like Wyatt's "They flee from me." The deserted mistress is also a familiar figure in the verse of all sentimental poets, from Ovid's *Heroides* to Tennyson's "Mariana." Most of these poems

are more pathetic than creative, just as the plaintive whimper-
ings of many rejected poets clarify why they suffer the repulse
they now bemoan. With few exceptions such poems do not
deserve our attention here. They lack creative and evolving
expression of a kind that would help our discussion.

On the other hand, some of the more virile and imaginative
poets have found inspiration to develop a more impressive
poetic pattern when placed in this situation of a failed love
relationship. They have done so because instead of abject
negation they have rallied their spirits to challenge and attack
the causes of their defeat, much as Wyatt does at the end of
"They flee from me." This mood of indignation gives vigor to
their writing, and the argumentative brace they seek to give
their feelings lends creative interest to their ideas. The key
theme in this vein is an assault on the attitudes of women
toward love. It may be that the creative energy which these
authors normally directed toward the realization of passionate
sexual desire is sublimated into a purposeful anger unknown
to more anemic writers. It is revealing that most of these
poems presuppose that the lover has succeeded to some extent
in winning his lady's love in the past. The plaintive laments
censured and dismissed earlier are usually the handiwork of
lovers who have totally failed in their aspirations, which leaves
them with little right to complain. The dynamic theme of rejection thus narrows itself to an attack on the folly and fickleness of women.

The least dramatic form that the theme can take is an ingenious sequence of comparisons which picturesquely illuminate the nature of woman. A typical epigram is quoted in
The Return from Parnassus:

> Quid pluma leuius? Flamen. Quid flamine? Ventus.
> Quid vento? Mulier. Quid muliere? Nihil.[54]

[54] *The Parnassus Plays*, ed. J. B. Leishman (London, 1949), p. 201.

(What is lighter than a feather? Flame. What than flame?
Wind. What than wind? Woman. What than woman?
Nothing.)

This kind of thing could be spun out into elaborate patterns
or condensed into epigrams based on various images; but the
theme lacks real diversity in this form, with the exception of
Horace's magnificent fifth ode of Book i, where the watery
fluctuations of Pyrrha's temper are translated into the seas of
which Horace, as an experienced pilot, affects to take leave.
This *tour de force* was never surpassed by any of Horace's
imitators or translators, though these include poets of the stat-
ure of Milton.

Much more interesting from our point of view than most
such witty poetic assessments of women are the curses called
down on the heads of stubborn or fickle women by their re-
sentful lovers. Though Horace once again occupies a conspicuous position in the tradition, one can see the germ of it lurking
in an epigram ascribed, a little unexpectedly, to Plato:

Ἡ σοβαρὸν γελάσασα καθ᾽ Ἑλλάδος, ἥ ποτ᾽ ἐραστῶν
   ἑσμὸν ἐνὶ προθύροις Λαῒς ἔχουσα νέων,
τῇ Παφίῃ τὸ κατόπτρον· ἐπεὶ τοίη μὲν ὁρᾶσθαι
   οὐκ ἐθέλω, οἵη δ᾽ἦν πάρος οὐ δύναμαι.

(She that laughed so disdainfully at Greece, she that once
kept a swarm of young lovers at her door, Lais offers this
mirror to the Paphian because she has no wish to see herself as she is, and cannot see herself as she was.)[55]

The dexterity of the epigram lies not in its explicit content but
in its implied moral. One whose beauty spurs her pride may
expect finally to scorn herself. While Horace's use of this
theme is much better known than Plato's, it is cruder, longer,
less individualized:

[55] *Greek Elegy and Iambus,* trans. J. M. Edmonds, ii, 8-9.

O crudelis adhuc et Veneris muneribus potens,
insperata tuae cum veniet pluma superbiae
et, quae nunc umeris involitant, deciderint comae,
nunc et qui color est puniceae flore prior rosae
mutatus, Ligurine, in faciem verterit hispidam:
dices "heu," quotiens te speculo videris alterum,
"quae mens est hodie, cur eadem non puero fuit,
vel cur his animis incolumes non redeunt genae?" (IV, x)

(O thou, cruel still and dowered with Venus' gifts, when unexpected down shall come upon thy pride and the locks have fallen that now wave upon thy shoulders, and the bloom that now outvies the blossom of the crimson rose has faded, Ligurinus, and changed to shaggy visage, then as often as thou gazest in the mirror on thy altered features, thou shalt say: "Alas! why lacked I as a lad the purpose that I have today? Or why to my present spirit do not my rosy cheeks return?")[56]

The poem has not gained in vividness by dramatizing a particular relationship, and the forecast of merited ruin is weaker than Plato's demonstration of its effective arrival. The power of the argument for a boy is also weaker than for a woman because, while a beautiful woman normally declines irrevocably into a less beautiful one, a beautiful boy may well mature into a yet more attractive man, along the lines, for example, of Alcibiades. In one of his elegies (III, xxvii) Propertius indeed conserved the timing of Horace's poem but also the female figure of Plato, including the mirror theme to enforce the concern with physical beauty. Nevertheless, Horace's ode was the more popular model for later poets. Lesser lyricists merely translated Horace, as did Bembo in a well-known sonnet and Sherburne in a shorter lyric. Ronsard, however,

[56] Horace, *Odes and Epodes*, Loeb edn., trans. C. E. Bennett (London, 1947), pp. 324-325.

showed more independence and graciousness in his celebrated sonnet:

Quand vous serez bien vieille, au soir à la chandelle,
Assise aupres du feu, devidant et filant,
Direz, chantant mes vers, en vous esmerveillant:
"Ronsard me celebroit du temps que j'estois belle."
    Lors vous n'aurez servante oyant telle nouvelle,
Desja sous le labeur à demy sommeillant,
Qui au bruit de Ronsard ne s'aille resveillant
Benissant vostre nom de louange immortelle.
    Je serai sous la terre et, fantôme sans os
Par le ombres myrteux je prendray mon repos;
Vous serez au fouyer une vieille accroupie,
    Regrettant mon amour et vostre fier desdain.
Vivez, si m'en croyez, n'attendez à demain:
Cueillez dés aujourdhuy les roses de la vie.[57]

(When you are really old, in the evening sitting by candlelight near the fire winding and spinning, you will say, singing my lines with wonder: "Ronsard praised me when I was beautiful." Then you will not have a servant hearing such words who, already half asleep with the work, will not waken at the sound of Ronsard's name, blessing your name in immortal praise. I shall be beneath the earth and, a phantom without bones, asleep in the myrtles' shade; you will be by the hearth, a bent old woman, lamenting my love, and your fierce disdain. Live, if you will believe it from me, do not wait for tomorrow: pluck the roses of life from this day on.)

The anticipated scene of beauty's decay is evoked here with the same attention to concrete detail that gives immediacy to Plato's miniature episode. The melancholy future is made the

[57] Cohen, I, 260.

immediate present of both poems; the actual beauty of the women lies lost in the poems' past. For his vaguer future scene Horace fails to catch such vivid details as does Ronsard's night setting, the candlelight, and the tedious wool-spinning (all probably ingeniously redeployed from Tibullus, I, iii). These details are as brilliantly invoked as Plato's vision of the revulsion of the aged courtesan from her own mirror. In the French sonnet the poet emerges, moreover, as a distinct character, which he fails totally to do in either the Horatian ode or the epigram. Ronsard's complacent and justified satisfaction in his poetic prowess is firmly communicated but offset tactfully by his sense of his own mortality. Only the abrupt reversion to the "carpe diem" admonition in the last two lines may seem unnecessarily conventional and awkward. In most other ways Ronsard's sonnet is much more complex than the classical poems: the relation is more completely communicated; the status of the poet is boldly asserted; and the chronology moves easily between the differing time perspectives of Greek and Latin poems. However, Ronsard is indebted for his success at least partly to his classical masters.

Ronsard was not the only Renaissance poet to exploit these effects of Horace and Propertius. Wyatt, twenty years Ronsard's senior, had also woven the theme dexterously into his censorius song "My lute awake!" After establishing the context of betrayal in an address to his lute, Wyatt deftly switches his remarks to the lady herself:

> Prowd of the spoyll that thou hast gott
> Of simple hertes thorough loves shot,
>   By whome, vnkynd, thou hast theim wone,
> Thinck not he haith his bow forgot,
>   All tho my lute and I have done.
>
> Vengeaunce shall fall on thy disdain,
> That makest but game on ernest pain;

Thinck not alone vnder the sonne
Vnquyt to cause thy lovers plain,
　　All tho my lute and I have done.

Perchaunce the lye wethered and old,
In wynter nyghtes that are so cold,
　　Playnyng in vain vnto the mone;
Thy wisshes then dare not be told;
　　Care then who lyst, for I have done.

And then my chaunce the to repent
The tyme that thou hast lost and spent
　　To cause thy lovers sigh and swoune;
Then shalt thou knowe beaultie but lent,
　　And wisshe and want as I have done.[58]

We are back in Horace's time sequence, looking toward the future, but Wyatt's intense indignation, powerfully enforced by a sense of moral propriety lacking in Horace's poem, transcends the Roman poet's emphasis. The word "vengeaunce" thunders out at the start of the second stanza quoted. The next is equally vivid—the setting of the mistress in bed during a winter's night is focused by the simple sensory detail of "that are so cold." There is also a careful psychological stroke in "Thy wisshes then dare not be told" which stresses a loss of mental poise in the woman matching her physical decline. Both these effects are hinted at in other odes of Horace, triumphing over faithless and now actually decayed women; but, as a whole, Wyatt's poem is a bold and free rendering of the classical tradition, less compact and effective than Ronsard's, but clearly superior to Bembo's free translation. Wyatt's distinctive contribution remains his sense of love as a function of man's moral sensibility—an awareness alien to Horace and most pagan love poets and often denied, as here, to Ronsard.

[58] Muir, p. 50.

On the other hand, the Petrarchan tradition outside England lacked the vulgar energy that Wyatt shares with the most overpowering of Horace's odes, that denouncing Lyce (IV, xiii).

Wyatt's poem is an important precedent (another is Ovid's *Ibis*, 153-158) for the culmination of this kind of traditional reproach or threat which comes in Donne's poem "The Apparition." This is a brilliant caricature of the familiar attitudes of the indignant lover. Wyatt had warned the lady not to think that her cruelty would pass "unquit," even though Wyatt might cease his complaints. Donne takes up this theme:

> When by thy scorne, O murdresse I am dead,
> And that thou thinkst thee free
> From all solicitation from mee,
> Then shall my ghost come to thy bed,
> And thee, fain'd vestall, in worse armes shall see;
> Then thy sick taper will begin to winke,
> And he, whose thou art then, being tyr'd before,
> Will, if thou stirre, or pinch to wake him, thinke
> > Thou call'st for more,
> And in false sleepe will from thee shrinke,
> And then poore Aspen wretch, neglected thou
> Bath'd in a cold quicksilver sweat wilt lye
> > A veryer ghost than I;
> What I will say, I will not tell thee now,
> Lest that preserve thee'; and since my love is spent,
> I'had rather thou shouldst painfully repent,
> Then by my threatnings rest still innocent.[59]

The poem is a triumph of poetic ingenuity, and by that very fact it is not to be taken too seriously. In it the tradition of cursing an intransigent mistress is made ridiculous by a conscious exaggeration that reveals the mere resentment of the lover's attitude. Donne deftly mingles Ronsard's condition as

[59] Grierson, p. 43.

a "fantôme sans os" with a practical development of Wyatt's
jibe at his mistress, "thy wishes then dare not be told," to produce a Rabelaisian melodrama. But the ending of Donne's
monologue almost deliberately exposes the artifice of the
whole situation. Donne's lover starts expecting to die from his
lady's scorn, but concludes that, since he no longer loves her,
he will conceal the horror of his ghostly curse in order to avoid
compelling her to love virtuously now. As he no longer loves
her any more, why should her scorn still turn him to a ghost?
The inconsequence of the speech is one of its most picturesque
touches, but it hardly permits one to treat this lover as seriously as the one in Wyatt's poem "My lute awake." In fact,
as we shall see, the hint of burlesque in Donne's poem suggests that passionate resentment of a mistress' behavior, such
as led to the dire prophecies of earlier poets, is already too
naïve a sentiment to be acceptable in seventeenth-century cir-
cles. There are few later poems which treat vehement curses
of fickle women as a suitable vehicle for poetic and psychological insights. A new, more complex vehicle would be needed
for the subtlest thought of the times. In the recapitulation,
on a more immediate level of experience, of such classical
forms of lyric expression as the lover's admonition to his aloof
beloved, a recapitulation leading often to parody and finally
to abandonment of the convention, we have an illustration of
the evolution of sensibility which it is our purpose to demonstrate. In due course we shall see with what new formulas
such classic situations were replaced.

[v i]

The ultimate conclusion of love affairs is frequently a repudiation of the mistress, but this gesture often implies equally
a flight from love in general. The lover's flight itself almost
invariably ends in further humiliation, a recommencement of

the sequence of love relationships which we have been tracing. Bearing this in mind poets have added a third subject to the themes of witty images for fickleness and of open denunciation of the betrayer. The third, most introverted reaction to female inconstancy illustrates how the beginning of one cycle grafts on to the end of the previous one. The pathetic vacillations of Catullus in the later stages of his love for Lesbia are a good illustration of how a lover's revulsion and renewed desire coexist during a period of disillusionment with women. "Odi et amo" has become proverbial. The detailing of such tortures of indecision has since been a fertile topic for poets. In one of his longest love poems Catullus outlines the lover's agonized self-debate in his most elaborate model for these future love poets:

> nam quaecumque homines bene cuiquam aut dicere
>   possunt
>   aut facere, haec a te dictaque factaque sunt;
> omnia quae ingratae perierunt credita menti.
>   quare cur te iam amplius excrucies?
> quin tu animum offirmas atque istinc teque reducsi
>   et dis invitis desinis esse miser?
> difficilest, longum subito deponere amorem.
>   difficile est, verum hoc qualubet efficias
> una salus haec est, hoc est tibi pervincendum;
>   hoc facias, sive id non pote sive pote. (LXXVI, 7-16)

(For whatever kindness man can show to man by word or deed has been done by you. All this was entrusted to an ungrateful heart and is lost: why then should you torment yourself now any more? Why do you not settle your mind firmly, and draw back, and cease to be miserable, in despite of the gods? It is difficult suddenly to lay aside a long-cherished love. It is difficult; but you should accomplish it, one way or another. This is the only safety, this you must carry through, this you must carry through whether it is possible or impossible.)[60]

Catullus' wavering attitudes in successive poems dramatize vividly what is here focused in a single dialogue, significantly with himself—the uncertainty about Lesbia which he faced in real life. Ovid's cruder observations on the subject in the *Amores* seem to carry less the painful authority of experience:

> Multa diuque tuli; vitiis patienta victa est;
>   cede fatigato pectore, turpis amor!
> scilicet adserui iam me fugique catenas,
>   et quae non puduit ferre, tulisse pudet.
> vicimus et domitum pedibus calcamus amorem;
>   venerunt capiti cornua sera meo.
> perfer et obdura! dolor hic tibi proderit olim;
>   saepe tulit lassis sucus amarus opem. (III, xi a, 1-8)

(Much have I endured, and for long time; my wrongs have overcome my patience; withdraw from my tired-out breast, base love! Surely, now I have claimed my freedom, and fled my fetters, ashamed of having borne what I felt no shame while bearing. Victory is mine, and I tread under foot my conquered love; courage has entered my heart, though late. Persist, and endure! this smart will some day bring thee good; oft has bitter potion brought help to the languishing.)[61]

Each of these Latin poets commits himself firmly to one attitude; but behind the self-admonition is a deep-rooted resistance to the intended abandonment of love. And in other apparently contemporaneous poems of each poet the self-disciplining attitude has been given up. This tension is inter-

[60] Loeb edn., trans. F. W. Cornish, pp. 154-157.
[61] Ovid, *Heroides and Amores*, Loeb edn., trans. G. Showerman (London, 1931), pp. 488-489.

esting, but the reader has no doubt in either of the passages quoted as to where the resolution of the poet lies. Despite the effort involved, both poets are seeking to achieve a kind of equilibrium in the resolved state of mind they describe. In this they are followed by a poem linked to Petronius Arbiter, though this solution shows more sophistication. The poet suspends the problem of disillusionment by preventing its development:

> Foeda est in coitu et brevis voluptas,
> et taedet Veneris statim peractae.
> non ergo ut pecudes libidinosae
> caeci protinus irruamus illuc
> (nam languescit amor peritque flamma);
> sed sic sic sine fine feriati
> et tecum iaceamus osculantes.
> hic nullus labor est ruborque nullus:
> hoc iuvit, iuvat et diu iuvabit;
> hoc non deficit incipitque semper.[62]

Ben Jonson translates this faithfully and neatly:

> Doing, a filthy pleasure is, and short;
> And done, we straight repent us of the sport:
> Let us not then rush blindly on unto it:
> For lust will languish, and that heat decay.
> But thus, thus, keeping endless Holy-day,
> Let us together closely lie and kisse,
> There is no labour, nor no shame in this;
> This hath pleas'd, doth please, and long will please;
>   never
> Can this decay, but is beginning ever.[63]

The classical poet's views of the tensions imposed by sexuality are the most sophisticated available in classical love poetry;

[62] Waddell, p. 15.   [63] *Ben Jonson*, VIII, 294.

but they differ in every way from those of typical Renaissance poets, who would find the classical poet's calculated physical diagnosis and solution quite incompatible with their more elevated views and spiritual expectation of love. When Shakespeare encounters the identical problem he cannot solve it with the materialist, physiological efficiency of the pagan poet. The warping of the Renaissance mind by the contrary forces of Christian morality and sensual desire releases an incandescent heat missing from the pagan poems. Shakespeare's sonnet is nevertheless indebted to the tense opening of the classical poet's otherwise facile poem:

> The expense of spirit in a waste of shame
> Is lust in action; and till action, lust
> Is perjured, murderous, bloody, full of blame,
> Savage, extreme, rude, cruel, not to trust,
> Enjoy'd no sooner but despised straight,
> Past reason hunted; and no sooner had
> Past reason hated, as a swallow'd bait
> On purpose laid to make the taker mad;
> Mad in pursuit and in possession so;
> Had, having, and in quest to have, extreme;
> A bliss in proof, and proved, a very woe;
> Before, a joy proposed; behind, a dream.
>   All this the world well knows; yet none knows well
>   To shun the heaven that leads men to this hell.[64] (cxxix)

The tone of this poem has all the authenticity of Catullus, or of Keats's sonnet to Fanny, but it also conforms closely enough to the pattern of the classical poems we have just discussed for significant differences in the attitudes of the two ages involved to emerge clearly.

The persistence of archaic strains in other, even later lyric

[64] Craig, p. 492.

poets is illustrated by Jonson's translation and analogous poems such as Herrick's minute and complacent lyric:

> I'le dote noe more, nor shall mine eyes
> againe
> maintain
> my former Jealousies,
> If I can feare
> noe more her haire
> to fetter mee, twill bee the best
> the noblest Trophy I can reare
> unto my rest:
> Thus perish in mee all my fire of Lust
> only a just
> desire keepe heat in mee
> to bee
> A looker on yet still Liue free.[65]

Such callow self-confidence was incompatible with the committed nature which increasingly characterized Renaissance man after the explosion of intense feelings we call the Reformation. It is from such intense and subjective sources of feeling as the puritans drew on that the volcanic flow of Shakespeare's epithets surges out in his sonnet—springing from a collision of will with experience that is inconceivably violent for classical poets, whose sole cause for concern was a clash not between ideal and fact, but between desire and expediency. By Shakespeare's time the human character has acquired a moral complexity and an energy which, when consciously present at moments of crisis, provoke pangs much more excruciating than the innocent sufferings of Catullus. Neither Catullus nor any classical poet could sustain the intensity of Shakespeare's resentment against ungovernable sexual desire and yet also conserve the high note of generalization, which

[65] Martin, p. 442.

prevents the poem from degenerating into Keatsian incoherence (both of which virtues stem from a deeper sense of moral order than was perhaps possible to a pagan). Horace has Shakespeare's bitterness on occasion; Lucretius talks of sensual love with the same hostile lucidity; but the conjunction in Shakespeare's sonnet of these attitudes, polarized in classical times, illustrates a diversification of the powers of the human mind almost unknown before the sixteenth century. Mr. Sullivan might have claimed with T. S. Eliot that the schizophrenia latent in this kind of duality hardly justifies a feeling that it represents an unmistakable advance from the finite concerns of ancient love poets. However, the potentialities of such new dimensions have not yet been fully discussed here though we have hinted at some of their virtues. So far we have been content merely to recognize that the study of poets' presentations of the self-evident facts of love affairs does show an elaboration of human awareness of their character. The consequences of this elaboration do not lie in simple projection of classical motifs into further permutations such as we have seen but in the addition of a whole new range of human relationships to which classical themes have only a marginal relevance.

[v i i]

With Shakespeare's acid concluding couplet we return unmistakably to the starting point of this chapter. His sonnet is in fact a hostile account of the sexual urge governing all the situations we have discussed. It was suggested in the first chapter that the number of these situations was necessarily finite because, in Aristotle's terms, a lover either has or has not a mistress who does or does not love him to his satisfaction. Though the occasions by which these possibilities may be illustrated are endless, the basic permutations they permit remain standardized, and, while our account in this chapter is in no sense exhaustive, it does fully illustrate the primary possibilities of such themes. It would be hard to find many traditions of the love lyric dating from classical times which cannot be quickly orientated in relation to the topics discussed. It is also true that a marked consistency is apparent in the pattern of evolution of these topics in postclassical times. In the earlier versions of each theme the area of human volition is smaller and the importance of the given facts of each situation is correspondingly more decisive. This means that the earliest poems have a distinct simplicity of mood, with a vividness and clarity of basic detail often lacking in later verse.

These qualities explain Arnold's desire to return to the classics. Arnold, having lost his bearings amidst the complexities and massed data of modern life, hopes to find in the decided sentiments and factual disciplines of classical themes a means of reorientating himself in relation to the basic issues of the human situation. He cannot control the vast potentialities of attitude and circumstance that the accumulated European tradition offers to modern writers. In the Renaissance, on the other hand, the sense of real choice to be made between the pagan and the Christian traditions, or between physical and metaphysical considerations, permits the love poets of the time a freedom to maneuver denied to the classical writers. However, the kind of choice required is not yet so complex as merely to stupefy the poet's mind as does the modern sense of cultural relativity.

In considering the topic of a future mistress, for example, Renaissance poets at their best were better able to define the status and nature of their desires than the classical authors, because the elaborate and unclassical dissection of rarefied states of mind had been practiced by the scholastic philosophers. Though sensual desire is accepted by the Renaissance poets with an almost pagan frankness wholly alien to medieval theologians, it is nevertheless defined in psychological terms that minimize the dangers of misunderstanding the nature of that desire. In the matter of a future mistress the Renaissance poets disassociate the theme from any arbitrary physical predictions and thus give play to subtler, more authentic motives for attraction, such as the need for mutual affection that Donne defines in "Aire and Angels." Equally, in our next topic—the documentation of the lover's sensation in the presence of his mistress—Dante liberated the convention from a mere detailing of physical symptoms and, by developing these into moral ones, showed that the effect of love is more accurately described in psychological terms. He verges here on a conscious discussion of "sublimation." This new intellectual level of analysis in love poetry allows Petrarch, Sidney, and Donne to approach the character of this phase of love more objectively, effectively analyzing its mechanical nature and its social and psychological dangers. The later poets are again more alert to the complexity of the condition and its consequences because Christian dialectic affords a more elaborate mechanism for describing human motives than was available to classical writers and had accustomed literate men to sustain elaborate logical connections from a primary observation or assertion. In relation to the plea for indulgence, Renaissance poets are better at consecutive argument than their prototypes but less at ease in seeking simple sensual satisfaction. When they do justice to the moral awareness of their times and earnestly deflect its imperatives, even if their pleas remain sensual in aim, they are obliged to pay much more scrupulous attention to the attitudes of the women they seek to seduce. Their relationship with women, in literature at least, is thus more exacting, richer in potentialities, and demands a fuller participation of their own personalities than was customary in classical times, when pederasty alone normally brought intellectual equals together in an emotional relationship.

Even the sensual dreams of Renaissance men are more compelling than those of pagan sensualists. The Renaissance lyric poets' powers of fantasy seem greater than their remoter predecessors', and therefore more dangerously seductive unless controlled by a sharp sense of true and false. This necessarily moral sense cannot but heighten the consideration of the lover for his mistress as well as secure him from risking something like schizophrenia. In the context of a much more spiritual view of love, many of the older physical images and patterns of amatory verse cease to carry the full weight of the lover's personality as he tends to express it in his love affairs. If one recognizes that love is not simply the gratification of sensual desire, the failure of the mistress to live up to expectation is not to be handled adequately by a blistering curse, any more than the possession of her body would of itself be wholly satisfying.

Our final impression of lyric poets' treatment of these primary situations of love must thus be that many of them cease to turn on precise physical data, or elementary choices. Some lyric situations decline in importance and all are regularly spiritualized by Renaissance intellectual awareness. The rise to popularity of secondary topics such as those in poems about involuntary separation and absence is an indication that the texture and evolution of a relationship are felt to be much more important than the need for practical consummation of sexual desire. The result is not simply an advance in discrimination and range of potentiality in love as it is practiced. It might even be argued that since much of the finer awareness is conditioned by Neo-Platonism, the classical period was already capable of such sensitivity insofar as it is anticipated by the *Symposium*. However, it is not true that Platonism was correlated with love between the

sexes in classical times, nor that physical desire and its consummation were normally associated with a stable, socially
and spiritually significant relationship before the Renaissance.
C. S. Lewis has convincingly demonstrated in *The Allegory
of Love* the importance of Spenser's adjustment of the
adulterous passions of courtly love to the socially more viable
institution of marriage. It remained for Renaissance lyricists
to complete the diversification of the relations between the
sexes by assimilating them at a practical level to the analytic
subtleties which Plato had admitted primarily to homosexual
relationships. In general Spenser's verse is in harmony with
this tendency because of his Neo-Platonic views. However,
the lyrics of Wyatt, Ronsard, Donne, and later poets excel
Spenser's in dramatic illustration of the fact that their mistresses are not simply persons but personalities as well. They
see more uniformly that women are best understood not as
patterns of sensations, even if governed by high principles,
but as patterns of volition, merely exploiting rules of conduct
for self-clarification, and dependent on sensation chiefly as
a medium of communication not as an end in itself. Spenser
often delights in his future wife's beauty for its own sake,
though in the second canto of the first book of *The Faerie
Queene* he recognizes the dangers of this attitude, in the
story of Fradubio. But most of the poets we are interested in
scarcely ever bother even to note the prettier details of their
mistresses' complexions. Such uniformity of outlook shows
why this body of lyric verse, from which on the whole
Spenser is excluded, has its own distinctive importance and
unity.

For classical poets, therefore, sexual love is best defined as
the physical satisfaction of sensual desire. For the Renaissance poets this attitude is still possible; but for those who
are reasonably alert to contemporary taste love is a tension
of mental attitudes far exceeding in scope the initial sexual

urge and its motivations. The Renaissance poets are thus capable of dramatizing that analytic psychology which appears first in such psychological treatises as those of Ebreo, Varchi, Elyot, Bright, Burton, and others. But the poets present these new possibilities with a dramatic vividness and actuality that first suggest that people may reasonably expect to behave in harmony with them in real life.

···-ᔆ CHAPTER III ᘓ-···

THE NEW STYLE

[i]

S T Y L E undergoes a progression no less marked than that of the climactic situations just discussed. This evolution effects its own transformation of traditional lyric forms, though usually this is in harmony with the social aspects of their development. In matters of poetic technique or taste the utility of tradition remains considerable. Few effects evolve spontaneously, and many of the most characteristic features of later lyrical expression prove to have interesting analogies and prototypes in classical literature. An evolution is traceable in each of the typical resources of lyricism, though in practice all have their combined and irregular bearing on any particular lyrical tradition. A study of the development of several of these aspects of lyrical style will illustrate the limitations of our primarily sociological analysis of literature in the previous chapter.

In addition to words' literal meanings in a poem, the volume, pitch, tempo, and tone with which they are spoken is of great importance. Few aids are given the reader to help him detect this auditory pattern, but his responses to vocal customs effectively specify the kinds of emphasis required by the poet, as Cicero confidently asserts, "quod ea sunt in communibus infixa sensibus neque earum rerum quemquam funditis natura voluit esse expertem" ("because these [skills] are rooted deep in the general sensibility, and nature has decreed that nobody shall be entirely devoid of these faculties").[1] The stress patterns of individual words are obvious examples of this communal awareness; but more elaborate

---

[1] Cicero, *De Oratore* (III, 195), Loeb edn., trans. H. Rackham (London, 1942), II, 154-155.

systems of stress overlie those of individual words. Each language has its own syntactically determined rhythms for distinguishing clearly the function of the sentence as a whole, be it statement, negation, assertion, question, order, apostrophe, or exclamation. By throwing distinctive stress on key words in an appropriate sequence, speakers identify the intention of their sentences. Statement, as the normal form of syntactical pattern, is usually the least characterized by this defining stress. The others all require more energy to communicate their identity and are associated with more intense feelings on the part of the speaker. It was readily divined by poets that these more emphatic forms of syntax carried their emphasis and emotional tension automatically, whenever the appropriate sequence was reproduced. Poets often indulge in the calculated introduction of such emotionally charged patterns as negatives, questions, orders, and exclamations, even where the situation and literal sense do not exact them. Such forms are used as emotional "colors" to enliven the movement and increase the impact of lyrics, and their detailed application in this way is even discussed formally under the heading "Efficacia" in his *Poetics* (III, xxiv) by the Renaissance rhetorician Scaliger ["Est et in Apostrophe, et in interrogatione tante efficacia" ("there is much force in apostrophe and interrogation")].

The simplest and most obvious use of such marked cadences is to catch the reader's attention at the start of a lyric. This effect is hardly a discovery of Renaissance rhetoricians and lyricists. Energetic poets from the earliest times have known how to jar the reader into attention by such effects as the opening of Rufinus' epigram:

Μήτ᾽ ἰσχνὴν λίην περιλάμβανε,
      ("Don't embrace a skinny woman . . . ")[2]

[2] *Greek Anthology* (v, 37), Loeb edn., trans. W. R. Paton, I, 146-147.

or Nicarchus' equally brusque admonition opening another *Greek Anthology* epigram:

Τῆς μητρὸς μὴ ἄκουε, Φιλουμένη·
("Don't listen to your mother, Philumena . . . ").[3]

More dazzling perhaps is Ovid's impassioned opening to one of his elegies:

Esse deos, i, crede—fidem iurata fefellit,
et facies illi, quae fuit ante, manet! (III, iii)

(Go on, believe that there are gods—she swore and has failed her oath, and still her face is fair, as 'twas before!)[4]

The aggressive blasphemy here is merely a calculated prelude to the familiar lover's denunciation. But from it the poem receives a surge of energy that it never loses, particularly since, with quaint inconsequence, Ovid later musters several more imperatives, this time addressed to the gods whose existence he has just denied. Ovid's elegy contains altogether six questions and six exclamations, mostly addressed to the gods. By this rhetorical device he manages to sustain the vigorous movement suitable to a mood of indignation. Ovid is not alone in using such devices, they are an essential part of Horace's stock in trade, and both poets look back to Catullus. The first ten poems of Catullus printed in standard editions are his most famous, and all begin with premeditated emphasis. Three open with imperatives, three with questions, and four with vocatives.

There is neither novelty nor larger meaning to be derived from focusing a study of syntactical rhythms simply on these opening cadences of love lyrics, though there is a form of *aubade* in which the lover's startled curse, leveled at the disturber of his love-making, constitutes the major effect of

[3] *Ibid.* (v, 40), pp. 148-149.
[4] *Heroides and Amores*, Loeb edn., trans. G. Showerman, pp. 456-457.

the poem. The value of syntactical formulas is more complex
than such a pyrotechnic device would suggest. With the
ancients, indeed, such an opening flourish was where the
value of a syntactical formula as a "color" revealed itself
most explicitly. However, by degrees (as with the repeated
"Pone me" at the end of Horace's ode "Integer vitae . . . ")[5]
it was recognized that a complex syntactical pattern could
extend to govern the structure of a whole poem more completely than by chance imperatives and exclamations alone.
Ideally the rhetorical effects should rise naturally from the
content of the lyric. Thus from the earliest times certain
themes are probably favored because they permit of distinctive or picturesque syntactical patterns, rather than because
they offer an opportunity for any serious or personal meaning.
This is particularly evident in poets' search for flattering
illustrations or "explanations" of the beauty of their
mistresses.

One of the Anacreontic poets had amused himself by revealing the fickleness of lovers through the proclamation of
love as a runaway. Meleager turned the device to good
rhetorical effect in flattering his mistress with his neater
epigram, quoted in *The Greek Anthology*:

Κηρύσσω τὸν Ἔρωτα, τὸν ἄγριον· ἄρτι γὰρ ἄρτι
    ὀρθρινὸς ἐκ κοίτας ᾤχετ᾽ ἀποπτάμενος. . . .
καίτοι κεῖνος, ἰδού, περὶ φωλεόν. Οὔ με λέληθας,
    τοξότα, Ζηνοφίλας ὄμμασι κρυπτόμενος.   (v, 177)

(Lost! Love, wild Love! Even now at dawn he went his
way, taking wing from his bed. . . . But wait! there he is
near his nest! Ah! little archer, so you thought to hide
from me there in Zenophila's eyes!)[6]

5 (I, xxii), Loeb edn., trans. C. E. Bennett, pp. 64-65.
6 Loeb edn., trans. W. R. Paton, I, 212-213.

The quaintness and artifice are evident, but there is rhetorical finesse in opening in the tones of a town crier proclaiming a runaway. Less artificial, as we might expect, is Catullus' version of such a pursuit, which runs to a full twenty lines. Catullus pleads with Camerius, a boy whom he loves, to reveal his whereabouts:

> Oramus, si forte non molestumst,
> demonstres, ubi sint tuae tenebrae. (LV)

(I beg you, if I may without offence, show me where is your dark corner.)[7]

Catullus claims to have scoured Rome in pursuit of the boy, even to the point of carrying his inquiries to the demimondaines, where the traditional flattering allusion reappears in the self-advertisement of one of the girls:

> "Camerium mihi, pessimae puellae!"
> quaedam inquit, nudum reduc[ta pectus],
> "en hic in roseis latet papillis."

("Give me my Camerius, you wicked girls!" One of them, baring her bosom, says, "Look here he is, hiding between my rosy breasts.")

The analogies with Meleager's epigram are evident—the dramatically framed quest, the pursuit of an attractive but willful boy, the answering idea that he is really Love and concealed in feminine beauties. But Catullus buries these effects in the exposition of the more elaborate situation involving the boy, in which his own feelings appear to be seriously involved. He treats the search realistically, and the girl who answers his inquiries does so incidentally, playing on Meleager's conceit only to permit herself the opportunity

---

[7] Loeb edn., trans. F. W. Cornish, pp. 62-63.

of enticing Catullus. Though the Greek epigram is merely ingenious, Meleager's point is nevertheless the same as the Roman beauty's—to offer a pleasing explanation (in the presence of love) for female attractiveness.

Ausonius explains Bissula's beauty with similar ingenuity, but his rhetoric sounds less spontaneous and therefore less memorable:

> Bissula nec ceris nec fuco imitabilis ullo
> naturale decus fictae non commodat arti.
> sandyx et cerusa, alias simulate puellas:
> temperiem hanc vultus nescit manus. ergo age, pictor,
> puniceas confunde rosas et lilia misce,
> quique erit ex illis color aeris, ipse sit oris.

(Bissula, whom no wax nor any paint can imitate, adapts not her natural beauty to the shams of art. Vermilion and white, go picture other girls: the artist's skill cannot so blend you as to match this face. Away then, painter, mingle crimson roses and lilies, and let that color which they give the air be the very color of her face.)[8]

The admonition first to the colors and then to the painter (advising painters long remained a familiar poetic motif—it still flourished in the seventeenth century) gives the epigram a certain emotional rhythm and direction. But the device does not rise as dramatically from the subject as either Catullus' inquiries in the course of his real search or those of Meleager's artificial one. Meleager had handled Ausonius' motif more deftly if more coyly in a graciously oblique compliment in *The Greek Anthology*, beginning:

> Ἀνθοδίαιτε μέλισσα, τί μοι χροὸς Ἡλιοδώρας
> ψαύεις, ἐκπρολιποῦσ᾽ εἰαρινὰς κάλυκας; (v, 163)

[8] Loeb edn., trans. H. G. Evelyn White, I, 220-221.

(O flower-nurtured bee, why dost thou desert the buds of spring and light on Heliodora's skin?)[9]

Ausonius himself probably noted the effect, for he else-where[10] admonishes his painter to "imitate the Attic bees" in ransacking flowers for the tinctures to portray Ausonius' little slave girl. And Ronsard a thousand years later is equally sensitive to Meleager's quaint but gracious compliment, beginning with a similar question, intended only to permit a later gracious assertion on the part of the poet:

> Où allez-vous, filles du Ciel,
> Grand miracle de la Nature,
> Où allez-vous, mousches à miel,
> Chercher au champs vostre pasture?
> Si vous voulez cueillir les fleurs
> D'odeur diverse et de couleurs,
> Ne volez plus à l'avanture.
>   Autour de ma Dame halenée
> De mes baisers tant bien donnez,
> Vous trouverez la rose née,
> Et les œillets environnez
> De fleurettes ensanglantées
> D'Hyacinthe et d'Ajax, plantées
> Pres des lyz sur sa bouche nez. . . .[11]

(Where are you going, daughters of heaven, great wonder of nature, where are you going, honey bees, to seek your pasture in the fields? If you want to gather flowers of varied scent and color, do not fly at random any more. Round about my lady, perfumed with my carefully bestowed kisses, you will find the rose born, and violets ringed

[9] Loeb edn., trans. W. R. Paton, I, 204-205.
[10] Loeb edn., I, 222-223.
[11] Cohen, II, 714.

with florets stained by the blood of Hyacinth and Ajax, growing close to the lilies born in her mouth. . . .)

Ronsard's poem compacts almost all the effects of the earlier poems about searches and comparisons into a firmly shaped line of cadence—a question followed by a counter-argument to the anticipated answer. There is not quite the same intimacy of tone as Catullus musters, but the movement of Ronsard's poem is much more distinctive, and the Renaissance delight in such rhetorical formulas appears in the way in which English writers restlessly experimented with this particular effect.

Drummond uses it as an incidental motif in the course of a poem with a truly Elizabethan magnificence of style within the syntactical frame:

> What Pincell paint? what Colour to the Sight
> So sweet a Shape can show? the blushing *Morne*
> The Red must lend, the *milkie*-Way the White
> And *Night* the Starres, which her rich Crowne adorne,
>   To draw her right: But then, that all agree,
>   The *Heauen*, the Table, *Zeuxis Ioue* must bee.[12]

The movement is easy and effective but, like the poised episode of the girl's attempt to seduce Catullus, the vividness of the particular passage is buried in less cadentially disciplined writing. It is left to Shakespeare to crystallize a syntactical pattern such as that sustaining all these poems, while refusing characteristically to drown the formula in a lush mass of conventional metaphor. By transposing the theme to a much more analytic level, he playfully affects to destroy the very effects for which his poem offers the perfect structure —the search to explain beauty's attraction:

[12] Kastner, I, 129.

Tell me where is fancy bred
Or in the heart or in the head?
How begot, how nourished?
      Reply, reply.
It is engender'd in the eyes,
With gazing fed; and fancy dies
In the cradle where it lies.
Let us all ring fancy's knell:
I'll begin it,—Ding, dong bell.
      Ding, dong bell.[13]

The poem is rhetorically dazzling, as well as playfully skeptical. The opening questions with their brisk imperatives are succinctly answered, and the answer projected into a judgment leading in turn to a somewhat sardonic affectation of mourning.

Nothing better illustrates the perfect poise of Shakespeare's syntactical structure here than the attempts of the next generation of poets to recapture it, as in the following poem:

Tell me where the beauty lies—
In my mistress? or in my eyes?
Is she fair? I made her so.
Beauty doth from liking grow.
Be she fairer, whiter than
Venus' doves or Leda's swan,
What's that Beauty if neglected,
Seen of all, of none respected?
Then tell my mistress that I love her,
Think her fair, cause I approve her.[14]

The poem is as subtle in thought as Shakespeare's, but little known because the poet, while recognizing the resonant and varied syntactical pattern of Shakespeare's lyric, has failed

[13] Craig, p. 518.
[14] *English Madrigal Verse 1588-1632*, ed. E. H. Fellowes (Oxford, 1920), p. 581.

completely to sustain the effortless conversational and syntactical evolution of Shakespeare's sentences. A similar difficulty impairs a significantly anonymous seventeenth-century Anacreontic lyric, which nevertheless catches Catullus' natural movement:

> Amid the myrtles as I walked,
> Love and my sighs thus entretalked:
> 'Tell me,' said I in deep distress,
> 'Where may I find my shepherdess?'
> Then, 'Fool,' said Love, 'knowst thou not this?
> In everything that's good she is;
> In yonder tulip go and seek,
> There thou shalt find her lip, her cheek. . . .'[15]

Here the assurance with which the sequence of dialogue is handled illuminates the lack of syntactical flow in the previous poem, but the poise of the question and answer is smothered by the narrative opening. The same kind of experiment is made by several other Stuart poets, such as Townshend and Edward Herbert, who each make similar errors. Herbert comes closest to bringing off the effect, though he also buries it in more awkward lines:

> Tell us at least, we pray,
> Where all the beauties that those ashes ow'd
> Are now bestow'd.

> Doth the Sun now his light with yours renew?
> Have Waves the curling of your hair?
> Did you restore unto the Sky and Air,
> The red, and white, and blew?
> Have you vouchsafed to flowrs since your death
> That sweetest breath?[16]

---

[15] *Wit's Interpreter* (London, 1655), p. 103.
[16] Lord Edward Herbert, *Poems,* ed. G. C. Moore Smith (Oxford, 1923), p. 33.

The rhythmic flow has been very deftly redeployed to suit a pantheistic funeral elegy. The repeated questions are massed cunningly, and the poet has even recaptured the cosmic range of Drummond's imagery. The artifice of such apostrophes as Meleager's or Ronsard's is scarcely felt—solemn occasion and marked cadence go hand in hand. Yet all these effects are screened by their undistinguished context.

The striking rhythmic potentialities of this search to define the fascination of a mistress were only fully displayed when Carew drafted his enormously popular version of the tradition:

> Aske me no more where *Ioue* bestowes,
> When *Iune* is past, the fading rose:
> For in your beauties orient deepe,
> These flowers as in their causes, sleepe.
>
> Aske me no more whether doth stray,
> The golden Atomes of the day:
> For in pure love heaven did prepare
> These powders to inrich your haire.
>
> Aske me no more whether doth hast,
> The Nightingale when May is past:
> For in your sweet dividing throat,
> She winters and keepes warme her note.
>
> Aske me no more where those starres light,
> That downewards fall in dead of night:
> For in your eyes they sit, and there,
> Fixed become as in their sphere.
>
> Aske me no more if East or West,
> The Phenix builds her spicy nest:
> For vnto you at last shee flies,
> And in your fragrant bosome dyes.[17]

[17] Dunlap, p. 102.

While not so subtle in thought as Shakespeare's lyric (though some of the material may have been derived from his Sonnet 99), the poem is clearly the one of all that we have so far discussed which most consciously exploits a syntactical formula. That this interest of Carew's was shared by his contemporaries appears in the fact that the poem was perhaps the most imitated one of the century, and this in an age whose poets copied each other freely. It exists in several versions, and was reprinted in numerous anthologies of the time. It was copied, distorted, and parodied endlessly. One of the most successful and original poems related to it is one by Henry King which begins:

> Tell me no more how fair she is,
>   I have no mind to hear
> The story of that distant bliss
>   I never shall come near:
> By sad experience I have found
> That her perfection is my wound.
>
> And tell me not how fond I am . . .[18]

Even two hundred years later a major English lyric poet like Tennyson could not forget Carew's insistent cadence and did justice to its distinctiveness by an ingenious redeployment of the sentence structure, in a lyric toward the end of *The Princess*:

> Ask me no more: the moon may draw the sea;
>   The cloud may stoop from heaven and take the shape,
>   With fold to fold, of mountain or of cape;
> But O too fond, when have I answer'd thee?
>   Ask me no more.
>
> Ask me no more: what answer should I give?
>   I love not hollow cheek or faded eye:

[18] Saintsbury, III, 173.

Yet, O my friend, I will not have thee die!
Ask me no more, lest I should bid thee live;
    Ask me no more. . . .[19]

Both King's and Tennyson's versions of the formula are obviously very different poems from Carew's and the earlier lyrics, yet they illustrate the dynamism of a syntactical cadence. Carew's poem earned its pre-eminence from the confident insistence on a sentence structure both energetic and, as the earlier examples show, entirely appropriate to the occasion of the poem—a poet's wonder at the enigmatic beauty of his lady. That Carew knew exactly what he was doing is shown by his relentless reiteration, not of feeling nor of image, but simply of phrasing. Once read, it is branded on the reader's mind with the same finality as the theme of that analogous piece of virtuosity, Ravel's "Bolero." Carew takes the formula "Tell me where," which had become merely conventional, and renews it by that process of reversal which is becoming increasingly familiar as a mode of memorable emphasis in the Renaissance. The negative "Ask me no more" gives the poet a larger assurance and authority than the necessarily naïve tone of the implied inquiry "Tell me." Such tentative questions lack the sonorous tones of Carew's confident assertions. It is noteworthy that one of the more successful uses of the "Tell me" formula is Cartwright's "Tell me no more of minds embracing minds,"[20] which matches Carew's poem with an opening, negative imperative and goes on to mass informed assertions.

We have seen here how the theme of a search, essentially for ways to explain the charms of a mistress, leads to the coinage of a sequence of sentences of unique cadence, first outlined by Shakespeare and then so defined by Carew that later

[19] *Poems of Tennyson 1830-1870* (Oxford, 1912), p. 342.
[20] W. Cartwright, *Comedies, Tragi-Comedies, with Other Poems* (London, 1651), p. 246.

poets were able to borrow the formula for poems (such as Tennyson's) unrelated to the topic associated earlier with the sentence pattern. This effect is obviously pursued with greater awareness by the Renaissance poets than the classical ones—among whom can scarcely be found a single analogy for Carew's triumphant insistence on his pattern. What remains to be shown is that the exploitation of such cadential patterns was a method of ordering lyrics fully developed and generally recognized by English seventeenth-century poets.

An exactly parallel sequence was established by the author of *The Song of Solomon,* a popular source of exotic effects for Renaissance poets. The Authorized Version translates the passage, "Turn away thine eyes from me, for they have overcome me . . ."[21] and Drayton versifies it as "Oh turne away thine eies, for they have wounded me. . . ."[22] The original goes on to speak of the charms of the mistress. Other poets appear to have noticed the passage before Drayton. A Renaissance Latin poet, Crottus, has a poem, "Ad Myrtalem," which includes the following lines:

> Formosissima Myrtale
>   Ah conde haec labia, hos purpureos sinus,
> Haec fulgentia sidera;
>   Conde has aureolas, oro, papillulas,
> Spirant quae undique cinnama,
>   Aura quae niuei pectoris, improbos
> Ignes et faculas cient,
>   Et mentem feriunt, et iecur vstulant.[23]

(Most beautiful Myrtale, ah, conceal these lips, this blushing bosom, these shining stars; hide, I pray, these gleaming little breasts, breathing spices everywhere, which

---

[21] Chapter VI, verse 5.
[22] M. Drayton, *Works,* ed. J. W. Hebel (Oxford, 1931), I, 16.
[23] *Delitiae Italorum,* I, 855.

with the gale of your snowy bosom stir up wicked fires and flames, and wound the mind, and inflame the passions.)

The effect was clearly cosmopolitan in its appeal, for Desportes exploits it clumsily in French also:

> Bref, toutes vos façons, beaux yeux, m'ostent la vie.
> Hé donc pour mon salut, cachez-vous, je vous prie!
> Non, ne vous cachez point, mais ne me tuez pas.[24]

> (In short, all your ways, O fine eyes, take my life away. Well then for my safety, conceal yourselves, I pray! No, do not conceal yourselves, but do not kill me.)

The persistence and popularity of this motif, defined by a few turns of phrase, is marked, even though up to this point in its development no poet had given it expression in a form disentangled from a smothering context which diminishes its effect. The English poets soon showed that they had the greatest awareness of its well-accented intonation: a crisp opening imperative expressing a picturesque resistance to the mistress, which led naturally to a titillating enumeration of the mistress' dangerously seductive charms. Drummond handles this movement primitively in one of his poems, but Drayton in "To his Coy Love" is more successful in sustaining the rhythm:

> I pray thee leave, love me no more,
>   Call home the heart you gave me,
> I but in vaine that Saint adore,
>   That can, but will not save me: . . .

> Shew me no more those Snowie Brests,
>   With Azure Riverets branched,
> Where whilst mine Eye with Plentie feasts,
>   Yet is my Thirst not stanched. . . .[25]

---

[24] P. Desportes, *Œuvres*, ed. A. Michiels (Paris, 1858), p. 165.
[25] Hebel, II, 372.

The dawning of a syntactical rhythm like that of Carew's poem is perceptible here. Instead of a simple question and answer, or just the reply to an implied question, there is here an elaborate play on imperatives and negatives, succeeded by a qualifying mood of plaintive explanatory statement rounded off by a neat antithesis. That this is not fortuitous appears from the duplication in the second stanza quoted. It might be argued that this grammatically defined pattern is only a substratum of a poem better defined by the images of too attractive female beauty; but Donne's "The Message" disproves this by breaking the image pattern while maintaining the syntactical one. It also radically modifies the apparent relationship between the lovers:

> Send home my long strayd eyes to mee,
> Which (Oh) too long have dwelt on thee;
> Yet since there they have learn'd such ill,
>   Such forc'd fashions,
>   And false passions,
>   That they be
>   Made by thee
> Fit for no good sight, keep them still.[26]

The second stanza reiterates the cadence, beginning:

> Send home my harmlesse heart againe,
> Which no unworthy thought could staine;
> But if . . .

There is a more than casual parallel of sentiment between Donne and Drayton, but the best correlation of the two poems is in the near identity of their syntactical organization. The verbs are less artificially massed by Donne but the exclamation which he introduces, like Crottus and Desportes, in his second line makes an effective substitute. The antithesis, in-

[26] Grierson, p. 39.

stead of being merely a contrasting rhythm with the same purport, externalizes in Donne's poem a complete counter-movement, leading back to an imperative matching but not contradicting the opening one. Donne's orchestration of the motif is more sophisticated than Drayton's, but it is the same motif; and Donne uses the syntactical structure of his stanza as the basis for the two successive stanzas just as Carew did. His last stanza, however, winds up the poem better than Carew's by boldly breaking the end structure of the cadence without modifying the sense, which gives the feeling of sustained resolution finally defined:

> Yet send me back my heart and eyes,
> That I may know, and see thy lyes,
> And may laugh and joy, when thou
>> Art in anguish
>> And dost languish
>>> For some one
>>> That will none,
> Or prove as false as thou art now.

To the already varied list of users of this particular sentence pattern can be added the name of Shakespeare, for the classic expression of the motif is probably the stanza sung in *Measure for Measure*; and Beaumont and Fletcher may possibly claim a place too, since a second stanza is added to that of Shakespeare's play in their *The Bloody Brother*. The two stanzas, rather interestingly from the point of view of their origin, together make up the total pattern of the lines from Crottus and Drayton that have been quoted, suggesting that the poem necessarily makes a complete unity in its longer form only:

> Take, Oh take those lips away
>> That so sweetly were forsworn,

And those eyes, like break of day,
  Lights that do mislead the Morn,
But my kisses bring again,
  Seals of love, though seal'd in vain.

Hide, Oh hide those hills of Snow
  Which thy frozen blossome bears,
On whose tops the Pinks that grow
  Are of those that *April* wears,
But first set my poor heart free,
  Bound in those Ivy chains by thee.[27]

The excellence of the poem is of complex origin, turning on many points of sound and meaning independent of any single, mechanical principle. But if we are analyzing the organization of the material, our earlier examples make it inevitable that we should feel a continuity of the established pattern: in the first six lines is a stanza opening with a repetition of imperatives and an exclamation and concluding with an antithesis, the whole movement recurring in each new stanza. Not only does this pattern project into the six lines of the second stanza but into the structure of all the stanzas written in conscious imitation of the poem as it appears in the later play. Such versions were produced by Strode, King, Carew, Kynaston, and Cotton, who all keep the syntactical form for their stanzas while varying the images and sentiments which they contain.[28]

We now have two analogous sequences showing a continuity based primarily on distinctive sentence rhythms. Both are extremely popular in the Renaissance period but lack many classical parallels, and in this ratio neither is uncharacteristic of such traditions. There is no point in multiplying these detailed studies, but the reader will discover readily that many

[27] *The Works of Francis Beaumont and John Fletcher,* ed. A. R. Waller (Cambridge, 1906), IV, 307.
[28] See my article "Take Oh Take Those Lips Away," *Studies in English* (Boston, 1960), IV, 214-222.

of the poems of the English Renaissance quoted in this book are based on a syntactical pattern recurring in successive stanzas, and frequently based on an explicit tradition including several poems. These examples include Waller's lyric "Go lovely rose . . . Tell her . . . ," Shakespeare's Sonnet 130, and Suckling's "Why so pale and wan, fond lover." Almost all of the examples in the remainder of this chapter show similar characteristics.

There is no necessary virtue aesthetically, or emotively, in constructing poems on the basis of a sequence of cadences governed by a syntactical pattern. Many poor poems are constructed in this way, but usually they are modeled on successful poems in which such a pattern is first consciously defined. Recurring syntax in successive stanzas is also not necessarily of critical importance in the Renaissance—one of its advantages is the purely utilitarian one that if the phrasing is approximately the same in each then the same musical setting, which was frequently provided for such lyrics, will serve for each stanza. A similar economy of effort in turn, no doubt, suggested the writing of new poems to fit the settings of old ones. This would certainly be an advantage of the close resemblance between Marlowe's "Passionate Shepherd" and the reply of Raleigh's nymph, not to mention Donne's equally standardized extension of the tradition in "The Baite." This Renaissance use of syntax always presupposes two things, a conscious awareness of the value and function of syntactical cadence in poetry and a capacity to exploit it habitually, which in no earlier age is quite as universal a skill among practicing poets. English poetry, at least, acquires a vivid clarity of cadence as a uniform attribute from about 1600 onward, a distinction which is rarely achieved before, even in the lines of Wyatt and Sidney, and which appears only intermittently in the poems of such major European writers as Sappho, Catullus, and Ronsard in any earlier tradition. Renaissance lyrics not only have a briskness and sureness equaled or surpassed only by a master craftsman like Horace, but the exact tone of a mood is caught so well that elaboration of vivifying detail is rarely needed. Many of the very best Renaissance poems are also the shortest for this reason, such as Shakespeare's "Tell me where is fancy bred." An accurate ear for the fall of words and a power to sum up a mood in an intonation give to much Renaissance poetry an immediacy of impact uncommon in classical Latin love poetry, where the protracted elegy was as common as the poised lyric for handling love topics. Without the awareness of cadence illustrated in the use of syntactical patterns, the Renaissance poets could never have given their poems the briskness that arrests attention and barbs the contents. Such vigorous tones as those renouncing convention, which were examined at the end of the first chapter, are directly attributable to the poets' mastery of these skills.

The relevance to the evolution of sensibility of this increasingly universal capacity for succinct and forceful lyrical expression, previously only in the power of the greatest poets, may not be immediately apparent. In practice it meant that most poets could swiftly create the dramatic situation without exhausting their skill. There is a greater margin of energy left for further creative impulse beyond the search for a firm statement of sentiment that is characteristic of much classical lyricism. When these lithe and pointed lyrics carry not only the weight of feeling of classical poetry but also the subtle insights derived from Christian thought, they accomplish something wholly new—immediacy of rhythm and complexity of allusion compactly expressed.

Because by training and instinct these poets readily dramatized feelings, they tended to concentrate on other aspects of the creative process—such as its intellectual range. Classical love poetry rises to abstraction only in general, impersonal statements and nowhere in the classical precedents for Carew's

"Ask me no more" do we find anything so philosophical as the end of his first stanza:

> For in your beauties orient deep,
> These flowers, as in their causes, sleep.

Carew can carry off the scholastic metaphysics of "as in their causes" because of the natural sound of his parenthesis—it is a triumph of manner. However peculiar the ideas in seventeenth-century poetry, the poems usually *sound* natural, or even conversational, not abstract or stiffly formal. Thus these poets acclimatized poetic dexterity and moral or metaphysical thought to tones approximating those of real speech. Their popularity further encouraged real speech to aspire to the subtleties of poetry, and by the end of the century Monsieur Jourdain's delight in speaking prose (in Molière's *Le Bourgeois Gentilhomme*) could no longer be shared by the more literate of the English upper classes, whose conversational epigrams were more like Renaissance lyrics than its prose. Restoration comedy echoes Restoration conversation as records of the remarks of Waller and Swift show. Wit was no longer confined to jocularity and abuse but was felt everywhere; courtship became an elaborate and lively exchange of values, at least as reflected in that of Mirabel and Millamant in *The Way of the World*, or in the love affairs of *Les Femmes Savantes*. Needless to say, lyric poetry with its verve and easy allusiveness merely fostered this process, but the universal familiarity of the literate with the work of the major lyric poets of the time confirms the importance of lyricism as a catalyst of subtlety in courtship. The lover of classical times would address his girl (or boy) less briskly and effectively simply because few of the literary models for courtship afforded by classical literature were both serious, intelligent, *and* natural. No Restoration lover lacked such conversationally viable resources. Perhaps this increased verbal facility further explains the success of amorists at the court of Charles II.

[ii]

If it is true that the cadence of Renaissance love lyrics is more distinctive than that of most earlier lyricism, it is also true that their accentuation of style is also more marked. Not that earlier poets failed to use words with great discrimination; no literature has excelled the Latin in its sense of calculated juxtaposition of words and phrases. But while Horace's poetry moves with hypnotic inevitability there is a consistency of firmly wrought texture about his verse that masks a talent as great if not greater than the virtuosity of the best Renaissance poets, whose stylistic explosions dazzle the reader much more than the Latin poet's style. There are few puns and paradoxes in Horace's writing. On the other hand, in epigrammatic writing, it is hard to judge who perpetrates the more outrageous plays on words, Martial or Herrick. Yet Martial's jokes rarely rise to serious meanings. This is one of his better lyrics:

Esse quid hoc dicam quod olent tua basia murram
  quodque tibi est numquam non alienus odor?
hoc mihi suspectum est, quod oles bene, Postume, semper:
  Postume, non bene olet qui bene semper olet. (ii, xii)

(How shall I explain this, that your kisses smell of myrrh, and that there is about you invariably some foreign odor? This is suspect to me, your being well scented, Postumus, always. Postumus, he is not well scented who always is well scented!)[29]

The poem is not merely amusing, the paradox is startling and meaningful. It has exactly the effect of Renaissance paradox, but, while in Latin and Greek such serious paradox is

[29] Loeb edn., trans. W. C. Ker, i, 116-117.

rare, in the Renaissance it is standard practice. Typically, Martial's poem, because it was so close to Renaissance taste, was frequently copied. Bonefonius' version, "Semper munditias . . . ," led to Jonson's "Still to be neat, still to be dressed," which turns the repeated "semper" of Martial into a syntactical color, borrowed in turn by a later poet who wrote "Still to affect, still to admire. . . ." Herrick also took up the idea in "Delight in Disorder." These poets were more serious than Martial, willingly forfeiting his pun to stress the thought behind the paradox that art's very success breeds suspicion. However, paradox, or its minor form, punning, was customarily used boldly by the Renaissance to make serious points.

Another classical paradox which the Renaissance elaborated, this time without loss of wit, is reflected in the lines with which Paulus Silentiarius begins an epigram in *The Greek Anthology*:

Μαλθακὰ μὲν Σαπφοῦς τὰ φιλήματα, μαλθακὰ γυίων
    πλέγματα χιονέων, μαλθακὰ πάντα μέλη·
ψυχὴ δ᾽ἐξ ἀδάμαντος ἀπειθέος· (v, 246)

(Soft are Sappho's kisses, soft the clasp of her snowy limbs, every part of her is soft. But her heart is of unyielding adamant. . . .)[30]

Silentiarius starts here with a fine rhetorical surge, typical of his epigrams, but his paradox is drowned in the flat recapitulations of his conclusion. Angerianus, a Renaissance Latin poet, shows more tact in the placing of his paradox, which is the climax of a poem comparing his mistress to her statue:

Haec glacialis hyems friget, glacialis et illa
    Friget hyems. Lapis haec scalptus, et illa lapis.
Sed non aequales sunt vna parte: quod illa
    Illa magis vento mobilis, haec stabilis.[31]

[30] Loeb edn., trans. W. R. Paton, i, 252-254.
[31] *Delitiae Gallorum*, ii, 747.

(An icily freezing winter is it, and an icily freezing winter
is she. It is sculptured stone, and she too is stone. But in one
respect they are not alike; for she, she is more variable than
the wind, it has stability.)

The control of the Renaissance Latin poet is better than that
of Silentiarius, and the concluding ratio is more challenging
because it does not present merely a somewhat obvious dis-
crepancy between physical and moral character as in Silentiarius, but an unexpected one between the mistress' own moral
attributes, which the physical comparison simply illuminates.
Nevertheless, it is James Shirley who perfects this particular
paradox in the following poem:

> I stood and saw my mistress dance
> Silent, and with so fixed an eye
> Some might suppose me in a trance,
>   But being asked why,
> By one that knew I was in love
>   I could not but impart
> My wonder, to behold her move
>   So nimbly with a marble heart.[32]

This is not, perhaps, a great poem, but its last words have a
calculated impact to which there are few analogies in classical
literature. The poem, to begin with, runs less sonorously and
more casually than Horace would let it, in easy conversational
rhythms, until it rises to a statement compressing all the meaning and tension into the ambiguities of the last five words. The
surprise is more absolute than any that classical literature
normally attempted. There is also a psychological complexity
involved, both here and in Angerianus, which is missing in
Silentiarius, for whom women remained, as for Horace, on a
lower moral and intellectual level than men. Shirley is not

[32] J. Shirley, *Poems* (London, 1646), p. 17.

merely being verbally witty in contrasting marble's associations with movement—he is really asking how the mental stiffness which he has found in his mistress could permit her to relax so freely in dance.

The effect was exploited among Shirley's contemporaries. John Hall shows almost equal virtuosity in handling the "marble mistress" conceit in another "occasional" poem with the same calculated effect as Shirley's. He begins "To Julia Weeping" with:

> Fairest, when thy eyes did pour
>   A crystal shower,
> I was persuaded that some stone
>   Had liquid grown;
> And thus amazèd, sure, thought I,
> When stones are moist, some rain is nigh.[33]

The image is ingeniously elaborated to sustain the psychological point, but after some gloomy thoughts in the second stanza, it is given decisive point in the final one:

> Yet I'll make better omens, till
>   Event beguile;
> Those pearly drops in time shall be
>   A precious sea;
> And thou shalt like thy coral prove,
> Soft under water, hard above.

The climactic ambiguity of the last line is beautifully calculated, for it was a commonplace that a tearful mistress ("under water") was softer than a serene one. The exposition of such paradoxical analogies is usually handled with more psychological finesse and more abstract intelligence by the Stuart poets, but also with a conscious exploitation of style more decisive even than that of *The Greek Anthology*.

[33] Saintsbury, II, 197. Text has "shall" in fifth line of the second stanza quoted.

The most economical illustration of the Stuart writers' heightened sense of how to make a word reverberate in climactic isolation is Herrick's tiny poem "Upon her Weeping":

> She by the River sate, and sitting there,
> She wept, and made it deeper by a teare.[34]

The faint formality of the first line's inversion and the rhyme alone distinguish the poem from prose—except for that single word "deeper." The river one feels first is not really "deepened" and the poem is thus satirical—a tear is after all only a very small quantity of water; but then one recognizes that a tear has often more significance than a whole river, which therefore becomes deeper because something really meaningful has been added to it, thus the poem is serious; yet, after all, the impression remains of nature as a large background against which mere human tears may well appear trivial. This virtuosity of meaning, and the pivotal role given to "deeper," show once more the refined sense of style and meaning of Stuart authors.

To vindicate fully these assertions of the superior control of style of Renaissance poets, it is fortunate that exactly the same sentiment is expressed by three poems, by Propertius, Marot and an English poet. Propertius briskly begins one of his elegies in this way:

> Quid iuvat ornato procedere, vita, capillo
>   et tenues Coa veste movere sinus?
> aut quid Orontea crines perfundere murra,
>   teque peregrinis vendere muneribus;
> naturaeque decus mercato perdere cultu,
>   nec sinere in propriis membra nitere bonis?
> crede mihi, non ulla tuae est medicina figurae:
>   nudus Amor formae non amat artificem. . . . (i, ii, 1-8)

[34] Martin, p. 251.

(What boots it, light of my life, to go forth with locks adorned, and to rustle in slender folds of Coan silk? Or avails it aught to steep thy tresses in the myrrh of Orontes, to parade thyself in the gifts that aliens bring, to spoil the grace of nature by the charms that gold can buy nor allow thy limbs to shine in the glory that is their own? Believe me, thou hast no art which can make your form more fair; Love himself goes naked and hates those that make a craft of beauty. . . .)[35]

There is a realistic familiarity of detail and an emotional color in these questions. Perhaps the sympathetic effects called the passage to Marot's attention. He typifies the attitude of Renaissance poets to the classics when he detaches this interesting theme from its less distinctive context. By framing his own poem to answer Propertius' criticisms in particular, he heightens its movement, and his sharper sense of debate gives it a unity and purpose lost in the rest of Propertius' elegy:

> Qui cuyderoit desguiser Ysabeau
> D'un simple habit, ce seroit grand' simplesse;
> Car au visage a ne sçay quoy de beau,
> Qui faict juger tousjours qu'elle est princesse:
> Soit en habit de chambriere, ou maistresse,
> Soit en drap d'or entier ou decouppé,
> Soit son gent corps de toile enveloppé,
> Tousjours sera sa beauté maintenue;
> Mais il me semble (ou je suis bien trompé)
> Qu'elle seroit plus belle toute nue.[36]

(Whoever would think of transforming Isabel with a plain dress, this would be very naïve; for she has in her face I know not what beauty, which makes it be judged always that she is a princess: whether in maid's dress, or mistress',

[35] Loeb edn., trans. H. E. Butler, pp. 4-7.
[36] Jannet, III, 31.

whether in whole cloth of gold, or slashed dress, or with her trim figure wrapped in linen always her beauty will be maintained; but it seems to me, unless I am much mistaken, that she would be most beautiful quite naked.)

Marot has surpassed his original by isolating its effects from a larger, less coherent whole, and by giving these effects aesthetic as well as logical direction. This he does by raising the sequence to a climax in the very last word. No classical poet shows quite this virtuosity, though in many such Renaissance poets as George Herbert the mastery of the technique is so automatic that it becomes almost conventional. The English poet's version of the theme is worthy of a countryman of Herbert:

> My love in her attire doth show her wit,
>   It doth so well become her:
> For every season she hath dressings fit,
> For winter, spring, and summer.
>   No beauty she doth miss
>   When all her robes are on;
>   For Beauty's self she is
>   When all her robes are gone.[37]

Like Marot, this poet has deftly turned the motive of Propertius' censure into the compliment it really suggests, but he has also condensed the poem still more, achieving thereby a more masterly and rapid articulation. There is none of the awkward detail or hesitant assertion of Marot. The English poet is in no doubt about the naked beauty of *his* mistress, but, while implying this knowledge, he does not refer to the subject with the faintly ungracious directness of Marot's conclusion. The English lyric rises almost in a single breath from gracious compliment to a wittily revealing yet tactful asser-

[37] *Speculum Amantis*, ed. A. H. Bullen (Oxford, 1889), p. 12.

tion completed only by the poem's very last word. Its virtues are those of many English contemporaries of the author.

Since all these poems have been light in tone, though not trivial, it is worth concluding our study of Renaissance verbal strategy by an illustration in the form of an epitaph, a challenge indeed to tact and style:

> The body which within this earth is laid,
> Twice six weekes knew a wife, a saint, a maid;
> Fair maid, chast wife, pure saint, yet 'tis not strange—
> She was a woman, therefore pleasd to change:
> And now shees dead, some woman doth remaine,
> For still she hopes, once to be chang'd again.[38]

By cunningly blending the satirical and paradoxical with a *finally* serious meaning, the poem becomes more memorable than many superficially more earnest epitaphs. Stylistically speaking it is a masterpiece of *double-entendre*, maintaining a logical theme of mockery that masks an earnest religious allusion to the resurrection in the last line. This epitaph by an anonymous poet is worth almost any epigram of Martial, chiefly because this poet's Renaissance contemporaries had developed the techniques of stylistic surprise to the point that these were recognized and practiced effectively by most poets, even minor ones.

The point of these various examples is to illustrate how, in that control of style which is most characteristically found in the paradoxical epigram, the English poets of the seventeenth century, even the comparatively minor ones, reveal a mastery possessed only by the greatest classical writers, just as the later poets also rival these classical writers in syntactical virtuosity. Perhaps in both types of achievement the real significance is more complex than simply the mastery of a poetic skill. The advantage of full mastery of an aptitude is not

[38] *Facetiae* (London, 1817), ii, 253.

simply that one achieves a greater perfection in terms of what is already known, but that, having turned what was once a painfully labored skill to the ease of instinct, one has a margin of uncommitted energy and awareness that modifies and develops those skills in totally new ways. What is most striking about Renaissance poets, in comparison say with Horace, is that Horace puts his full force into the eloquence of each line that he is writing. Later poets are concerned not simply with sustained perfection of expression but also with the special effects that will dazzle and overpower the reader's imagination. They have progressed from art to virtuosity. This detachment from the detailed texture of their writing is perhaps a form of latent irony, though not always so intended. But what should be sought in these later poets is less the ironic hints of detachment than the reflection of this surplus awareness in precise creative accomplishment of a kind which can be discussed factually and informatively.

[i i i]

In poetry we would expect the pivotal resource of metaphor to afford an ideal occasion to illustrate the realization of this potentiality. Such is indeed the case. Each time a classical image or pattern of images of some distinctness is set next to a closely related Renaissance one, a consistent ratio appears which reveals how the surplus awareness and skill has modified the original aim and achievement. This change in the later verse often results from the very existence of a model, which arouses more delicate critical responses than would be possible in giving painful birth to a wholly original motif. Since Martial was popular in the Renaissance and had some sense of the curt, distinctive patterns which later poets savored, his verse offers the best source of contrasts with that of later lyricists. Like them he often chopped off a small fragment from the work of an earlier poet and adjusted it to a more dramatic and highly focused pattern. In his *Metamorphoses* Ovid had written the quaint yet gruesome story of Polyphemus, Galatea, and Acis. Polyphemus' rustic plea to the sea nymph was one of the climactic points in the episode and this is how the uncouth Cyclops seeks to flatter his mistress in his own terms:

> Candidior folio nivei Galatea ligustri,
> floridior pratis, longa procerior alno, . . .
> lucidior glacie, matura dulcior uva,
> mollior et cygni plumis et lacte coacto, . . . (XIII, 789ff.)

(O Galatea, whiter than snow privet leaves, more blooming than the meadows, surpassing the alder in your tall slenderness, . . . more shining-clear than ice, sweeter than ripened grapes, softer than swan's down and curdled milk.)[39]

There are already traces of a syntactical pattern here in the rhetorical power of the heaped-up comparatives. There is also considerable deftness of characterization in this blunt flattery, gaily enameled with rural allusions. But Martial finds that effects such as these may be used independent of the bizarre courtship of the sea nymph by a monster. He uses them to evoke the charm of a dead slave girl, Erotion, whom he loved —a marked evolution in historicity and immediacy from most of Ovid's love poetry:

> Puella senibus dulcior mihi cycnis,
> agna Galaesi mollior Phalantini,
> concha Lucrini delicatior stagni,
> cui nec lapillos praeferas Erythraeos
> nec modo politum pecudis Indicae dentem
> nivesque primas liliumque non tactum;

[39] Ovid., *Metamorphoses*, Loeb edn., trans. F. J. Miller (London, 1926), II, 284-285.

quae crine vicit Baetici gregis vellus
Rhenique nodos aureamque nitellam;
fragravit ore quod rosarium Paesti,
quod Atticarum prima mella cerarum,
quod sucinorum rapta de manu gleba; . . . (v, xxxvii, 1-11)

(A maid, sweeter voiced to me than aged swans, more
tender than the lamb by Phalanthian Galaesus, more dainty
than mother-of-pearl of Lucrine's mere, before whom thou
wouldst not choose Eastern pearls, nor the tusk new polished of India's beast, and snows untrodden, and the unfin-
gered lily; whose locks outshine the Baetic fleece, the knotted
hair of Rhine, and the golden dormouse; whose breath was
fragrant as Paestan bed of roses, as the new honey of Attic
combs, as a lump of amber snatched from the hand; . . .)[40]

The kind of movement found in Ovid's lines is here isolated
from any elaborate context and given pride of place as the
major effect of Martial's poem, where its orchestration can be
more fully developed. Even Martial is diffident about trusting
entirely to such a single effect and emotion, as is Horace in
his famed second epode praising rural life, which turns out to
be the sentimentality of an urban usurer. Martial finishes his
lyric with a satirical allusion to the bereaved widower of an
heiress. However, Martial effectively shows that the effects
can stand by themselves, supported primarily by the cumulative force of conventional allusions massed in a single unified
movement. The Renaissance recognized something distinctive
in this relentless flow of imagery.

But while a lesser poet, Salmonius Macrinus, simply produced a Latin elegy approximating to Martial, Jonson did
much more in the final flourish of "Her Triumph":

[40] Loeb edn., trans. W. C. Ker, i, 322-323.

Have you seene but a bright Lillie grow,
　Before rude hands have touch'd it?
Have you mark'd but the fall o'the Snow
　Before the soyle hath smutch'd it?
Have you felt the wooll o'the Bever
　　　Or Swans Downe ever?
　Or have smelt o'the bud o'the Brier?
　　　Or the Nard in the fire?
　Or have tasted the bag o'the Bee?
O so white! O so soft! O so sweet is she![41]

Here the parallelism and cumulative sequence of Martial have
been used more consciously and definitely—this passage is
the poem's climax, not an effect to be dispersed in satire.
Metaphor is more severely regulated by syntax not only
for vocal effect but also for logical emphasis. The attempt
reads, without pedantry, like an attempt at formal definition.
The mounting pressure of meaning does not crumble away
under the pressure of irrelevant effects as in Martial. It is
clinched by the final, brief, and emphatic generalization
summarizing the implications of the images, which Martial
was content to leave confusedly if picturesquely assembled.
Now it may be that the control of imagery by tone and logic
is a failure in sensibility, but I think that Sullivan and Shelley,
even Arnold and Eliot, might well have hesitated to assert
this without qualification. We are left with the interesting
fact that only professional Latinists know of Martial's poem,
and no one has ever picked out the Ovidian fragment for
particular praise. But Jonson's poem was not only popular in
its own day—being both copied and parodied—it is still
enthusiastically sung on concert platforms throughout the
world. The changes rung on the stanza by Jonson's contem-

[41] *Ben Jonson*, viii, 134.

poraries were, of course, very varied. Some poets added extra stanzas modeled on Jonson's conclusion or excised the latter from the earlier stanzas to stand, with extensions based on the syntactical or logical pattern of the original, as a complete poem. Other poets inverted syntax and imagery in downright ridicule, rather in the style of Shakespeare's Sonnet 130. There is unmistakably something distinctive and wholly original in the poem's clarity of sequence which marks a development in sensibility. The poem also certainly rallied an enthusiastic interest, like Carew's lyric, which shows that both poets had managed to bring contemporary taste into focus in a way few earlier poems quite did.

Both the poems show a disciplined pattern of imagery, though Jonson's conclusive generalization is missing in Carew's; but it is worth adding a third illustration to show how many poets had come to approach the discovery and development of imagery on a highly systematized pattern, whether primarily syntactical as in Carew, logical as in Jonson, or even mathematical, as in the following example. Wotton's famous poem "To his Mistress the Queen of Bohemia" begins with a ratio reiterated in the imagery of every succeeding stanza:

> You meaner *Beauties* of the *Night,*
> That poorly satisfie our *Eies*
> More by your *number,* then your *light,*
> You *Common-people* of the *Skies;*
> What are you when the *Moon* shall rise?[42]

Without considering the fragmentary precedents for the ratio in Sappho, Horace, Petrarch, and Shakespeare, we can be sure of the inherited nature of this imagery by comparing

[42] *Metaphysical Poetry,* ed. H. J. C. Grierson (Oxford, 1921), p. 24. Mr. J. B. Leishman argues convincingly that Grierson's "Sun" in line 5 should be "Moon" as printed here. See his article, "You Meaner Beauties of the Night," *Library,* xxvi (1945), 99-121.

it with effects in a poem by Muretus, "Ad Noctem, Sidera, et Auroram, de Dominae Pulchritudine" ("To the Night, Stars and Aurora, of his Lady's Beauty"):

> Vos quoque lucentes Aethrae radiantis ocelli
>   Quorum alta assiduo templa canore sonant,
> Non pudor est, oculis vbi scintillantibus illa
>   Cedere tot vestras lampadas vna iubet?[43]

(You also, the shining eyes of the gleaming heaven, by whose constant song the high heaven rings, does it not shame you when she alone orders your so numerous lamps to yield to her sparkling eyes?)

This was not the only available contemporary source for Wotton's effects since in *Il Pastor Fido,* Guarini had written:

> Trà queste ella si staua,
> Si come suol trà violette humili
> Nobilissima rosa; . . . [44]

(Among these she was standing like a most noble rose among humble violets; . . .)

This is echoed in Wotton's third stanza:

> You *Violets,* that first apeare,
> By your *pure purpel mantels* knowne,
> Like the proud *Virgins* of the *yeare,*
> As if the *Spring* were all your own;
>   What are you when the *Rose is blowne?*

Muretus is, of course, Wotton's primary source, for the Latin poem provides the syntactical pattern for Wotton's— an opening apostrophe "You that . . . ," "Vos quoque . . . ," followed by a statement, and finally a question "What are

[43] *Delitiae Gallorum,* ii, 754.
[44] B. Guarini, *Il Pastor Fido* (Venice, 1621), p. 68.

you when . . . ?" "Non pudor est, . . . ubi . . . ?" Having
chosen this organization for his stanza, Wotton then finds
that certain classic images can be adjusted to the structure,
for which Guarini is only one obvious source among many.
There thus emerges in the successive stanzas of the final
poem a sense of order and emphasis which none of the
sources, including even Muretus, had shown. Imagery, while
remaining prominent and even suggesting the recurring ratio
of one to a group, is ultimately subjected to an ordering
principle more deliberate and systematic than any known in
earlier eras, but yet sufficiently subtle, flexible, and diversified to avoid monotony or vulgar artifice. Once again a poem
boldly illustrating this technique achieved enormous contemporary success and was favored by later anthologists.

By now it is possible to generalize more freely about
imagery in Renaissance lyricism and Stuart poetry in particular. Its status remains high. Varied and even challenging
imagery is much cultivated as is seen in poems such as
Donne's "The Flea," or "Valediction: forbidding mourning."
In fact, the images in these two startling poems are mostly
derivative. What makes them distinctive is the poet's novel
intellectual mastery over the articulation and purpose of his
images in each case. In the latter poem, a deathbed, the
precession of the equinoxes, the tensile properties of gold,
and the motion of compasses are deftly juxtaposed by a
process of disciplined parallelism akin to that of Jonson and
Wotton in the poems just discussed. The poet accumulates a
series of images which are strictly analogous in a way that
lends force to the poem's climactic assertion, either avowed
as in Jonson or implicit as in Wotton. What is new in Stuart
verse is not the so-called metaphysical imagery, which per-
vades nearly all Renaissance lyricism, but the power to discipline any image to a logically or rhythmically significant end.
This power is not the attribute merely of either metaphysical

or cavalier poets—a poor enough distinction anyway. It is the attribute of Stuart society as a whole that it started to speak more coherently and systematically not only of astronomy and other mathematical sciences, not only of theology, but also in courtship and even in flattery. When popular poets show this power it is surely proper to assume that contemporary sensibility has advanced with them.

[iv]

Its disciplined but conventional imagery suggests that ratiocination is becoming the prime feature of such Renaissance lyricism. This is not the case. It is truer to say that the requirements of logical thought are increasingly fulfilled by Renaissance lyricists than that logic becomes their primary interest. With this in mind it is worth discussing the evolution not only of syntactical, stylistic, and image patterns in these lyrics but also of traditional thought patterns. The disciplines by which familiar intellectual motifs in lyricism are regulated prove to be no less thorough than those governing other resources in Renaissance lyricism. To recognize this does something to show late Renaissance verse is not merely cerebral but also factual and exploratory as well. A typical intellectual motif which illustrates this is the popular affectation of systematically identifying one's mistress with either a goddess or, less blasphemously, with an incarnation of some heavenly ideal. In classical times poets were not given to Platonizing in love poetry—their sensibility did not readily assimilate intellectualism to heterosexual love. When they wished to flatter a woman they invoked the beauty of an appropriate goddess, who might be said to function as a crude approximation to a Platonic idea. Thus Rufinus wrote:

Ὄμματ᾽ ἔχεις Ἥρης, Μελίτη, τὰς χεῖρας Ἀθήνης,
τοὺς μαζοὺς Παφίης, τὰ σφυρὰ τῆς Θέτιδος.   (v, 94)

(Thou hast Hera's eyes, Melite, and Athene's hands, the breasts of Aphrodite, and the feet of Thetis.)[45]

There was a Christian version which began as a tactful simile, but matured in more profane times into a metaphor. Dante's madrigal may well be a prototype:

> Poichè saziar non posso gli occhi miei
> Di guardare a madonna il suo bel viso,
> Mirerol tanto fiso,
> Ch'io diverrò beato, lei guardando,
> A guisa d'angel che, di sua natura
> Stando su in altura,
> Devien beato sol guardando Iddio . . . .[46]

(Because I cannot satisfy my eyes with looking at the beautiful face of my lady, I stare with wonder so fixedly that I shall become exalted watching her, as an angel, in its own way supported on high, becomes beatified seeing God . . . .)

The Christian motif is a little more elaborate and technical than the pagan one, and in this it resembles most Neo-Platonic versions of the theme. However, Catullus does give us a glimpse of later Neo-Platonic extravagances when he writes:

> Lesbia formosast, quae cum pulcherrima totast,
> tum omnibus una omnis surripuit Veneres. (LXXXVI, 5-6)

(Lesbia is beautiful: for she possesses all the beauties, and has stolen all the graces from all the women alone for herself.)[47]

[45] Loeb edn., trans. W. R. Paton, I, 172-173.
[46] Ballata IX; Moore, p. 182a; not certainly Dante's.
[47] Loeb edn., trans. F. W. Cornish, pp. 162-163.

There is only a step from this to Petrarch's suggestion that
Laura is nature's earthly ideal of beauty:

> In qual parte del ciel, in quale idea
>   Era l'essempio onde natura tolse
>   Quel bel viso leggiadro, in ch'ella volse
>   Mostrar qua giú quanto là su potea?[48] (CLIX)

(In what zone of heaven, in what ideal was the model
whence nature drew that beautiful face, full of grace, in
which she sought to show down on earth how much she
might be capable of up there in heaven?)

The step is nevertheless decisive; one assertion is merely
enthusiastic in its appraisal, the other is systematic and metaphysical. Petrarch sounds less spontaneous but richer in potentialities because a new level for amatory debate, the philosophical, has been introduced. Many poets did little, in
following Petrarch's lead, to develop the creative potentialities of such philosophical allusions in love poetry. Two
centuries later Desportes was still writing, with a flatness he
shared with other Neo-Petrarchans:

> Sur la plus belle Idée au ciel vous fustes faite
> Voulant nature un jour monstrer tout son pouvoir,
> Depuis vous luy servez de forme et de miroir
> Et toute autre beauté sur la vostre est portraite.[49]

(On the most beautiful idea in heaven were you modeled
one day when nature wanted to show all its resources, and
since then you serve it as pattern and mirror, and all other
beauty is copied from yours.)

There is nothing here that carries the tradition forward. The
question in Petrarch's poem gives a faint pulse to its rhythm

---

[48] Carducci, p. 245.   [49] Michiels, p. 110.

but Desportes has lost even this. Only the explicitness of the philosophic allusion remains. The poem is nevertheless helpful as an illustration of the profoundly intellectual climate of the most sophisticated love-making at the time.

In this context more creative poets could not avoid intellectualizing their loves. Shakespeare was hardly an unreserved Platonist, but we find him writing in this vein with full mastery of the Platonic machinery:

> What is your substance, whereof are you made,
> That millions of strange shadows on you tend?
> Since everyone hath, everyone, one shade,
> And you but one, can every shadow lend.
> Describe Adonis, and the counterfeit
> Is poorly imitated after you;
> On Helen's cheek all art of beauty set,
> And you in Grecian tires are painted new:[50] (LIII)

He returns to the theme in Sonnet 106, and Drummond also found it irresistible:

> My Minde mee told, that in some other Place
> It elsewhere saw the *Idea* of that Face.[51]

Even Donne hardly varied the idea in "The Good-morrow":

> If ever any beauty I did see
> Which I desir'd, and got, 'twas but a dreame of thee.[52]

In themselves, because they follow closely the frigid Petrarchan model, there is little to praise in most of these uses of the motif identifying the mistress with an Idea. But there is something very curious about the theme if it is scrutinized in the light of the everyday experience to which Donne's poem alludes. He appears covertly to be excusing himself for

[50] Craig, p. 480.   [51] Kastner, I, 6.
[52] Grierson, p. 7.

previous and premature love affairs by claiming that they resulted from pursuit of approximations to his mistress' beauty in other women. It is an ingenious argument, worthy of Donne, but it is quite out of accord with the somewhat priggish attitudes of Petrarch when he is seeking to ingratiate himself with Laura.

The affected identity of mistress and idea proves, in fact, a double-edged compliment to many of the ladies involved when it is set in a context of earnest love-making, which was how most English poets used it. Shakespeare led the way, not unexpectedly, by taking advantage of an allusion somewhat like that which we noted in his *Sonnets*. In *Love's Labour's Lost* (IV, iii, 60) a lover addresses a sonnet to his "heavenly" mistress as if she were above morality and he beneath it, merely to justify the demands of expediency:

> Did not the heavenly rhetoric of thine eye,
> 'Gainst whom the world could not hold argument,
> Persuade my heart to this false perjury?
> Vows for thee broke deserve not punishment.
> A woman I forswore; but I will prove,
> Thou being a goddess, I forswore not thee:
> My vow was earthly, thou a heavenly love;
> Thy grace being gain'd cures all disgrace in me. . . .[53]

This poem could not have been written by a classical poet, for he would lack the dialectical skill and resources. It could not be written by a Dante or a Petrarch or a Desportes because they were only introducing dialectic to verse and kept a formal manner befitting the solemn context from which the ideas were taken. But by 1600 English poets, as we see, were not merely thinking scholastically in easy verse, they were deploying metaphysics and theological distinctions in the service of dramatic situations wholly alien to the narrower

[53] Craig, p. 116.

sympathies of their predecessors. Shakespeare's lover argues that his new love, like that of God, is too important to take account of lesser allegiances, and that the breaking of these may be overlooked if his new mistress will, like the Christian God, give him "grace" (a neat pun). The argument is only superficially jocular—Romeo's casual abandonment of Rosaline for Juliet shows what Shakespeare has in mind. The idea is thus pursued not simply for the argument's sake but to resolve the tension resulting from the same sense of tainted integrity in changing loves that worried Donne a little in "The Good-morrow" and concerned him much more in "Loves Deitie." In less impressive poems the metaphysical motif systematically identifying a woman with a goddess or idea exists for its own sake—unlike such poems Shakespeare's sonnet is not merely a piece of virtuoso flattery. It conforms superficially to the pagan tradition identifying the mistress with a goddess, which preceded the Platonic motif of her as an idea, but redeploys its meaning to suit more directly personal ends with the almost cynical ingenuity more commonly associated with Donne.

The theme of the incarnated idea proved equally susceptible to distortion in the service of a dramatic situation, without risking the offense to religious sentiments which Shakespeare's cynical and punning view of grace offered. Carew uses the theme with a precise gallantry in his poem "To a Lady Resembling my Mistress," which manages to confess an attraction in another woman analogous to that of his mistress without compromising his own integrity:

> To Lead, or Brasse, or some such bad
> Mettall, a Princes stamp may adde
> That valew, which it never had.
>
> But to the pure refined Ore,
> The stamp of Kings imparts no more

Worth, than the mettall held before.

Only the Image gives the rate
To Subjects; in a forraine State
'Tis priz'd as much for its owne waight.

So though all other hearts resigne
To your pure worth, yet you have mine
Only because you are her coyne.[54]

The argument is plausible. However, there is an undertone of self-exculpation in its very virtuosity, which cleverly obscures some difficult facts. First, it implies that the attractions of Carew's first love are not unique. It also ungraciously assumes, to justify Carew's admitted attraction to her, that the lady addressed is a mere copy of the poet's mistress, outwardly at least. There is no doubt that the argument is defensive rather than merely ingenious and amusing. Take away the attraction to another woman, which is what really demands some such vindication as the assertion of resemblance, and there is little point in the poem. However, after the preliminary display of virtuosity, the confession that the second lady has Carew's heart passes happily almost unnoted. In Petrarch and Desportes the actuality of such an immediate and distinctive situation is missing, and the thought is sustained in their poems merely by its uninspired flattering intention.

Thus, what distinguishes the poems of Shakespeare and Carew from their earlier models is not the process of argument, but the development of a distinctive and once neglected possibility in love poetry, the existence of a previous or succeeding attraction to the supposedly climactic one on which most poets normally focus their exclusive attention. This theme affords an interesting challenge to the imposing moral and psychological patterns of love which the Renais-

54 Dunlap, p. 27.

sance had elaborated, serving to focus and exercise fully the best resources of the lyric poet. The most striking effect of Renaissance poetic virtuosity on conventional patterns of love-making may therefore lie, not in distinctive imagery or thought, but in subjecting previously available resources to new and challenging situations not yet explored by lyricism. Classical love poetry tended to concern itself with the primary issues of love, not the delicate marginal discriminations which increasingly attract the attention of seventeenth-century Stuart poets. It is perhaps a significant revelation of differing values that the defense of his changed affections would never seem necessary to a classical love poet. Only the unsolicited fickleness in his mistress would demand discussion, because it directly touched his continued sensual satisfaction.

With the Stuart poets it is quite otherwise. The theme of vindicated fickleness demands their most considered attention as a pivotal issue for the now much more self-conscious and intellectually consistent love poet. The concern with the demands of a practical issue clearly governs the intellectual virtuosity of Lord Edward Herbert's conclusion to his brief lyric on inconstancy:

> Inconstancye, noe synn will proue
> Yf wee consider that wee Love
> But the same beautye in another fface
> Lyke, the same Bodye, in another place.[55]

This is a sardonically frank exposition of the argument Carew is really using—but it does show a *need* for self-vindication, which is more important and primary than the ratiocination that satisfies it. Even here, despite the abstraction of the thought, the poem is concerned with the potential demands of a precise situation, which the ingenious lover will find

[55] Moore Smith, p. 119.

more disturbing than the mere obligation to flatter governing Petrarch and his followers when handling the topic of beauty. The same sense of the illumination of original and demanding situations is found in other typical Stuart applications of the intellectual content of the motif we are tracking—that is, the linking of woman's beauty with an ideal essence. Sir Robert Howard's poem "To the Unconstant Cynthia" shows a more fashionably suave use of it, neatly ballasted with affected piety:

> Tell me once, dear, how does it prove
>   That I so much forsworn could be?
> I never swore always to love,
>   I only vowed still to love thee:
> And art thou now what thou wert then,
> Unsworn unto by other men?[56]

There is considerable ingenuity in the argument, but what is achieved is more than a sense of triumphant logic, it is the accurate analysis of an equivocal situation, an analysis that logic merely serves, not justifies. Lovelace duplicates Howard's methods more brutally in forswearing a woman whose treachery to her own nature consists simply in growing old and ill-favored, but it is Stanley who shows how the argument for frank promiscuity could be vindicated by the logical resources borrowed from Platonism and theology:

> Wrong me no more
>   In thy complaint,
> Blam'd for inconstancy;
>   I vow'd t' adore
>   The fairest Saint,
> Nor chang'd while thou wert she:
> But if another thee outshine,
> Th' inconstancy is only thine. . . .

[56] *Unfamiliar Lyrics,* ed. N. Ault (London, 1938), p. 244.

None (though Platonic their pretence)
With reason love unless by sense.

> And He, by whose
> > Command to thee
> I did my heart resign,
> > Now bids me choose
> > A Deity
> Diviner far than thine; . . .

> 'twere as impious to adore
> Thee now, as not t' have done't before.[57]

This is another version of the same situation, with the poet using Shakespeare's logic to vindicate a new attachment rather aggressively, to the eclipsed and repudiated beauty. And here again, clever though the argument is, it is the rather unpleasing situation that exacts primary attention. The poem's brusqueness and cruelty may well alienate the reader despite its logical finesse. Thus the same intellectual motif succeeds or fails in a poem depending on the interest and importance of the situation to which it is subordinated. Novelty of situation rather than of argument or even of insight is the key to the character of much Renaissance lyricism. Poets do not so much discover new techniques as demand new functions from old resources. The perversion of Platonic arguments to alien ends is a salutary illustration of this.

[v]

Renaissance poets extend vastly the range of topics customarily handled by writers of love lyrics. These new topics show certain consistent patterns. They tend to reflect the day-to-day life of lovers more than the climactic moments of love. Occasional poetry flourished at the expense of heroic

---

[57] Saintsbury, III, 113.

emotion, which in turn became increasingly conventional in its expression. Even on a more serious level, incidental anxieties rather than the facts of consummation increasingly preoccupy poets. The female readers' genteel expectations of the more casual kinds of poetry encouraged ingenious improvisations on such routine occasions as the mistress' dancing, walking, sickness, or admiring herself in the mirror or in a variety of less conventional but still hardly serious activities, such as those described in Waller's poems about a lady playing with a snake, or cutting trees in paper. It might seem that the apparent triviality of these topics implies folly in both author and readers. Yet the pompous charge of the eighteenth and nineteenth centuries that poets such as Herrick and Waller frittered away their talents on trivialities is not borne out by modern psychiatry. This branch of medicine has seen in the most superficial details of conduct a wealth of meaning which vindicates the elaborate analysis by Renaissance poets of topics which seem at first sight hardly to demand it. Johnson may well ridicule Waller's poem about a lady playing with a snake, but no Jungian would find the theme trivial, and no critic has ever found the version of this topic framed by an exact contemporary of Waller's, John Milton, contemptible. In this light, Waller's poem becomes a little more startling and meaningful, for one sees that Waller recognizes these overtones in addressing this "fair Eve." His famous poem "On a Girdle" appears equally slight, but in fact it is a striking rationalization of a theme that goes back to the *Anacreontea*—preoccupation with some intimate object associated with one's mistress. Waller identifies the sentiment at its most gracious, with consummate accuracy and understanding. Herrick's more morbid fascination with clothes is also closely related to the theme, and his poems are profoundly interesting to modern students of fetishism, though they are less successful as poetry the more pathological they become. Nevertheless, his poems are often illuminating and picturesque when seen as methods of ingenius sublimation or transference of emotions which might otherwise threaten his emotional stability.

Such topics form a category whose importance is by no means diminished as the individual subjects become slighter. On the other hand, Renaissance poets develop the documentation of many serious aspects of love relationships which earlier ones either neglected or failed to recognize. The Renaissance lyrics offer thus a kind of systematic "meteorology" of the spiritual climate of sexual love, analogous to Herbert's exposition of that of religious feeling. The serious vindication of fickleness which we have examined is one example of a group of lyrics doing this; poems about separation, absence, and death in love affairs form another group whose subjects were only intermittently handled by classical poets, despite one conspicuous series of examples in Ovid's somewhat mechanical and undistinguished *Heroides*. (By contrast one thinks of Donne's four distinctive "Valedictions.") Poems dealing with such topics are particularly interesting as illustrations of how characteristic of Renaissance lyricism is its concern with previously unfamiliar or at least unfashionable topics. This rather unclassical theme of impediments to love shows as well as any the decisive widening of scope in the choice of topics for love poetry in the Renaissance.

The theme of lovers' separation was certainly recognized by classical poets, but it was almost synonymous with that of fickleness. It was also more characteristically a female than a male concern, at least as far as we can judge from the treatment of such figures as the abandoned Ariadne and Dido in the *Heroides*, a treatment which derives from Greek precedents such as Theocritus' second idyl. A kind of male version is indeed found in the treatment of Polyphemus in Theocritus' eleventh idyl and in Ovid's *Metamorphoses*, as well as in Virgil's second eclogue. However, these poems all presuppose betrayal as the premise of separation. To the ancients, with their strong sense of the here and now, life was little qualified by any larger spiritual sense, despite the aspirations of Plato's philosophy before it declined into the Pyrrhonism that his followers too often made of it. Absence was taken as a fatal obstacle to love, usually incurred to confirm a choice, and rarely seen as an incidental obstacle to be overcome. Horace does perhaps face the challenge hypothetically at the end of his famous ode "Integer vitae," which praises the power of virtue. Here the final assertion is more a mode of rhetorical coda than a serious analysis of the problem, but it has a movement very like that favored by the Renaissance:

> pone me pigris ubi nulla campis
> arbor aestiva recreatur aura,
> quod latus mundi nebulae malusque
>   Iuppiter urget;
>
> pone sub curru nimium propinqui
> solis in terra domibus negata:
> dulce ridentem Lalagen amabo,
>   dulce loquentem. (i, xxii, 17-24)

(Place me on the lifeless plains where no tree revives under the summer breeze, a region of the world o'er which brood mists and gloomy sky; set me beneath the chariot of the sun where it draws too near the earth, in a land denied for dwellings! I will love my sweetly laughing, sweetly prattling Lalage.)[58]

The passage is obviously a concluding flourish, linked with the body of the ode perhaps only by the implication that Horace's confidence in Lalage's love helps to give him the courage both to face the wolf whose flight chiefly makes him so proud and to brave the rigors of bad climates, apparently

---

[58] Loeb edn., trans. C. E. Bennett, pp. 64-65.

even ("pone *me*") if he is exiled from her. The separation remains only a convenient hypothesis subordinated to the poem's main purpose and there is no hint of a serious consideration of the practical difficulties of absence, such as, say, Ovid's exile from Rome and his family must have raised. However, Horace's self-confidence gives the sense of a love superior to circumstance, and this makes his poem one of the few classical treatments of the theme of affection transcending difficulties.

The writers of the Middle Ages were no happier in contemplating absence than were the pagan poets—but for them the physical presence of the beloved was no longer a prerequisite for the relationship to have value and expression. Though the anonymous English poet saw it differently:

> Christ, if my love were in my arms
> And I in my bed again,[59]

Walafried Strabo could write to his friend:

> Cum splendor lunae fulgescat ab aethere puro
> tu sta sub divo cernens speculamine miro,
> qualiter ex luna splendescat lampade pura
> et splendore suo caros amplectitur uno
> torpore divisos, sed mentis amore ligatos.
> si facies faciem spectare nequivit amantem,
> hoc saltem nobis lumen sit pignus amoris.
> hos tibi versiculos fidus transmisit amicus;
> si de parte tua fidei stat fixa catena,
> nunc precor, ut valeas felix per saecula cuncta.[60]

(When the splendor of the moon shines in the clear heaven, stand looking attentively beneath the fair sky how the

[59] *Early English Lyrics*, ed. E. K. Chambers and F. Sidgwick (London, 1921), p. 69.
[60] Waddell, p. 116.

moon's lamp shines clearly and unites in splendor two friends divided in body but linked in mind by love. If it is denied to your lover's eyes to see your face, this light may be a token of love which links us. Faithful love sends these verses to you; if on your side your faith stands as a fixed chain, then I pray that you may be happy for all the centuries.)

The ingenious bridge of the moon is less important than the strong chains of loyalty and faith which link the two men, and the poem shows in this stress on firmness and spiritual communion what a difference the sense of Christian metaphysics has made to the spiritual resilience of the whole range of human emotions. That this kind of enduring loyalty in the face of actual difficulties was increasingly current appears in a fifteenth-century English lyric, which shows some analogy to the amatory allusions in Horace's ode:

> Thogh I be far out of her sight,
> I am her man bothe day and night,
> And so wol be.[61]

The poet rejects absolutely his lady's proverb, "seldin seen is soon forgeten," and hopes that she will learn to love him best "evermore wherever she be." There seems little advance on this in Surrey's sonnet in which he consciously stresses Horace's syntactical pattern in typical Renaissance fashion:

> Set me whereas the sun doth parch the green,
> Or where his beams may not dissolve the ice, . . .
> Set me in low or yet in high degree; . . .
> Yours will I be, and with this only thought
> Comfort myself when that my hope is nought.[62]

[61] *Early English Lyrics*, p. 32.
[62] *Silver Poets*, p. 120.

The sterility of the poem is clear in its final, futile assertion of love for a merely unresponsive beloved. Like Horace's conclusion the subject is really more rhetorical than actual— Horace shows his self-confidence in daring the worst of distance and climate; Surrey advertises, not even his trust in his mistress, but his capacity for loyalty. Neither handles the demands of a real challenge to a substantial relationship as the medieval poets try to do.

It is curious to realize that Donne's "Valediction: forbidding mourning" takes up the Surrey theme in the famous compass image, which illustrates that sustained mutual awareness of loyal lovers during their separation that Strabo also registers. The crucial differences between Surrey and Donne lie in the occasion of the discussion of absence and the methods by which it is handled. Surrey is talking rhetorically about how he loves his mistress. As Walton notes in his *Life*, Donne gave his verses "to his wife at the time he then parted from her" because "her divining soul boded her some ill in his absence." Donne's arguments have a sense of urgency and relevance to a particular problem equally present in the medieval poet but not present in Surrey. Donne tries to confirm the stability and permanence of his love and to show that, as it does not depend on physical factors, absence does not touch it radically. It is interesting to see that Donne's poem is as much an "occasional" one as Waller's about the snake, or the paper tree. Surrey's poem is also occasional, but not in a way so directly related to an actual lover's problem. Further, the argument merely implicit in Surrey's poem has become fully evident and logically articulated by Carew's time, thanks to its explicit recognition by Donne. Carew can bluntly state the crucial fact in his poem "Upon Love's Ubiquity":

> Goe I to *Holland, France,* or furthest *Inde,*
> I change but onely Countreys, not my mind.[63]

[63] Dunlap, p. 123.

Many contemporaries of Carew surpassed him in analyzing the resistance of lovers to absence. Lord Edward Herbert, for example, noted perceptively the mutual intellectual penetration of lovers in "The Thought":

> If you do love, as well as I,
> Then every minute from your heart
>   A thought doth part:
> And winged with desire doth fly
> Till it hath met in a streight line,
>   A thought from mine
> So like to yours, we cannot know
> Whether of both doth come or go,
>   Till we define
> Which of us two that thought doth ow.[64]

The passage is interesting as an attempt to define the mental communion between lovers, but it is awkward and unmemorable because it lacks the verve this chapter has attributed to the best Renaissance lyricism.

John Hoskins had succeeded better, before Herbert, in a poem which opens with a challenge:

> Absence hear my protestation
>   Against thy strengthe
>   Distance and lengthe,
> Doe what thou canst for alteration:
>   For harts of truest mettall
>   Absence doth joyne, and time doth settle.[65]

From this rhetorical challenge Hoskins modulates deftly to an intimate validation of his self-confidence by way of the assertion of the virtue of intellectual communion enforced by absence:

[64] Moore Smith, p. 43.
[65] *Metaphysical Poetry*, p. 23.

By absence this good means I gaine
   That I can catch her
   Where none can watch her
In some close corner of my braine:
   There I embrace and kiss her,
   And so enjoye her, and so misse her.

The poem is a dexterous blend of sensuous longing and intellectual awareness for which there is no precedent in Horace or any premedieval poet. The evolution of mood in this last stanza is particularly assured in its expression. It shows how much closer to everyday experience and flow of feelings such love poets were getting, in their treatment of topics that were themselves closer than many to the routine concerns of lovers.

We see the same processes at work in Lovelace's three poems on absence. The most famous one is also that most precisely focused on a particular and precisely defined situation, "To Althea, from Prison." True, the barrier here between the lovers is only an iron grating, but Lovelace finds means to transcend not only this but all the material barriers to his freedom, by means more fully expressed in one of his two poems to Lucasta on absence, "Going Beyond the Seas":

   Though seas and land betwixt us both,
      Our faith and troth,
     Like separated souls,
    All time and space controls:
   Above the highest sphere we meet
   Unseen, unknown, and greet as angels greet.[66]

There is an elusive principle lurking here, one deeply embedded in medieval and Platonic mysticism, but the argument may be easily rationalized as based on the confidence given to separated lovers by their mutually assured and always self-

[66] Howarth, p. 246.

conscious affection. The elusive connection which survives distance is this common knowledge of a sustained attitude; and in this matter the third Lovelace poem on another occasion of separation, "To Lucasta, Going to the Wars," offers a clinching argument for the theory by demonstrating the lover's integrity:

> Yet this inconstancy is such
> As you too shall adore;
> I could not love thee, dear, so much,
> Lov'd I not Honour more.[67]

The exact and unfamiliar (though realistic) nature of the event is again the decisive feature of the poem. "In Prison," "Going to the Wars"—such wholly localizing titles illustrate the immediacy and primacy of the situation governing each poem, and many of the most memorable late Renaissance love lyrics have this novel, "occasional" character.

It is worth noting that, in the pursuit of such topical immediacy, poems on separation were not confined to physical separation. Marvell's "Definition of Love" implies something more like a social barrier rather than a physical one, since he "quickly might arrive" where his attentions are fixed. He uses the same arguments, of lovers' spiritual affinity being able to defy worldly barriers, that were used by Donne and Lovelace. But the most distinctive situation to which these arguments were ever applied is probably that in Cartwright's poem "To Chloe who Wished Herself Young Enough for Me." Cartwright argues that the lovers' true maturity dates only from their first mutual understanding and delight in each other and that it is this spiritual age which counts. Again the situation, precise and realistic rather than fanciful, is the decisive and original feature of the poem as literature. Yet the topic is one which has been clearly of interest and importance

[67] *Ibid.*

to real lovers as the number of such alliances suggests. It was left until the time of seventeenth-century poets like Waller, Marvell, Sedley, and Etherege (not to mention Prior shortly afterwards) for love lyrics to canvass exhaustively every permutation of Cartwright's theme and discuss not simply a mistress who is too old but the charm and pathos of one who is too young for the tempted lover. In the classical poets who dealt with approximately the same topic, notably Anacreon and Horace, the typical reaction was simply to turn the theme into an occasion for another argument for or against early sexual consummation. The Renaissance poets reviewed this possibility, but also explored other more gracious (and, in their society, more practical) approaches to the situation with subtlety and accuracy. The crude and universal impetus of sexuality is a notably subdued element of their poems, while the logic of the particular situation is explored fully. It is typical of the age that this particular topic should be thoroughly discussed by five conspicuous English poets within half a century or so, while all the classical poets together offer only two or three poems about it, none of which investigates the subject subtly from the point of view of the truly discriminating lover himself. Such a concern with precise and immediate situations is a frequent characteristic of Stuart love poetry.

[vi]

Since it is being asserted that the monochrome picture of love presented by the ancients is brightened into a dazzling array of possibilities by the prism of Renaissance sensibility, this chapter on the new style in lyricism may well conclude its detailed discussion by showing what happened to two highly literary conventions superior in complexity to any of the individual strands of poetic skill hitherto examined. Because the

skills and perceptions which they involve defy neat characterization, these themes illustrate fully the dramatic evolution
and extension of European sensibility between classical and
Renaissance times. The two themes are less unrelated than
polarized versions of the same theme—the relation between
lovers and nature. One is focused on the man devoted to winning his lady,[68] and the other upon the mistress who com-
mands a lover's respect and that of everything around her.
The two figures about whom the appropriate patterns crystallized in classical times were the Cyclops Polyphemus and
Aphrodite herself. These markedly antithetical figures govern
two closely related traditions which survive the disappearance
of the nominal characters at a fairly early date, though the
names do periodically recur in later but more traditional
treatments of the themes.

Polyphemus was probably first conjured into the role of a
clumsy rustic wooer by the Greek poet Philoxenus. He used
the figure of the one-eyed monster to ridicule a myopic tyrant
who had condemned the poet for seducing one of the court
singers. Versions of the pattern appear in Theocritus and
Virgil, but Ovid preserves the original pattern in pristine
clarity in his *Metamorphoses*. The original satirical flavor survives here only in the realistic evocation of Polyphemus' rural
origins by means of the gifts with which he seeks to tempt
the lady of his choice, the sea nymph Galatea, and the instinctively rural imagery with which he ornaments his speech.
All the classical versions of the pattern run to the considerable
length of an elegy, but all consciously distinguish the invitation to accept the lover from other conventional arguments
for love, to which it is closely related, by the careful evocation
of a bucolic setting for the temptation. The only analogous
motif in the Middle Ages appears in a slight poem beginning:

[68] For an extended discussion of this theme, see the author's article
"Polyphemus in England," *CL*, XII (1960), 229-242.

Iam, dulcis amica, venito,
quam sicut cor meum diligo;
Intra in cubiculum meum,
ornamentis cunctis onustum.

Ibi sunt sedilia strata
et domus velis ornata,
Floresque in domo sparguntur
herbeque fragrantes miscentur. . . .

Ego fui sola in silva
et dilexi loca secreta:
Frequenter effugi tumultum
et vitavi populum multum. . . .[69]

(Come now sweetheart, whom I love like my own heart; enter my room rich with many furnishings. There are couches to sit on, a home ornamented with drapery, and flowers spread in it mixed with sweet-smelling herbs. . . . I have been alone in the wood and sought out secret places; I fled often from noise and avoided the crowds. . . .)

The poem is interesting because of its innocent tone, echoing the naïve hopes of Polyphemus; but if it is comparable to the earlier pleas in this way it must also be noted how the theme has lost most of its marginal details. The plea is given in its most economical form yet, and with a sharper cadence, seen in its opening imperatives boldly set in short lines. Already the Middle Ages is paring down lyric statement to its essentials in a way almost standardized in the best Renaissance lyrics. The speaker is no grotesque such as Ovid had pictured him, nor even the courtier faintly disguised as a shepherd of Virgil's second eclogue. He is the author himself, just as we find the speaker to be in an interesting but clumsy elegy of Muretus:

[69] Waddell, p. 144.

Scire cupis quae sit votorum summa meorum,
  Et qua praecipue vivere sorte velim?
Non ego tecta mihi Phrygiis innixa columnis,
  Diuitis aut auri pondera mille petam; . . .
Sed tecum longae traducere tempora vitae,
  Securumque tuo semper amore frui . . . .
Tecum ego per montes, tecum per deuia tesqua,
  Et curram nullo per loca tacta pede . . . .
Balnea non illic, non sunt populosa theatra,
  Non quicquid mentes sollicitare potest,
Sed nemora et placido currentes murmure riui,
  Demulcensque rudi carmine pastor oues.[70]

(You wish to know what may be the height of my desires, and in what manner I would particularly like to live? I do not seek roofs supported with Phrygian columns or weighted with priceless gold and riches; . . . but with you to pass the extent of a long life and to enjoy your love always in security. . . . With you I would wander in the mountains, with you along winding paths and in places never touched by foot. . . . Neither yonder baths, nor are crowded theatres anything the mind can desire, but woods, and rivers flowing with soft murmurs, and the shepherd soothing his flock with rustic songs.)

This Renaissance poem has the ring of Horace's famous second epode upon the joys of rural life, but instead of being ironically attributed to an urban usurer it is here a veiled invitation to rural dalliance offered by a lover who is treated quite seriously throughout by the author.

As we have seen with other effects studied in this chapter, it is left to an English poet to strip away the various surface patterns into which the motif has been shaped, until the essential structure underlying the various poems in which it

[70] *Delitiae Gallorum*, ii, 740.

appears becomes clear. Marlowe's "Passionate Shepherd" catches the economical resonance of the medieval lyric and also the urban nostalgia for the country of Horace and Muretus. One sees the distinctive movement of the medieval poet in Marlowe's opening stanza, and the aristocratic myth of the elegists in his second:

> Come liue with mee, and be my loue,
> And we will all the pleasures proue,
> That Vallies, groues, hills and fieldes,
> Woods, or steepie mountaine yeeldes.
>
> And we will sit vpon the Rocks,
> Seeing the Sheepheards feede theyr flocks
> By shallow Riuers, to whose falls
> Melodious byrds sings Madrigals. . . .[71]

Despite Marlowe's title the speaker is in no sense the quaint rustic that his prototype was, but a sophisticate like Virgil's "shepherd" who finds bucolic fantasy a useful mode of attaining his desires. The lover hardly appears in a servile role in this pretty landscape. Thus we see in Marlowe's poem both the increasing normalization of curious myths and the replacement of bizarre and merely physical data by sophistication of style and sentiment. Marlowe's poem is briefer, more decisive and memorable, as well as truer to the writer's own nature than the original Cyclops myth, and even than most other versions of the motif.

Needless to say the poem was rapidly copied, reversed, and satirized. Raleigh answered the argument in realistic terms but in the same syntactical pattern. In "The Baite" Donne copied the invitation in harsher, more satirical tones, while transposing the pastoral convention to a piscatory one. Mar-

---

[71] C. Marlowe, *Works*, ed. C. F. Tucker Brooke (Oxford, 1910), p. 550.

lowe even parodied himself in *The Jew of Malta* (ll. 1806 ff.)[72] in ways which return the motif to something like Philoxenus' satirical purposes—Ithamore hopes to entice the tricky courtesan, who finally eludes his affections, by temptations more rhetorical but scarcely more effective than those of Polyphemus. Cotton and Herrick also duplicate the Passionate Shepherd's invitation. Cotton does so twice, once in piscatory form, once in a charmingly localized Derbyshire version. Herrick makes his insipid plea in a simpering style which contrasts sharply and significantly with the lush, authentic color of Ovid's account. Townshend strikes a stern moral note in his version, inditing the flashy seductions of urban life while offering the worthy severities of rustic integrity. However, it is no distortion to see in Comus' lyrical temptation of the Lady a climactic illustration of the motif's deployment in the Renaissance. Here the economy of Marlowe's lyric is deliberately sacrificed to the masterly focusing of the central theme by a subtle dialectic, so that it harmonizes with the fullest moral and intellectual frames of reference of the time. The seductive sprites of "Il Penseroso" and "Arcades" clearly inherit many of the virtues of Polyphemus, but the latest "Genius of the Woods" urges his now ominous arguments for the Lady's reconciliation to his bucolic orgies with a brilliance that leaves far behind all previous appeals to accept Nature's blessings and the suit of the giver. Comus inherits Milton's own youthful delight in rural nature and argues vividly and subtly for the acceptance of those indulgences that earlier poets, perhaps less consciously committed to Nature than Milton, had presented from the lips of Polyphemus so much less dynamically.

An illustration of the almost infinite permutations of the motif so characteristic of the restless energy of Renaissance lyricism, is that Ronsard's orthodox version of the story in his

[72] *Ibid.*, p. 289.

eclogue about Polyphemus, "Le Cyclops Amoureux," provides inspiration for Donne's "Twicknham Garden." Ronsard's eclogue is an elaborate rhetorical excursus in which the frustrated Polyphemus seeks consolation by identifying himself with the insentient nature around him, in the same striking way that characterizes the lover in Donne's poem. If "Twicknham Garden" is read in the light of the Polyphemus-Galatea tradition, there is a basic resemblance between the situation in the poem and in the tradition. Though the character of the English Renaissance poem seems to clash with the bizarre classical theme, Donne has simply transcended the local peculiarities of the prototype. He has not rejected the basic pattern, but normalized it. Both Donne's lover and Ronsard's Polyphemus have retired to a rural sanctuary to complain of their loves, each being the victim of a woman loyal to another. The crucial difference lies not in the facts but in the lovers' reaction to them. In classical versions the Cyclops or his counterpart is coolly and accurately portrayed with a firm massing of local color. In Ronsard, despite a bulky recapitulation of this kind of detail, various new notes of subjective feeling emerge. And in "Twicknham Garden" the defeat of the Cyclops has been wholly transmuted into a vivid study of the mood of a rejected lover, for which the factual circumstances are only a preliminary definition. The poet's sensitive communication of the texture of wholly subjective reactions, as opposed to the detailing of the traditional concrete facts of rural gifts and pleasures, is distinctively the mark of late Renaissance lyricism. Even the false charm of Marlowe's picture of rural life, so sharply censured in Raleigh's equally one-sided reply, is maintained in the true negative to such wishful thinking, which lies in Donne's record of the world's actual condition despite his lover's subjective despair. While Marlowe's lover sees all nature green and golden with his hopes, Donne's manages to see the fertility of the spring even though it conflicts with his mood. Here, thanks to Ronsard, who also exploits the contrast, he surpasses both Marlowe's and Raleigh's insights but preserves their memorable concision, poise, and energy, which in turn were absent from Ronsard's eclogue and earlier elegies. Donne thus liberates feeling from the "pathetic fallacy" in a way which neither Marlowe nor Raleigh did in their poems. Such a rectification was quite inconceivable to classical poets, as even the sentimental defect was hardly consciously current among them. Thus we see an almost endless permutation of practical or fanciful possibilities realized by the pens of Renaissance poets, where only a single quaint tradition existed in classical times. And almost all the later permutations are marked by strong rhythmic flow, a stress on the normal social nature of the situation, and a subtle exploitation of interesting subjective moods.

The alternative, feminine theme focuses nature not on the aspirant lover but on the triumphant beauty of the mistress. In its earliest form the allusion was no flattery of a woman but a tribute to a fertilizing principle. The birth of Aphrodite is thus described in Hesiod's *Theogony*:

> ἐκ δ' ἔβη αἰδοίη καλὴ θεός, ἀμφὶ δὲ ποίη
> ποσσὶν ὕπο ῥαδινοῖσιν ἀέξετο· (1, 194)

(And came forth an awful and lovely goddess, and grass grew up about her beneath her shapely feet.)[73]

And in Lucretius' *De Rerum Natura* Venus is credited with similar powers as the incarnation of the natural principle of harmony which calms and fertilizes all earthly things:

> te, dea, te fugiunt venti, te nubila caeli
> adventumque tuum, tibi suavis daedala tellus
> summittit flores, tibi rident aequora ponti
> placatumque nitet diffuso lumine caelum. (1, 6-9)

[73] Hesiod, *Theogony*, Loeb edn., trans. H. G. Evelyn White (London, 1936), pp. 92-93.

(Thou, goddess, thou dost turn to flight the winds and clouds of heaven, thou art thy coming; for thee earth, the quaint artificer, puts forth her sweet-scented flowers; for thee the levels of ocean smile, and the sky, its anger past, gleams with spreading light.)[74]

Theocritus had already shown in one of his *Idylls*[75] how the attributes of the goddess might flatteringly be redirected toward mere mortal women. Two shepherds are made to assert that their sweethearts exert divine influence on the crops, flocks, and climate wherever they go, and Virgil uses similar effects in his seventh eclogue. An interesting extension of the motif occurs when Martial seriously, and Juvenal sarcastically,[76] applied the conceit to their emperors, whose frank claims to divinity invited such flattery. This kind of affectation might seem incompatible with Christian views, but, as similitudes between the Christian God and the poet's chaste mistress declined into metaphor (and hence into blasphemy) about Petrarch's time, the attribution of the fertilizing, harmonizing powers of the pagan goddess to a woman again becomes conventional. Petrarch grants Laura exactly the effect of Hesiod's Aphrodite and Lucretius' Venus.[77] Ronsard follows the pattern, but it is in English that the theme really reaches full expansion. To take just one variant—Donne, Waller, and Cowley all describe the desire of fish to sacrifice themselves to the mistress just as Martial and Juvenal had shown animals happy to die for Caesar.

The fullest expansion of the motif came in the "promenade poem," whose movement is hinted at in Hesiod's lines. The divinity, now become the poet's mistress, walks through her

[74] Lucretius, *De Rerum Natura*, ed. and trans. C. Bailey (Oxford, 1947), I, 176-177.

[75] VII, 57ff.

[76] *Epigrams*, IX, xxxi, 5, and *Satires*, IV, 69, respectively, in the Loeb editions.

[77] CLXV; Carducci, p. 252.

garden or a landscape, spreading her beneficent influence everywhere. Tasso's *Rime d'Amore* provided one source of this motif for Stuart poets, in the poems inspiring Strode's "On Chloris Walking in the Snow." However, it also seems likely that Ronsard's complimentary elegy to the queen who befriended him, the ill-fated Mary Stuart, affords another conspicuous Renaissance model for later poets, since his poem fuses all the earlier allusions into a coherent and memorable whole. He describes the widowed Queen of France pensively pacing through the gardens at Fontainebleau:

> pensive, et baignant vostre sein
> Du beau crystal de vos larmes roulées,
> Triste marchiez par les longues allées
> Du grand jardin de ce royal Chasteau
> Qui prend son nom de la source d'une eau.
> Tout les chemins blanchissoient sous vos toiles, . . .
> Lors les rochers, bien qu'ils n'eussent point d'ame,
> Voyant marcher une si belle Dame,
> Et les deserts, les sablons, et l'estang
> Où vit maint cygne habillé tout de blanc,
> Et des hauts pins la cyme de verd peinte,
> Vous contemploient comme une chose sainte,
> Et pensoient voir, pour ne voir rien de tel,
> Une Déesse en habit d'un mortel
> Se promener, quand l'Aube retournée
> Par les jardins poussoit la matinée,
> Et vers le soir, quand desjà le Soleil
> A chef baissé s'en-alloit au sommeil.[78]

(. . . thoughtful and bathing your bosom with the fine crystal of your fallen tears, sadly you used to walk by the long avenues of the great garden of this royal palace which

[78] Cohen, II, 294.

takes its name from a spring. All the paths whitened beneath
your clothes, . . . while the rocks, although they lacked
souls, seeing so fine a lady walk, and the bare spaces and
the fine sands, and the pool where dwells many a swan
clothed all in white, and the high pines with their green-
painted tops, all gazed at you as something sanctified, and
thought they saw, as they had seen nothing similar, a goddess clothed as a mortal walking when the returned dawn
sent morning through the gardens, and toward the evening
when the sun already lowered his head and was going to
sleep.)

The poem masses many more precise details and proves
infinitely more acceptable than the frigidly conceited verses
of Petrarch and Marino on analogous occasions, if only because a sense of mood and veiled simile softens the allusions
brazenly offered as the truth by the Italian poets. Even the
whitening of the paths near the queen may simply be the
optical effect of their contrast with her mourning. The con-
ventionalities which the Petrarchans had made of the various
classical motifs are focused effectively on a highly particularized and actual situation—the promenade of the widowed
Mary Stuart through the gardens of Fontainebleau. Literary
traditions and conventions here coalesce in the celebration of a
particular historical event in which the poet is firmly involved,
for Ronsard lived for some time in Scotland and was a close
associate of the Scots queen. Her bereavement and later return to Scotland were for Ronsard a loss not only of a
patroness but also of a sympathetic audience. His personal
concern for his lady ironically seems more authentic than the
supposedly more passionate attachments of Petrarch and
Marino. Certainly if one seeks an attractive alternative to
Ronsard it is rather to Chiabrera than the Petrarchans that one
turns for such elegant and playful effects as distinguish his

airy lyric to his celestial mistress. Chiabrera's lyric is typical of the Renaissance in its boldness of line and economy of materials:

> Ove gira un guardo solo,
>   indi a volo
>   ogni nuvolo sparisce;
> ove ferma un poco il piede,
>   là si vede,
>   che ad ogn'or l'erba fiorisce.[79]

(Wherever she glances once, there every cloud takes flight and disappears; wherever her foot rests an instant, hour by hour the grass flourishes.)

The English poets caught up the manner of both Ronsard and Chiabrera. A charming if less exaggerated equivalent of the latter's poem is Congreve's "Where'er you walk," but the former sets a precedent for almost every major seventeenth-century English poet. Waller's poem about Sacharissa walking in the gardens at Penshurst may well have led the way for such poets as Cleveland and Hammond, not to mention a host of lesser versifiers who hymned their ladies' power over nature. However, it is Marvell who carries the theme forward to the verge of something revolutionary in "Appleton House," probably under the direct influence of Cleveland's "On Phillis Walking in the Morning." When the "young Maria" finally appears at the end of the poem she exercises a magnetism over nature which far surpasses the quaintest excesses of the poets preceding Cleveland and is of a radically different character from the effect Ronsard ascribes to Mary Stuart, and de Viau to his analogous heroine in "La Maison de Silvie." Marvell writes, with an exaggeration far surpassing the conceits of Marinismo:

[79] G. Chiabrera, *Canzonette Rime Varie Dialoghi,* ed. L. Negri (Turin, 1952), p. 127.

'Tis *She* that to these Gardens gave
That wondrous beauty which they have;
She streightness on the Woods bestows;
To *Her* the Meadow sweetness owes;
Nothing could make the River be
So Chrystal-pure but only *She*;
She yet more Pure, Sweet, Streight and Fair,
Then Gardens, Woods, Meads, Rivers are.[80]

Though there is a logical structure here reminiscent of Jonson's last stanza in "Her Triumph," Marvell's extravagant assertions seem to clash with the tendency to regularize themes and their treatment that has been stressed as a characteristic of late Renaissance lyricism in this chapter. Marvell's views bizarrely resemble those of Hesiod and Lucretius speaking of their goddesses when he describes the supremacy of Maria over nature. Earlier Renaissance "promenade poems" had made the relationship one of incidental respect on the part of nature. Marvell, however fanciful his nominal intention, still manages to suggest that the lady is a necessary principle for the survival of nature in its present form. But there is a significant difference between the mode of domination he suggests and those of the classical poets. To Hesiod and Lucretius the principles in Aphrodite and Venus were transcendent ones, or at least superior to the regulation of the human mind. In Marvell the principles inherent in Maria's nature are much more human ones, and their subject is less nature as a whole than man's share of it in gardens and carefully cultivated landscape. Nature is seen to be subject, at least in the gardens, to aesthetic and ethical values, and in this sense there is no metaphor involved in making Maria the genius of these gardens. From so happily endowed a personality as she possesses, the

[80] A. Marvell, *Poems and Letters*, ed. H. M. Margoliouth (Oxford, 1927), I, 80.

human mind derives its examples for action not only in general but in the development of the English landscape, which by the seventeenth century is as much under human discipline as any other area of man's activity. Thus the treatment of Maria as an archetype for nature is the humanist equivalent to the natural principle of fertility concealed behind the figures of the goddesses of Hesiod and Lucretius. Only the arbitrary flatteries of some early Renaissance poets who robbed goddesses of their attributes, without accepting a fully articulated temporal scale of values, falsify their own allusions.

It is not without significance that Marvell was a puritan, since puritanism was one of the great pressures to transpose metaphysical truth into psychological terms. One can see the elements of Marvell's correlation of Maria and nature in such a remark as Whichcote's, "The Truth of First Inscription is conatural to Man, it is the Light of God's Creation and it flows from the Principles of which man doth consist, in his very first make" (*The Evidence of Divine Truth*). Clearly then the perfections of Maria are an ideal model to be projected on a nature disordered by the Fall (if one accepts that particular explanation). Marvell's connection of human virtue and picturesque nature leads easily to the park landscapes of Pope's "Windsor Forest":

> Here hills and vales, the woodland and the plain,
> Here earth and water seem to strive again;
> Not chaos-like together crush'd and bruis'd,
> But, as the world, harmoniously confused.[81]

The last couplet echoes the effect of the Lucretian Venus, as well as Marvell's description of how Maria, as "Paradise's only map," regulates the world's "rude heap together hurled" into "more decent order tame." Thus Maria's relationship to her

[81] A. Pope, *Complete Poetical Works*, ed. H. W. Boynton (New York, 1903), p. 28.

setting is simply a picturesque illustration of man's impact on landscape, which leaves it "Nature still, but Nature methodised." It was left to Wordsworth, in his Lucy poems and those celebrating his sister, to break the supremacy of man in this ratio and leave a picture of a woman and nature mutually interpenetrated. This is a reasonable if remote projection of Whichcote's sentiment and Marvell's image of Maria in a responsive landscape. The consequence of this analysis is to see in "Appleton House" not a poem in which a lady is flattered by an artificial twisting of metaphysics so much as the condensation of metaphysical ideas and images into a more coherent and practical meaning. In this it conforms to the pattern of sophisticated and subtle but particularized experience that has been shown to be a characteristic prerequisite for Renaissance poetic technique at its best.

[v i i]

We can now summarize the impact of Renaissance lyricism on the traditions of European love poetry. The poets whose work we have examined have tended to exert positive pressures on the material they inherited from earlier periods and to extend that material in definite directions. In every aspect of creativity the later poets as a group show greater powers of control. Their material has become more malleable, not because human nature changed, but because European culture accumulated increasingly diversified tools with which to mold and discipline experience both in real life, to some extent, and conspicuously in poetry. Christian ethics, scholastic dialectic, and Platonic psychology were typical resources which left any poet who was familiar with them masterfully competent to deal with challenges such as the pressure to consummate every love affair sexually at an early point, pressures which most pagan poets perceived no means of modifying.

Love was seen more analytically and precisely, hence less passively by the later poets. Instead of an emotional principle governing men's lives in the arbitrary form of a divinity, such as the Aphrodite of Euripides, love comes to be an elaborate pattern of social situations demanding the same care and subtlety that the ancients devoted usually to politics and rhetoric rather than to religion and manners. Where such ancients as Ovid and Catullus had incidentally struck out quaint or forceful sparks of insight or expression in their poems, later poets studied each particular inspiration and modeled it to a detached and carefully poised unity whose meaning was not smothered by a sometimes fortuitous context, as it often was in their sources. It is the difference between a crowded frieze in low relief and a series of dramatic, but isolated statues in the round.

The difference, as we noted, is perhaps not simply that greater insight is shown by the later poets, since many of their ideas were hinted at by the earlier writers, but that the later poets inherited a more defined sense of purpose and an immeasurably vaster range and accumulation of materials by their later date in the tradition. Any of the best poems of Horace, Catullus, or Sappho might easily challenge comparison with the best Renaissance lyrics in many ways. But, as with Ronsard's poem to the bees, the Renaissance poems often draw on a wider range of resources than any comparable single classical poem, whatever its particular perfections, and the diversity of Renaissance poets as a group is incomparably greater than that of the classical authors. The classical writers tend to see love as a physically defined activity governed exclusively by sexual attraction or reaction and focused on the climax of physical consummation. This finite potentiality is also visible in one kind of lyric in the Renaissance, but only as one rather naïve or cynical pattern among a host of shades of behavior and situations, which gears the facts of love in the most diversified form to the full range of accepted human potentialities. Ovid's *Art of Love* and *Amores* may well offer a preliminary account of the potentialities and situations of love, but as a full or even challenging presentation these works are clearly inadequate for the post-Renaissance lover if he seeks to be fully aware of the problems and delights of relations between the sexes.

Though Renaissance lyricism continued to use techniques, motifs, and style familiar since classical times, the detailed use made of them differs markedly from that of any earlier period because they are exploited more deliberately and absolutely. Instead of rhetorical colors, syntactical patterns are often developed to the point that they determine the whole structure of a poem, and most lyrics show a refined sense of the relationship between sentence structure and mood. English lyrics in particular show a baroque sense of climax, surprise, and control of style. They plan the use of imagery with a care that is at least architectural, and sometimes almost mathematical in its logical symmetry and coherence. Even highly analytic thought processes themselves are subjected to a unifying sense of their function within the larger purpose of the poems. In fact all the resources of lyric expression appear not only fully mastered but adjusted with a craftsman's precision to combine in furthering a fully integrated unity, governed in many of the best lyrics by a very precise and challenging situation. It is in the accumulation of a wide range of immediate and practical situations, dissected with all the means lyric expression affords, that the character of Stuart love poetry can best be defined. The higher level of coherence within each lyric and the greater intellectual potential this unity reflects were not confined simply to certain aesthetic achievements of the kind just discussed. Under the pressure of such imaginative reconstruction the texture of everyday situations frequently changed and blossomed in the most unexpected ways, as we saw in our climactic illustrations of the Polyphemus and "promenade" poems.

Of course the fanciful, rhetorical, or sensual patterns of earlier eras survived and were even enhanced by subjection to the new intellectual resources of the times as they penetrated and modified the lyric tradition. The closeness to real life of the typical literary situations in more contemporary styles of love poetry allowed a freer exchange of qualities between actual and artificial. Renaissance love poets seem to speak increasingly in the historical roles and authentic accents of contemporary lovers as we see in the opening lines of Drayton's sonnet "Since there's no help, come let us kiss and part"; but the real lovers also normally speak increasingly like poets, as in the "prose" comedies of Wycherley and Congreve at the end of the century, which surely reflect the concern of their audiences with conversational finesse. This kind of conversational skill was almost the only cement which held together the fragmentary but dazzling literary careers of men like Waller. To bed a woman with a paradox on one's lips or die with an epigram were literary ideals to Donne and Cleveland, but they were requirements of fashion at the court of Charles II. Intelligence ceased to be the attribute primarily of theology, which became itself more emotional and secular under the influence of the Reformation. And, while religion became more down to earth, love and social intercourse also became even more subtly elaborate and philosophical. By keeping their analytic powers and ingenuity severely in the service of highly particularized situations, poets achieved that juxtaposition of factual and intellectual which Eliot mistakenly calls the fusion of thought and feeling. What happened was not that feeling became penetrated by intelligence but that, as we see in Donne's "The Sunne Rising," traditional or familiar situations of both classical poets such as Ovid and later ones such as the troubadours were presented in a more colloquial style, and often also more intelligently. The latter element in this combination ultimately gave sexual desire and its satisfaction less pre-eminence in love and intelligence more pre-eminence than in classical times, though scarcely more than in Dante. As the intellectual stringency and rarefication of orthodox scholastic theology may have encouraged the Protestant Reformation to exploit religious emotion as a counterforce, so Stuart aristocrats' intellectualization of love encouraged first libertinism, as we saw in Lord Herbert's little poem on inconstancy, then a sentimentality by way of reaction already visible in Herrick, and finally the passionate extremism of romanticism.

T. S. Eliot once deplored the consequences of the process that inevitably advanced intelligence at the expense of feeling, while he praised the virtues of that process's initiation. The need is not to lament the post-Renaissance "decline in sensibility," but to recognize the Stuart lyric tradition's best productions without approving that potential unbalance of psychological and aesthetic values which was remedied by the lyric tradition's later evolution. Augustanism and Romanticism are in fact counterweights to recurring defects (such as frigid eccentricity) within the sensibility of late Renaissance poetry itself, not digressions from its greatness. The best seventeenth-century love poetry is perfectly compatible with the instincts of both Augustan and Romantic writers, as is shown by the interest and even praise of it by notable poets and critics in each later era. The major achievements of Stuart lyricism now need to be defined in impartial terms that can be transposed freely into those of conventional modern judgments, both intellectual and moral. We have seen in detail the resources, both traditional and contemporary, of Stuart lyricism, but we have not yet established the many permanent and practical extensions of human sensibility that it illustrates, beyond the mere sophistication of effects in earlier traditions. If we can

show that Stuart lyricists were not only well-read and ingenious, which Eliot suggests, but came to possess new and
practical kinds of awareness, then their writings as a mass may
well achieve the status of a classic comparable to those of the
troubadours, or the wandering scholars. So far the character
of seventeenth-century English lyricism has been defined, but
its claim to greatness of psychological insight must now be
vindicated.

THE NEW ATTITUDES

[i]

DESPITE the subtler and more romantic relationships of a Catullus or a Propertius, when a pagan poet such as Horace encounters a stubbornly hostile mistress, his natural reaction is simply to warn her sharply of the uncertain yet finite nature of human life. To him the mere physical facts of experience are usually decisive in love affairs. Modest repulse and treacherous betrayal may well be equally agonizing because each constitutes a reversal of the desirable physical circumstances, one over which moreover the poet has no conscious control. Man is nothing but a passive subject of fate:

> Fortuna saevo laeta negotio et
> ludum insolentem ludere pertinax
>   transmutat incertos honores,
>   nunc mihi, nunc alii benigna. (III, xxix, 49-52)

(Fortune exulting in her cruel work, and stubborn to pursue her wanton sport, shifts her fickle favours, kind now to me, now to some other.)[1]

Stoicism and a smug sense of rectitude are Horace's only answer, in this ode to Maecenas, to the fluctuations of Fortune. Thus when Ligurinus proves unresponsive to Horace's affection, the poet can only make threats like "sometime you'll regret this."[2] There is little immediate satisfaction in the hope. On the other hand, there is something vulgar in the stale hatred with which Horace gloats over the ruin of a beauty who once, years before, repulsed him:

---

[1] Loeb edn., trans. C. E. Bennett, pp. 276-277.
[2] *Ibid.* (IV, x), p. 324.

Audivere, Lyce, di mea vota, di
audivere, Lyce: fis anus et tamen
 vis formosa videri
  ludisque et bibis impudens. (ɪv, xiii, 1-4)

(The gods have heard my prayer, O Lyce, aye, the gods
have heard it. Thou art becoming old, and yet desirest to
seem beautiful and joinest in the merriment and drinkest
hard.)[3]

The poem is memorable for its acidity, but it also vividly displays a mind wholly subject to the forces which play on it. For
such a lover there is no immediate escape from his situation
once it is explicitly established, though it is a poor satisfaction
to wait for Time's revenges. Earlier, in the face of untrust-
worthiness, the lover or even the moralist is simply incapable
of any reaction but indignation:

Vlla si iuris tibi peierati
poena, Barine, nocuisset umquam,
 dente si nigro fieres vel uno
  turpior ungui,

crederem. Sed tu simul obligasti
perfidium votis caput, enitescis
pulchrior multo iuvenumque prodis
 publica cura. (ɪɪ, viii, 1-8)

(Had ever any penalty for violated vows visited thee,
Barine; didst thou ever grow uglier by a single blackened
tooth or spotted nail, I'd trust thee now. But with thee, no
sooner hast thou bound thy perfidious head by promises than
thou shinest forth much fairer and art the cynosure of all
eyes when thou appearest.)[4]

Under the same circumstances Ovid could only affect atheism,
challenging his reader to "go on, believe that there are gods,"

[3] *Ibid.*, pp. 334-335.   [4] *Ibid.*, pp. 126-127.

if he can reconcile their existence with such feminine freedom to take advantage of lovers without penalty (*Amores*, iii, iii).

It may be argued that to this day authors have done no better. While the insidious delights in *The Sorrows of Werther* have been effectively exorcised by Flaubert's icy analysis in *L'Education Sentimentale*, there still seems to be no simple solution to the problem of frustrated affection available to the popular imagination; and the fate of the undergraduate population of Oxford in *Zuleika Dobson* is by popular taste merely extreme, not wholly inappropriate. Yet the Stuart poets resolved the whole question of misplaced affection, if we would only read them for their psychological insights and not just for their quaint verbal texture or their urbane poise and humor. It is not their metaphysical imagery and their wit that count ultimately, but the purposes served by such attributes. If the motives of love are in some sense spiritual, or at least psychological, a love affair is not governed merely by material facts; and it becomes thereby infinitely more viable, provided only that the lover knows how to apply the right intellectual pressure to his feelings. Stuart poetry confidently identifies the decisive issues of love's dramas as the thoughts of the lovers, rather than the physical events of their relationship. Such poetry refuses to accept the idea that love's inception and progress is simply a matter of physique or sensual indulgence. These primitive facts of sex provide merely the groundwork and raw materials of the final artifact, of which the real structure is conceptual.

[ii]

Of course, if what the Stuart poets have to say is accurate, their outlook can hardly be wholly novel. It is unlikely that earlier poets should have ignored a whole range of potentialities in so important a matter as sexual relationships. This anticipation is certainly present in classical works, though in rather unexpected forms having in common only an assumption that simple sexual desire based on physical attraction is not the only basis of sexual love. One may not find the following epigram from Martial in good taste, but it has interesting overtones:

> Petit Gemellus nuptias Maronillae
> et cupit et instat et precatur et donat
> adeone pulchra est? immo foedius nil est.
> quid ergo in illa petitur et placet? tussit. (I, x)

(Gemellus seeks marriage with Maronilla; he desires it, he urges her, he implores her, and sends her gifts. Is she so beautiful? Nay, no creature is more disgusting. What then is the bait and charm in her? Her cough [i.e., she will die soon].)[5]

This disconcertingly objective perspective on sexual relations is lacking in Horace's love poetry. Martial shows a sense of less mercenary, more refined motivations for an attachment when he writes:

> Uxorem quare locupletem ducere nolim
> quaeritis? uxori nubere nolo meae.
> inferior matrona suo sit, Prisce, marito:
> non aliter fiunt femina virque pares. (VIII, xii)

("Why am I unwilling to marry a rich wife?" Do you ask? I am unwilling to take my wife as husband. Let the matron be subject to her husband, Priscus; in no other way do woman and man become equal.)[6]

The paradox is amusing, but the psychological observation is accurately made and argues an insight which is of value both

---

[5] Loeb edn., trans. W. C. Ker, I, 36-37.
[6] *Ibid.*, II, 12.

to the success of the poem and to the understanding of sexual relations. The same process is still more subtly at work in Juvenal's sixth satire:

> sit formosa decens dives fecunda . . .
> quis feret uxorem cui constant omnia? malo,
> malo Venusinam quam te, Cornelia, mater
> Gracchorum, si cum magnis vitutibus adfers
> grande supercilium.

(Let her be handsome, charming, rich and fertile . . . yet who could endure a wife that possessed all perfections? I would rather have a Venusian girl for my wife than you, O Cornelia, mother of the Gracchi, if with all your virtues you bring me a haughty brow.)[7]

Here again the orthodox virtues of women prove less attractive than custom suggests, when scrutinized by an alert psychologist. And this process of sophistication was extended by some poets, chiefly those late Latin ones like Ausonius or decadents of the earlier empire such as Petronius Arbiter, in whom fitful gleams of new horizons can be seen. Martial indeed led the way briskly to new paradoxical revelations:

> Quaero diu totum, Safroni Rufe, per urbem,
>   si qua puella neget. . . . (IV, lxxi)
> (I have long been looking all through the city, Safronius Rufus, for a girl who says "No." . . .)[8]

—but he hastily assures one young woman who took him seriously that the "no" was only to be said once, "pernegare non iussi" ("I did not bid you to refuse for ever"). Only in a poem linked with Petronius is found an author who dares to suggest that physical consummation could be as fatal to love

---

[7] Juvenal, *Satires*, Loeb edn., trans. G. G. Ramsay (London, 1924), pp. 96-97.
  [8] Loeb edn., trans. W. C. Ker, I, 280-281; cp. IV, lxxxi.

as good health in an heiress or perfection in a wife, and he chose to delight in endless and unfulfilled expectation:

> Hoc iuvit, iuvat et diu iuvabit;
> hoc non deficit incipitque semper.[9]

(This has pleased, pleases and always will please; this never ends but is always beginning.)

Enough has been said to show that classical poets were not strangers to fancifulness or psychological sophistication in their selection of loves (or wives, at least). The plausibility of these vindications of eccentric choices was recognized by at least two conspicuous Latin poets, Ovid and Lucretius. Lucretius contemplates the delusions of lovers with unsympathetic contempt:

> Nam faciunt homines plerumque cupidine caeci
> et tribuunt ea quae non sunt his commoda vere.
> multi modis igitur pravas turpisque videmus
> esse in deliciis summoque in honore vigere.
>
> (IV, 1153-1156)

(For the most part men act blinded by passion and assign to women excellencies which are not truly theirs. And so we see those in many ways deformed and ugly dearly loved, yea, prospering in high favor.)[10]

He goes on to list some typical sophistries by which enamored wretches try to make the very defects of their loves praiseworthy: a girl who stammers is said to have a pretty lisp; a skinny girl is gracefully slender; a swarthy complexion becomes an exotic tan, and so on. One of Horace's satires notes the same curious tendency, but it is Ovid who turns this characteristic lover's misrepresentation from a folly to be laughed

[9] Waddell, p. 15.
[10] Bailey, ed. and trans., I, 420.

at in others to something like a virtue in himself. In the *Ars Amatoria*[11] he only half satirically counsels lovers to conceal defects in their loves from themselves, "nominibus mollire licet mala" ("you can soften defects with words"). He lists the delusions of Lucretius' lovers with approval, observing "lateat vitium proximate boni" ("let its nearness to a grace conceal a fault"). There is a conscious art in this exploitation of the quirks of human psychology to further an expedient love. In the *Amores* the theme ceases to have even faintly ironic overtones. Ovid proudly displays his virtuosity as a lover in a way that recalls the Anacreontic poet's joyful arithmetic when he totaled the loves he had enjoyed in various Greek cities:[12]

> non est certa meos quae forma invitet amores—
> centum sunt causae, cur ego semper amem. . . .
> Denique quas tota quisquam probet urbe puellas,
> noster in has omnis ambitiosus amor.
>
> (II, iv, 9-10, 47-48)

('Tis no fixed beauty that calls my passion forth—there are a hundred causes to keep me always in love. . . . In fine, whatever fair ones anyone could praise in all the city—my love is candidate for the favors of them all.)[13]

In the passage between the first two and the last lines quoted from his elegy Ovid almost exhausts the hundred possible vindications of love that he mentions. The effect is hardly very serious, but on the other hand the poet's satisfaction in his own intellectual power to manipulate the motives of sexual fascination to suit circumstances is quite evident. We have here at the very least a lover who might learn how to avoid being upset by a particular refusal or betrayal as Horace sometimes seems to be.

[11] *Art of Love*, II, 657, Loeb edn., p. 110.
[12] See pp. 10-11 above.
[13] *Heroides and Amores*, trans. G. Showerman, pp. 390-393.

It is noteworthy that while several classical poets use the pattern of virtuoso vindications of affection, the theme of a lover's plausibility was almost a commonplace in seventeenth-century verse. Donne's piquant "I can love both fair and brown" was endlessly copied and paraphrased. Other poets who followed Ovid's version include Jonson, Herrick, Cowley, Wither, Brome, and Flatman; the list could be extended considerably. In each of these cases the poets felt that the motif was no longer distinctive or vital enough to stand alone. They therefore adjust it to fit some new highly individualized purpose: Donne to satire, "I can love any, so she be not true"; Jonson to compliment:

> Fathers, and Husbands, I doe claime a right
> In all that is call'd lovely: . . .

Herrick to pathos:

> I have lost, and lately, these
> Many dainty Mistresses: . . .[14]

and so on. Such endless revisions and reapplications are typical of Stuart versifiers, whose relentless redeployment of earlier hints ensures the discovery of any interesting or unexpected potentialities latent in an idea or motif. The popularity of this particular theme, stressing an eager subjectivity in choice of love, indicates a certain tendency in taste no less than the traditions discussed in the previous chapter.

The difficulty with this particular tradition is that it is largely a flippant, or at best a light-hearted, one, which hardly invites the poet to draw to the full on his imaginative powers. As far as the classical poets are concerned, none of the uses of the theme appears to have much bearing on anything but a joyful promiscuity in love. We have to look carefully to find any serious love poems, comparable in tone to those of Catul-

[14] Respectively: Herford, VIII, 200; Martin, p. 15.

lus, in which this conscious subjectivity is exploited. An interesting epigram of Callimachus runs:

Ἔγχει καὶ πάλιν εἰπὲ "Διοκλέος." οὐδ᾽ Ἀχελῷος
κείνου τῶν ἱερῶν αἰσθάνεται κυάθων.
καλὸς ὅ παῖς, Ἀχελῷε, λίην καλός, εἰ δέ τις οὐχὶ
φησίν—ἐπισταίμην μοῦνος ἐγὼ τὰ καλά.

(Fill the cup and say again "To Diocles!" And Achelous knows not of his sacred cups. Fair is the boy, O Achelous, and very fair: and if any denies it may I alone know how fair he is!)[15]

Here the whole point of the poem is the quaintness of the sentiment, which minimizes the seriousness with which it is offered; but the occasion is infinitely more localized and actual than anything else in this vein that we have seen so far. There is all the data required for an authentic dramatic effect—the name of the boy, a precise occasion in the drinking of the toast, and an issue in the challenge to any person present who refuses to drink the toast. The lover's satisfaction in the isolation of his point of view is a much more earnest parallel to Martial's mercenary motives for choice. In view of the distinction of the Greek epigram, it is not surprising that Propertius, one of the favorite Latin love poets of the Renaissance, hoped to become the Latin Callimachus. However, it was a less conspicuous poet, Ausonius, who made the rationale of the Greek epigram fully explicit and sincere:

Deformen quidam te dicunt, Crispa: ego istud
  nescio: mi pulchra es, iudice me satis est.
quin etiam cupio, iunctus quia zelus amori est,
  ut videare aliis foeda, decora mihi.

[15] *Callimachus and Lycophron*, Loeb edn., trans. A. W. Mair (London, 1921), pp. 158-159; see note *a*.

(Some say that thou art deformed, Crispa: that I know not: for me thou art fair, 'tis enough since I am judge. Nay more, I long—for jealousy is yoked with love—that thou mayest seem to others ugly, comely to me alone.)[16]

This poem shows marked progress in the powers of psychological analysis of a situation in comparison with those of Callimachus, even though there is a decline in the vividness and immediacy with which the scene is presented. Ausonius' epigram presents the lover's perspective on the Lucretian evaluation of female beauty. Not only is the ugly mistress found beautiful but the lover is happy in the fact that he alone sees her beauty. This gives him greater security in his affection for her because she is less likely to find a rival for him.

All of these poems are superior in poise, vividness, and dramatic truth to the notorious lines of Tasso's "Sopra la Bellezza," from which, because of its burlesque character, the Renaissance poets probably did not derive the tradition of a lover attached to a woman despised by most men. Challenging Tasso as a rival for the earlier classical poets are the no less lively but more serious Renaissance poets of France and England. Marot equals the classical poets in their own manner:

> Vous perdez temps de me dire mal d'elle,
> Gens qui voulez divertir mon entente:
> Plus la blasmez, plus je la trouve belle;
> S'esbahit on si tant je m'en contente?
>> La fleur de sa jeunesse,
>> A vostre advis rien n'est ce?
>> N'est-ce rien que ses graces?
>> Cessez vos grans audaces,
> Car mon amour vaincra vostre mesdire:
> Tel en mesdict qui pour soy la desire.[17]

---

[16] Loeb edn., trans. H. G. Evelyn White, II, 206-207.
[17] Jannet, II, 192.

(You waste time speaking ill of her to me, you people who seek to change my intention: the more you censure her, the more beautiful I find her; are you surprised that I am so happy? The flower of her youth is nothing in your opinion? Are her graces negligible? Stop your gross audacities, for my love will triumph over your insults: the one who insults her really desires her for himself.)

This poem is less picturesque than that of Callimachus and not so analytic as that of Ausonius. It is, however, more authentic in the neat twisting of motives by the lover to justify his infatuation. Ausonius was glad not to risk a rival; but Marot's tone is sharper and more urgent, and his situation less hypothetical than Ausonius'. Slander of his mistress is no reassurance to this lover, whose anxiety sees even denigration as a rival's plot to distract his attention. The only relevance of Tasso's poem to this one is its nominal structure of logical argument in favor of an unattractive mistress. But the argument of the Italian poem, by frankly admitting the repulsiveness of the proposed beloved (as Marot does not), wholly falsifies the dramatic truth of the presentation. Tasso's ingenuity is no more help to the serious lover than Lucretius' insight into the psychology of love; both views would have to be reconciled to the convincing presentation of love for such a woman before their perceptions would become positive assets to the lover.

This fusion of actual and ingenious is the unique triumph of English poets of the seventeenth century. When Shakespeare frames the opening to his brief lyric "Tell me where is fancy bred?" he raises the issue that his own generation and the next tried to solve. In his Sonnet 130, Shakespeare refutes the conventional estimate of beauty by means of which lovers had previously vindicated their choice, to the amusement of the philosophers. Yet he sustains his delight in his mistress.

The decision is revolutionary, and it is the same decision that
Donne takes in "Aire and Angels." To seek to estimate the
physical beauty of one's mistress objectively, as the basis for
love, is to falsify the essential factor in the attraction, which
is a subjective attachment transcending external particulars.
Carew enlarges Donne's thoughts, though blurring the knowledge of Shakespeare's sonnet:

> Wonder not though I am blind,
>   For you must bee
> Darke in your eyes, or in your mind,
>   If when you see
> Her face, you prove not blind like me.
> If the powerfull beams that flye
>   From her eye,
> And those amorous sweets that lye
> Scatter'd, in each neighbouring part,
> Find a passage to your heart,
> Then you'le confess your mortall sight
> Too weake, for such a glorious light. . . .[18]

This certainly reflects Donne's dazzled sense in studying his
mistress's physique, but it fails to recognize fully the loss of
critical power that Shakespeare identifies in other lovers and
averts in himself. Even Ronsard had ruefully admitted that, in
his passion: "je ne puis discerner la laide de la belle" ("I cannot tell ugliness from beauty").[19] It was Henry King who
managed finally to vindicate the lover's sense of his mistress's
beauty without losing his critical power. His "Defence" manages to sustain all the positive qualities of the earlier poems,
without any vulgar delusions:

> Why slightest thou what I approve?
> Thou art no Peer to try my love,

[18] Dunlap, p. 33.   [19] Cohen, I, 292.

Nor canst discern where her form lies,
Unless thou saw'st her with my eyes.
   Say she were foul and blacker than
The Night, or sunburnt African,
If lik'd by me, 'tis I alone
Can make a beauty where was none;
For rated in my fancy, she
Is so as she appears to me. . . .[20]

King sees that it is a matter not of objective perception, but subjective satisfaction, that governs the lover's appreciation of his mistress. To associate this wholehearted appreciation with any one charm or even to vindicate one's satisfaction by any specific characteristics is to misunderstand the nature of the relationship. Another poet of the period showed how closely related Sonnet 130 is to this view by clarifying its meaning, at the price of losing its verbal color:

I know, as well as you, shee is not faire,
Nor hath the sparkling eyes or curled hair;
Nor can shee brag of vertue or of truth,
Or anything about her save her youth. . . .
All this I know, yet cannot choose but love her.
Yet am not blind as you and others bee;
Who think and sweare they little Cupid see
Play in their Mistris eyes; and that there dwell
Roses on cheekes, and that her brest excell
The whitest snow, as if that love were built
Of fading red and white, the bodies quilt.
And that I cannot love unless I tell
Wherein or on what part my love doth dwell.
Vain Hereticks you bee, for I love more
Than ever any did that told wherefore:

[20] Saintsbury, iii, 187.

Then trouble mee no more, nor tell me why,
'Tis! because shee is shee, and I am I:[21]

The conclusion may well seem fatal to analytic discussion, but it is actually a vindication of spontaneous choice, based entirely on the intuitive reaction to the other person, not on some arbitrarily specific and intellectualized motive. This is the logical outcome of a sensitive lover's reaction to the observations and censures of a critic such as Lucretius.

One has only to set this latest illustration against the earliest examples, drawn from classical writers, to see that the resources of love poetry have become enormously extended. The Stuart poet is quite able to sustain the dramatic intonation of Callimachus. His opening lines catch perfectly the tone of responsive resentment to some condescending advice from a well-meaning friend. The liveliness of tone is sustained by the lover's Shakespearean vindication of himself through an attack on naïve if no less impassioned lovers, with whom he classes his critics. When this lover's attitude toward his mistress is compared with the motivations offered by any of the classical poets, we find an enormous advance in subtlety of analysis. Ovid argues himself into love by misrepresenting physical peculiarities as charms; Horace, while indignant about Barine's fickleness, is puzzled that he cannot explicitly connect this hostile reaction with any sense of the impairment of her attractions. Neither poet understands that the lover's attitude necessarily and readily overrides both physical and moral defects of a specific kind, provided it finds a more basic sanction. The Renaissance poet by contrast recognizes neither distinctive beauty nor virtue in his mistress. He sees in her only one essential attribute—that their personalities are complementary. What the girl affords is not her indi-

[21] *Facetiae* (London, 1817), I, 225.

vidual looks nor her character but her nature seen in its unique relation to his. Since this poet can vindicate his mistress's fascination only by the fact of his love, not because of any intrinsic virtue that she possesses, the lyric expounds an attitude which is to some extent shared by Ovid and Horace, who both love unsuitable women, but an attitude with a rationale that their conscious minds clearly reject. For them the lover must have a conventional reason for his love, and Horace particularly is upset because trustworthiness proves inessential in Barine for her to keep her attractiveness. One is reminded of the difference between the Old and New Testaments. The former bases its judgments on the substantial facts of conduct, the latter on an attitude superior to historical events and based on a mutual and gratuitous recognition between God and the individual. Similarly, if on a lower plane, the Renaissance poet asserts that whatever reasons we give for sexual love are always secondary to a motivation that at first seems to elude objective analysis; and if we fail to recognize this elusive imperative we betray our own natures. The poet warns us of this danger:

> Vain heretics you be, for I love more
> Than ever any did that told wherefore.

This may still seem speculative and vague, so perhaps some authority should be invoked. We have already seen that Donne's "Negative Love" says exactly the same thing:

> I never stoop'd so low, as they
> Which on an eye, cheeke, lip, can prey,
>   Seldome to them, which soare no higher
>   Then vertue or the minde to'admire,
> For sense, and understanding may
>   Know, what gives fuell to their fire:
> My love, though silly, is more brave,

For may I misse when ere I crave,
If I know yet, what I would have.[22]

Donne's poem harmonizes closely with the thought of as serious a writer as Plotinus, who says that in the condition of psychological perfection man rejects all specific motives because these finite ideas involve a fragmentation of awareness that is incompatible with the mind's ideal poise. The lover finds his mistress stabilizing and satisfying for the same reason that Plotinus finds "the One" so, simply because an unspecified awareness of her delights him.[23] As soon as he becomes specific the balance is lost and irrelevance introduced. The real relation of particular attractions to the lover's intuitive appreciation was illustrated by the poem we noted in the previous chapter, modeled on a Shakespearean song:

Tell me where the beauty lies—
In my mistress? or in my eyes?
Is she fair? I made her so.
Beauty doth from liking grow.
Be she fairer, whiter than
Venus' doves or Leda's swan,
What's that Beauty if neglected,
Seen of all, of none respected?
Then tell my mistress that I love her,
Think her fair, 'cause I approve her.[24]

As Plotinus put it, in rather different circumstances, "desire generates intelligence."[25] This poem has come full circle without forfeiting the knowledge acquired in the process. The poet does not deny beauty to his mistress, but he insists

[22] Grierson, p. 59.
[23] See J. S. Harrison, *Platonism in English Poetry* (New York, 1903), pp. 153-155.
[24] Fellowes, p. 581.
[25] *Select Works of Plotinus*, ed. G. R. S. Mead (London, 1914), p. 295.

that only his satisfaction with her in some more basic way generates the awareness of these beauties that otherwise would go unappreciated. "Beauty" thus comes to mean "the assertions about a woman's nature made by her committed admirer to vindicate his judgment." The view taken here differs from that of Lucretius only in that what Lucretius thought was just a defect of lovers' judgments is accepted as the nature of all aesthetic evaluations, which can be confirmed only by inducing the same unpremeditated commitments in others as the reaction that first provoked the admirer's assertions. When King reproaches his critic for not seeing his sweetheart through a lover's eyes, he is exactly demonstrating the point of disagreement, not being willful. "If you love this girl, then these are the reasons you might give," he argues. His allusion to "sunburnt Africans" is not consciously grotesque but aesthetically apt. The comparison of ideals of female beauty in various societies shows that a standard of anatomical or moral character has nothing to do with the existence of love, but merely provides convenient excuses for it.

[iii]

The consequences of this pattern of thought are bizarre but illuminating when set against the background of Horace's warning to Ligurinus, his anger that Barine's charms are untouched by her fickleness, and his long deferred satisfaction in the wreck of Lyce's beauty. If the lover is truly affronted or betrayed and chooses to withdraw, there is, after his withdrawal, no distinction left for the mistress to pride herself on, since all her beauties are founded supposedly on his continued affection. This bald assertion obviously carries little conviction of itself, but it gains weight when it is systematically vindicated through application to the classic situations of love.

What, exactly, determines the lover's attraction to his beloved, if we reject all the limited reasons hitherto offered? The nearest classical analogy to "Negative Love" and similar Renaissance poems is Martial's epigram about his search for "the girl who says 'No.'" But Martial clearly does not really want such a woman always to refuse advances. The classical love poets saw things in simple terms. They wanted a girl to surrender herself physically to them, for this was their avowed standard of love. Betrayal meant simply physical union with a rival. Even suspended consummation was only a challenge to arouse the jaded appetite. In contrast to this extreme, "Neo-Platonic" and "spiritual" love were governed essentially by the rectitude of the beloved—the more or less complete impassivity of Beatrice, Laura, Stella, and the others was a logical manifestation of the disciplined mind and affections that were conventionally associated with the "Platonic" mistress. These are the two conflicting sets of objective attributes of classic loves which are repudiated by Stuart poets—physically exciting attractions are no less irrelevant than Platonic impassivity. Since the necessary characteristics of a lovable mistress do not lie in her own attributes they must lie in her relationship to some external factor. Some clues about its identity are found in classical verse. Thus the beloved in the following couplet is of a highly elusive nature suggesting the intangible mistress we are interested in:

Σύν μοι πῖνε, συνήβα, συνέρα, συστεφανηφόρει
σύν μοι μαινομένῳ μαίνεο, σὺν σώφρονι σωφρόνει.

(Drink with me, play with me, love with me, be wreathed with me; be wild when I am wild, and when I am staid be staid.)[26]

[26] *Lyra Graeca*, trans. J. M. Edmonds, III, 568-569.

What is postulated in this love affair is not a particular set of attributes of either mind or body, but a kind of relationship sustained by the lovers' power to adjust to the fluctuating requirements for its continuance. What is important is not the nature of the individual factors but the ratio maintained by their continual modification in the face of circumstance. Ovid's *Art of Love* hints at the same need, not for a particular form of conduct in those seeking love, but for an indifference to set responses:

> Comibus est oculis alliciendus amor.
> Odimus inmodicos (experto credite) fastus:
> Saepe tacens odii semina vultus habet.
> Spectantem specta, ridenti mollia ride:
> Innuet, acceptas tu quoque redde notas. . . .
>   (III, 510-514)

(By gentle eyes must love be enticed. I hate immoderate haughtiness [believe one who knows]; a silent face oft holds the seed of hatred. Look at one who is looking at you, return a pleasant smile; if he beckons, acknowledge and return his nod. . . .)[27]

It might almost be possible to say that these lines reject any patterns of behavior independent of a particular occasion and its requirements. This is clearly one of the virtues of the "occasional" love poetry of the seventeenth century, which increasingly substitutes the matters of everyday experience for the now conventional subjects and attitudes which it inherited from classical and Neo-Petrarchan love poetry. However, even though classical poetry was less constricted by such traditions than some later imitators of it, comparatively few classical poems register the fluctuating circumstances of actual love while stressing the continuity

[27] Loeb edn., trans. J. H. Mozley, pp. 154-155.

of the crucial reciprocated response in the lovers. The Middle Ages was also only occasionally aware of the need for reciprocity rather than specific endowments in a mistress, and this imaginative effort was the product of the more creative Latin versifiers rather than the courtly vernacular singers. Though the poet of this poem in the Benedictbeuern manuscript ends a slave of passion, he opens hopefully and vivaciously by repudiating orthodox views:

> Volo virum vivere viriliter,
> diligam, si diligar equaliter.
> sic amandum censeo, non aliter.
> hac in parte fortior quam Jupiter
> nescio precari
> commercio vulgari;
> amaturus forsitan
> volo prius amari . . . . [28]

(I want a man to live in manly fashion, I shall love if I am equally beloved. I approve of loving thus, not otherwise. I hold myself superior in this to Jupiter, that I will not plead with base entreaties. Should I love, I wish first to be loved.)

The subtlety of the poet lies in discountenancing censure of his supposedly excessive demands by a conclusion in which he surrenders all his pretensions and admits he is in love, though with a lady somewhat more amenable than the conventional courtly mistress. His point is well made despite its unorthodoxy. To fall in love with a woman not well disposed toward one is an anomaly that degrades love to the level of a most trivial and casual relationship, or to mere vulgar sensuality. In "Loves Deitie," Donne deplores the fashion of those who have "sunk so low as to love one which

[28] Waddell, p. 228.

did scorn," though rather like the medieval poet he finds it discreet to claim that he has fallen victim to the very error which he censures. Suckling later copies him in jibing at the frustrated "passions" of lovers such as Petrarch and Sidney.[29] One Renaissance Latin poet, Andreo Dactius, dryly makes the same point in the reverse situation, when he observes to a lonely youth:

> Scis quare te nullus amat? Quia despicis omnes:
>   Quaeris amatorem Candide? Primus ama.[30]

(You want to know why no one loves you? Because you disdain everyone: if you seek to be loved, Candidus, you must first love.)

And even the frigid Desportes rises to some sense of true reciprocity:

> Je ne suis point de ceux qu'en doubte il faut tenir,
> Afin que leur ardeur dure en sa violence;
> La seule affection peut mon feu maintenir,
> Qui s'éteint aussitôt que j'entre en méfiance.[31]

(I am not at all one of those who has to be kept in doubt so that their passion maintains its vigor; mere love can sustain my flame, which dies as soon as I become uncertain of you.)

All these poets are aware that reciprocity in love is important, but this remains simply one attitude among many possible ones for them. Only by degrees does the view that love is essentially a mutual sympathy become consciously incompatible with all others. This emergence of a conscious and even philosophical coherence is another striking attribute of English Renaissance lyricism. An assertion of Campion's in

[29] Howarth, p. 192.   [30] *Delitiae Italorum*, I, 890.
[31] Michiels, p. 397.

Rosseter's *A Book of Airs* would surely have startled any classical poet and many later ones by its confident absolutism:

> Thou art not fair for all thy red and white,
>   For all those rosy ornaments in thee.
> Thou art not sweet, though made of mere delight,
>   Nor fair, nor sweet, unless thou pity me.
> I will not smooth thy fancies. Thou shalt prove
> That beauty is no beauty without love.[32]

The poem continues in this paradoxical vein, each stanza urging the reciprocation of the poet's love in terms that invoke comparably sophisticated motivations to the one quoted. The contrast between the quoted stanza and any classical plea for love reveals a complete change in perspective, and an enormous advance in subtlety of thought. While in classical times psychological patterns were approached, if at all, through material considerations, now material facts are wholly subordinated to psychological concerns. Another poem in one of Campion's collections of lyrics makes the point even more sharply. The argument is so original and elliptic that the reader's mind, like that of the mistress probably, is staggered by the mental agility of the supposed lover:

> Other beauties others move,
>   In you I all graces find.
> Such is the effect of love
>   To make them happy that are kind.
>
> Women in frail beauty trust.
>   Only seem you fair to me;
> Yet prove truly kind and just,
>   For that may not dissembled be.[33]

To do justice to the thought behind the poem demands a synthesis of Platonic idealism in the style of Milton's *Comus*

[32] Fellowes, p. 590.   [33] *Ibid.*, p. 344.

and parts of *Paradise Lost* with a modern sense of solipsistic philosophy. Milton argues that virtue perfects man totally, physically as well as spiritually, and as far as modern skeptical thought is concerned it remains true that the response to kindness may well be an induced sense of the beauty of the benefactor, which resists any objective challenge. But the argument may be reduced to the simple statement that any expression of graciousness has a beauty that effectively modifies the primary physical attributes of its possessor. What Campion's poem says, is simply that she who is kind is attractive, and in turn is so loved that she is happy and thus may become yet more beautiful. The argument is hardly that of self-delusion. We have come a long way from Lucretius and even from Ovid.

Waller characteristically expresses the whole pattern with elegant lucidity in "To Flavia." He bluntly admonishes Flavia from the start that,

> 'Tis not your beauty can engage
> My wary heart;[34]

and after rejecting equally "the graces of a well taught mind" as the governing attraction, just as did Donne in "Negative Love," Waller concludes:

> No, Flavia! 'tis your love I fear;
> Love's surest darts,
> Those which so seldom fail him, are
> Headed with hearts;
> Their very shadows make us yield;
> Dissemble well, and win the field.

One notices at once the skeptical insight of the last lines, which show a greater awareness than Campion's poems that even psychological virtues are potentially suspect. The para-

[34] Thorn Drury, I, 125.

dox of fearing a woman's love more than the fascination of
her beauty is as beautifully weighed and poised as anything
we have encountered, and the light dash of cynicism in the
conclusion gives a perfect hint of astringency to the whole.
Few poets can more discreetly surprise us than Waller when
he warns us against the fatal attraction, not of beauty nor of
wit, but of the gracious and sympathetic woman. What would
Horace have made of *this* warning, one wonders . . .

It must be urged that this view of love as exclusively based
on a mutual sympathy wholly independent of other attributes
was not that of a few subtle eccentrics. It is the theme of
many major poetic debates in Stuart love poetry, whose most
conspicuous examples are at least as popular and fashionable
as the tradition stemming from Marlowe's "Come live with
me and be my love." A pivotal poem in such a sequence is
one of those memorable lyrics with which the works of
George Wither are, somewhat unexpectedly, studded. The
poem probably borrows its syntactical structure from an earlier
one in the manner of other classic Stuart lyrics, but there is
no mistaking the finality of Wither's shaping of the poem's
movement. It seems to offer an answer to Horace's ode
puzzling over the continued powers of fascination of the
fickle Barine:

> Shall I wasting in despair
> Die because a woman's fair?
> Or make pale my cheeks with care
> 'Cause another's rosy are?
> Be she fairer than the day,
> Or the flowery meads in May,
> > If she thinks not well of me,
> > What care I how fair she be?[35]

[35] G. Wither, *Poetry*, ed. F. Sidgwick (London, 1902), I, 138.

Wither goes on with this analysis, firmly rejecting each particularization of a woman's virtues both physical and mental if they fail to synchronize with a sympathetic attitude toward her lover. He summarizes his argument in the last stanza with typical Stuart precision:

> Great, or good, or kind, or fair,
> I will ne'er the more despair;
> If she love me, this believe,
> I will die, ere she shall grieve:
> If she slight me when I woo,
> I can scorn and let her go.
>   For if she be not for me
>   What care I for whom she be?

Wither's poem clarifies Donne's poem "Negative Love." What Donne looks for in a mistress is what Wither predicates—neither beauty, wit, nor virtue of any special kind, merely responsiveness to her lover. And the opening question and answering refrain of Wither's poem were echoed again and again in the miscellanies of the seventeenth century, always to the same effect—why worry about a woman's beauty if what makes her most attractive—graciousness—is missing?

It is amusing to compare a short poem by Patrick Carey with the Ovidian elegy mentioned earlier in which the Roman lover prides himself on the virtuosity of his self-deceptions in advancing his love affairs. Carey, knowing this delusiveness of beauty, discounts it—and finds himself without a single woman who understands the true discipline of love:

> There's no woman, but I'm caught
> Whilst she looks with kind eyes on me;
> If I love not then, the fault
> Is unjustly cast upon me:

They are to be blam'd, not I,
If with freedom still I hover;
Were I us'd but courteously
I should soon become a lover.

Did I anyone exclude
For her dye, or for her feature,
I should grant myself a rude
Mannerless, hard-hearted creature:
But since I except 'gainst none
By whom I am not contemnèd,
If I can't find such a one,
Pray tell, who's to be condemnèd? . . .[36]

The satire is witty and idealistic, clashing markedly with the trivial promiscuity of Ovid and of his Anacreontic master. There is no mistaking the source of the overtones in the last lines quoted—the conclusion of Wyatt's "They flee from me," a poem whose inquest on past love heralds the English poets' critical alertness to values in love:

But syns that I so kyndely ame serued
I would fain knowe what she hath deserued.[37]

The virile music of Wyatt's ironic indignation re-echoes through most of the seventeenth-century lyrics we have quoted, for Wyatt's note of gentlemanly but often affronted indulgence leads the way for later distinctive attitudes. Again and again Wyatt anticipates the easy responsiveness of the Stuart gallants to the advances of love, only to be more bitterly disillusioned than they. Compare Carey's calm appraisal and challenge with Wyatt's analogous but less cunningly barbed resentment:

Wyth seruing still
This have I wone

[36] Saintsbury, II, 456.   [37] Muir, p. 28.

For my godwill
To be vndone; . . . [38]

Wyatt lacks the resilient intelligence of the later poets, having in this much in common with Horace; he therefore lacks the means to sustain his responsiveness unqualified by the bitterness of failure. Though the possession of such intelligence may ultimately betray the poet into cool cynicism this is better than the blunt emotion or mere Horatian indignation of many of Wyatt's poems.

To see what the seventeenth century could produce at its most alert, if at its most ominously cool, we can compare its lyrics with Wyatt's most original lyric beginning:

Madame, withouten many wordes
Ons I ame sure ye will or no;[39]

and ending

Yf it be yea, I shalbe fayne;
If it be nay, frends as before;
Ye shall an othre man obtain,
And I myn owne and yours no more.

The bluntness of the challenge rightly provoked a contemptuous reply in a poem by another hand, which took the woman's part. The miniature debate anticipates the Stuart poets' elaborate canvassing of possible attitudes, which fragmented the old solemn and elaborate medieval *débats* about love into a thousand flashing lyrics. One can see at once how fully Wyatt's aspirations have been intellectually articulated, and endowed with an easy flexibility of attitude, in the following poem:

If at this time I am derided
And you please to laugh at me,
Know I am not unprovided

[38] *Ibid.*, p. 146.   [39] *Ibid.*, p. 25.

Every way to answer thee,
Love, or hate, what ere it be.

Never Twinns so nearly met
    As thou and I in our affection,
When thou weepst my eyes are wet,
    What thou lik'st is my election
    I am in the same subjection.

In one centre we are both,
    Both our lives the same way tending:
Do thou refuse, and I shall loath,
    As thy eyes, so mine are bending,
    Either storm or calm portending.

I am careless if despised,
    For I can contemn again;
How can I be then surprised,
    Or with sorrow, or with pain,
    When I can both love and disdain.[40]

It is not a soothing poem, and Barine would probably have felt less flattered if Horace's censure had taken this form. Ovid had in fact noted in his *Ars Amatoria* some hints for this as a line of attack for the hopeful lover:

Cede repugnanti: cedendo victor abibis:
    Fac modo, quas partes illa iubebit agas.
Arguet, arguito; quicquid probat illa, probato;
    Quod dicet, dicas; quod negat illa, neges. (II, 197-220)

(Yield if she resists; by yielding you will depart the victor; only play the part she bids you play. Blame if she blames; approve whatever she approves. Affirm what she affirms and deny what she denies.)[41]

[40] *Choice Drollery* (London, 1656), p. 9.
[41] Loeb edn., trans. J. H. Mozley, pp. 78-79.

But Ovid's advice had been to a lover already attracted by a woman's beauty and bent on securing her consent to love-making. The anonymous English poet, on the contrary, cares little for his mistress's charms if the responsiveness which the Ovidian lover had earlier used to win such beauty is not her own essential attribute. The Stuart poet's indifference to physical attributes can be explained only by the seventeenth-century recognition that beauty is the reflection of the lover's affection, and that this in turn depends on sympathetic consideration of his love by the mistress. If the lady is kind she will win his love and will seem beautiful, if not she will appear unattractive because of her harshness, and he will not risk involvement with her. The symmetry of the lyric's conceptions reflects an intellectual assurance and a sophistication of values that neither Ovid nor Wyatt can rival. However, like Wyatt, the unknown poet prefers to place his thoughts in the isolation of a short lyric instead of running them together with a heterogeneous flow of ideas such as characterizes the *Ars Amatoria*. More noteworthy still, while Ovid loads his verse with lush and piquant detail, imagery, and allusions, the seventeenth-century Englishman carries the spareness of imagery, already visible in Wyatt's brisk conversational style, to the point that it is hard to detect any figures of speech or conventional poetic "colors" at all. The first stanza, for example, is wholly devoid of ornament or image. This conversational plainness and force are the typical products of that sense of syntactical cadence so necessary to the aural experiments and traditions examined in the last chapter. If a poem has a lilt and energy to it there is no need of imagery to focus the attention or dramatize the issues. However, this very plainness has its ominous qualities. The severity of this poem's texture risks the charge of over-detachment, which in turn may appear likely to be fatal to that free expression of sentiment that the speaker desires. The poet's loss of individuality matches that of Donne's anticipated mistress. The impassivity is founded on an ideal of love closely allied to Donne's in "The Good-morrow" and perhaps, more generally, to the Christian view of grace—"ask and it shall be given you; seek and ye shall find." All that counts here is the will to salvation, not the endowments of mind and body. A readiness to respond to his love assures the mistress, by this view, of the passionate devotion and admiration of her aspiring lover. It is interesting once more to find two such distinct resources as theology and amatory *expertise* advancing together. Clearly, to fragment and compartmentalize the advance of human awareness is misleading.

[iv]

Among the Latin elegists it is not Ovid, with his love lore and picturesque data, who most completely illustrates those facets of human personality that were so assiduously cultivated in the late Renaissance. Ovid is essentially a poet to be treasured by the eager and exotic poets of the earlier wave of enthusiasm for the classics—by a never-aging Marlowe or a youthful Shakespeare. For the increasingly sophisticated amorists of the Caroline courts it was Propertius who most nearly anticipated the half willful, half cynical note that marked the declining stages of the Stuart dynasty. When the disillusioned Propertius turns on Cynthia, it is with sarcastic lucidity without parallel in other classical amorists:

> Falsa est ista tuae, mulier, fiducia formae,
>   olim oculis nimium facta superba meis.
> noster amor tales tribuit tibi, Cynthia, laudes.
>   versibus insignem te pudet esse meis.
> mixtam te varia laudavi saepe figura,
>   ut, quod non esses, esse putaret amor; (iii, xxiv, 1-6)

(False, woman, is the trust thou puttest in thy beauty; long since the partial judgment of mine eyes hath made thee overproud. Such praise of old my love bestowed on thee, and now it shames me that thou hast glory from my song. Oft did I praise the varied beauty of thy blending charms, and love deemed thee to be that which thou were not.)[42]

It confirms the association of Propertius with the Restoration gallants that his amatory excesses conclude with a new devotion to good sense in this poem:

Mens Bona, si qua dea es, tua me in sacraria dono!

(Good sense, if there is such a goddess, I devote myself to your shrines.)

This elegy is one of the most ingenious and original that Propertius wrote. It shows great psychological agility in presenting an angry lover capable of exploiting, in his revenge, the flimsiness of those same subjective values which in the first instance vindicated his attachment. The unusualness of this line of thought is seen in the fact that another Propertian elegy[43] about fickleness relapses into conventional resentment and pursues the rejected mistress with the familiar bitter prophecies of future ugliness. These conform exactly to the conventional pattern by assuming that a woman's beauty has an objective character, with which few Stuart poets would choose to credit it.

However, there is another elegy of Propertius which displays some of the cool virtuosity of the later ages in a way that proved an ideal model for Stuart poets. Propertius reacts differently from Horace when confronted by the fickleness of his mistress. His revenge is ingenious. He will take his praise elsewhere:

haec merui sperare? dabis mihi, perfida, poenas;
et nobis aliquo, Cynthia, ventus erit.

[42] Loeb edn., trans. H. E. Butler, pp. 256-257.   [43] III, xxv.

inveniam tamen e multis fallacibus unam,
    quae fieri nostro carmine nota velit. (II, v, 3-6)

(Did I deserve to look for this? Faithless one, I will pun-
ish thee, and the wind shall bear me, Cynthia, to some
other haven. Though all womankind be deceitful, yet out of
so many I shall find one that will be glad to be made famous
by my song.)[44]

But worse, he will devote his talents to her ruin—not by
physical violence, but by reversing the effect of his poetry,
which had previously served to foster her reputation for charm
and beauty and will now destroy it:

    hic tibi pallori, Cynthia, versus erit.

(This verse will drive the color from thy cheek, Cynthia.)

The threat is ingenious, but it failed to find an imitator even
among the earlier Renaissance poets. Ronsard, indeed, censured Hélène for failing to be grateful to the poet whose attentions had raised her to reputation, and Donne in "Elegie
VII" lamented that his love, once "Natures lay Ideot," was
now betraying him, though it was he who had,

        with amorous delicacies
Refin'd thee into a blis-ful Paradise.
Thy graces and good words my creatures bee;
I planted knowledge and lifes tree in thee,
Which Oh, shall strangers taste?[45]

But neither poet fully mastered the potentialities of the lover's
subjective view of his mistress's nature as a weapon to keep
her true to him. It was left to Carew in "Ingrateful Beauty
Threatened" to bring the warning of a fickle woman to its full
maturity as an immediately effective psychological weapon,

[44] Loeb edn., trans. H. E. Butler, pp. 76-77.
[45] Grierson, p. 80.

rather than a wishful hope for her future ruin. Carew's poem is another of the peaks of Renaissance creativity and deserves the most careful attention:

> Know *Celia*, (since thou art so proud,)
>   'Twas I that gave thee thy renowne:
> Thou hadst, in the forgotten crowd
>   Of common beauties, liv'd unknowne,
> Had not my verse exhal'd thy name,
> And with it, ympt the wings of fame.
>
> That killing power is none of thine,
>   I gave it to thy voyce, and eyes:
> Thy sweets, thy graces, all are mine;
>   Thou art my starre, shin'st in my skies;
> Then dart not from thy borrowed sphere
> Lightning on him, that fixt thee there.
>
> Tempt me with such affrights no more,
>   Lest what I made, I uncreate;
> Let fooles thy mystique formes adore,
>   I'le know thee in thy mortall state:
> Wise Poets that wrap't Truth in tales,
> Knew her themselves, through all her vailes.[46]

The poem is a masterly fusion of earlier effects. The outline is approximately that of Propertius' elegy, the first stanza matches the thoughts of Ronsard, the second those of Donne; but the last has a conscious authority that has been called "insolent," yet is surely a proper reaction to the lady's earlier insolence to her lover. It is important to stress that what is involved is not simply a poet's pride in his craft, it is the sense of the power of a lover's affection to confer a distinction on its source far superior to that source's intrinsic virtues. The poem turns as much on a point of applied psychology as upon a poet's

[46] Dunlap, p. 17.

vanity. The loss of a lover subtly diminishes the attractions of a beautiful woman—this is the assertion that is made by Carew, and he vindicates this view in another poem, "Didain Returned":

> Hearts, with equall love combind,
>   Kindle never dying fires.
> Where these are not, I despise
> Lovely cheekes, or lips, or eyes.[47]

These views verge on the theories of Neo-Platonism found in the philosophical works of Ficino, Leone Ebreo, and others; but there is a crucial difference between these philosophical works, which were also popular at the court of Henrietta Maria, and the poems in which their thought is reflected. The philosophers argued for theories, poets such as Ronsard, Donne, and Carew projected these theories into everyday experience. They used the theories not for their own sakes but to illuminate essential features of the dramatic situations that they visualized in their lyrics. Carew's poem to his "Ingrateful Beauty" is not Neo-Platonic, but simply psychological in its concerns. There is no reason to assume that the relationship involved here is supersensual. Because Neo-Platonism gave to heterosexual love an apparatus for analysis superior to the facts of sensual experience, the earlier Stuart poets like Donne freely describe their love with its assistance, when they are concerned with psychological considerations. It is interesting that, as the ideas vindicated by "Platonic" arguments became established, the Platonic terminology that first justified the attitudes withered away. By 1660 Pembroke and Ruddier's collection of poems could easily assert:

> Why should thy look requite so ill,
>   all other Eyes,
> Making them Pris'ners to thy will,

[47] *Ibid.*, p. 18.

Where alone thy beauty lyes:
When men's Eyes first look't upon thee,
They bestowed thy Beauty on thee.[48]

The poem goes on to illustrate the arbitrariness of male preference. Preference for a particular racial color, it argues, is a random choice made independently of the full potentialities of an individual:

To touch white Skins is not Divine,
Ethiops Lips are soft as thine.

Clearly what started as mercenary choices in Martial and willfulness in Tasso is soon to become the freedom from convention of a world governed by relativist values. The eccentricity of Margaret Metroland (in *Decline and Fall*) in choosing a Negro lover is heralded by these specious seventeenth-century poems in which the free range of human choice is first vindicated.

A year after the Pembroke and Ruddier collection, Alexander Brome warned "a Coy Lady" of the liberation of lovers from naïve credulity in the objectivity of what they admired. Two hundred years before the rationalization of the idea by psychoanalysts Brome seems to be describing the symptoms of "projection"—the imposition of preconceived patterns, for whatever reason, on an object which does not necessarily match them:

I prithee leave this peevish fashion,
　Don't desire to be high priz'd.
Love's a *Princely*, noble passion,
　And doth scorne to be despis'd.
Though we say you're fair, you know,
We your *beauty* do bestow,
For our *fancy* makes you so.

[48] W. Herbert, Earl of Pembroke and B. Ruddier, *Poems* (London, 1660), p. 77.

Don't be proud 'cause we adore you,
　We do't only for our pleasure,
And those parts in which you glory,
　We by *fancy* weigh and measure.
When for *Deities* you go,
For *Angels*, or for *Queens*, pray know,
'Tis our *fancy* makes you so.[49]

If it is suggested that the poem adds little to Ovid's analogous
elegy it must be noted that while in the classical formula
what was involved was the reconciliation of the lover with the
particular attributes of his mistress, the woman in this poem is
shown to be admired for no reason outside the lover's consciousness. Her objective characteristics, beyond her responsiveness on a psychological level, are completely ignored, yet
this view is offered without the faintest trace of that Neo-
Platonism that first justified indifference to physical attributes.

[v]

By means of such an awareness of the force of the individual imagination love poets were able to achieve the most
surprising revisions of classical topics. It is this sense of the
extension of the potentialities of a given situation that is the
distinctive feature of the Renaissance. On the one hand it
could be argued that a true choice of reactions became possible with the awareness of the existence of alternative attitudes to love, both pagan and Christian, but better still it
could be argued that lovers were offered increasingly civilized
ways of coping with the explosive situations generated by
sexual attraction. Horace would curse his fickle mistresses,
while Propertius would simply tell Cynthia's misdeeds to
others, ruining her by her own actions. But some of the subtler
Renaissance poets found it necessary neither to denounce nor

[49] A. Brome, *Poems* (London, 1661), sig. D5.

even to resent fickleness in their loves. They discovered that
the fact itself was fatal both to their affections and to the
beauties with which these were associated. Thomas Beedome
shows an intermediary stage in the evolution from Horace's
pattern, in his poem "Question and Answer." This starts in
the Horatian mode, predicting the woman's rueful incredulity,
once her beauty fades, that it ever existed. However, this
familiar theme is obviously inadequate to express the poet's
increasing sense that the whole process is not a temporal but
psychological one. Note the curious change of tense in this
stanza which succeeds the prediction of her future disbelief
in her own beauty:

> Yes, yes, I know thou wilt, and so
> Pitty the weaknesse of thy scorne
> That now hath humbled thee to know,
> Though faire it was, it is forlorne,
>   Love's sweetes thy aged corpse embalming not,
>   What marvell if thy carkasse, beauty, rot?[50]

The eagerness of tone, the usual distinction of Stuart verse, is
manifest in the repeated "yes" and the final question. The
whole poem has Horace's harshness but avoids his sense of
defeat. Rather the rejected lover holds the advantage. He
pities the mistress whose ill-advised harshness has brought
on her the frank revelation of her necessary misfortune once
she has betrayed him. This pity is vindicated by an argument
apparently Platonic but again perhaps simply psychological:

> Then shall I live, and live to be
> Thy envie, thou my pitty; say
> When e'er thou see mee, or I thee,
> (Being nighted from thy beauties day)
>   'Tis hee, and had my pride not wither'd mee,
>   I had, perhaps, beene still as fresh as hee.

[50] T. Beedome, *Poems* (London, 1928), p. 5.

> Then shall I smile and answer: true thy scorne
> Left thee thus wrinkled, slack't, corrupt, forlorne.

The wavering tenses in the first stanza and the futurity of this one show a lack of assurance in the promptness of the realization of this startling assertion, but the profound credit given to mental attitudes in the nature and preservation of beauty is unmistakable, and time enters not as the deciding factor but as a mere catalyst to the psychological process.

Thomas Stanley, though more brittle in style, was more fully the master of these effects, which Beedome perhaps merely derived from him. Stanley's "The Self Cruel" shows a mastery of challenging paradox in handling the fatality of pride to beauty:

> Behold how thy unthrifty pride
>   Hath murder'd him that did maintain it!
> And wary souls, who never tried
>   Thy tyrant beauty, will disdain it:
> But I am softer, and that me
> Thou wouldst not pity, pity thee.[51]

This conclusion is beautifully handled, the reversal of expectation being an exact illustration of the Stuart poets' extension of psychological awareness in comparison with the more direct and naïve reactions of classical poets. But Stanley elucidates the whole pattern of feeling in another poem, "The Deposition," which shows that a new range of reactions was now consciously available:

> Though when I lov'd thee thou wert fair,
>   Thou art no longer so;
> Those glories all the pride they wear
>   Unto opinion owe;
> Beauties, like stars, in borrow'd lustre shine;
> And 'twas my love that gave thee thine.

[51] Saintsbury, III, 145.

The flames that dwelt within thine eye
Do now, with mine, expire;
Thy brightest graces fade and die
At once with my desire;
Love's fires thus mutual influence return;
Thine cease to shine, when mine to burn.

Then, proud Celinda, hope no more
To be implor'd or woo'd,
Since by thy scorn thou dost restore
The wealth my love bestow'd;
And thy despis'd disdain too late shall find
That none are fair but who are kind.[52]

One detects echoes of both Donne's "Elegie VII" and Carew's "Ingrateful Beauty Threatened," but there is a neatness in Stanley, an assured sense of the precise articulation of human relationships, which neither of the earlier poets displayed. Though both are better poets than Stanley, it is significant that, while they were able effectively to communicate flashes of insight that distinguished them from their exact contemporaries, only a few years later a lesser poet such as Stanley moves among equally subtle patterns of motive and values with cool competence. The turbulence of Donne and the elegant incisiveness of Carew have both been lost, but there remains, as a permanent acquisition for the literate poet, a sense of how completely the pale light of experience is transmuted by the prism of a sensibility tinctured with self-awareness.

Later poets show interesting projections of Stanley's patterns. Cotton, for example, defines the concept with a disturbing explicitness. His assertions have a hallucinatory absoluteness which suggests how completely sensibility was in the ascendant over factual experience at the onset of an age supposedly

[52] *Ibid.*, p. 130.

governed by good sense. His "Valediction" to a "perfidious maid" includes these stanzas:

> Methinks thou'rt blemished in each part,
> And so, or worse than others are,
> Those eyes grown hollow as thy heart,
> > Which two suns were.
>
> Thy cheeks are sunk, and thy smooth skin
> Looks like a conquest now of Time,
> Sure th' had'st an age to study in
> > For such a crime.
>
> Th' art so transform'd, that I in thee,
> (As 'tis a general loss) more grieve
> Thy falling from thyself, than me
> > Fool to believe![53]

Cotton is urging the relativity of beauty, in terms not merely of the observer's own love and that of an impartial observer but also of the lover's choice of perspective. If his moral awareness is called into play adversely, the virtues of a woman's physical beauty appear sensibly diminished. Cowley rationalized this process neatly but without vividness in his "Not Fair":

> So since, against my will, I found thee foul,
> > Deform'd and crooked in thy soul,
> My reason straight did to my senses show,
> > That they might be mistaken too:
> Nay, when the world but knows how false you are,
> > There's not a man will think you fair;[54]

It is a measure of the virtuosity of the concluding assertion that it has the same ring of willfulness as Horace's ode to Lyce

[53] C. Cotton, *Poems*, ed. J. Beresford (London, 1923), p. 177.
[54] A. Cowley, *Poems*, ed. A. R. Waller (Cambridge, U.K., 1905), p. 74.

but advances several distinct degrees deeper into the world of conscious subjectivity. Horace delighted in the fact that Lyce's beauty and good taste had faded in time. Cowley manages to convince himself that the whole process is instantaneous. Clearly such subjectivity may be dangerous if it gets out of control, but it unquestionably remains a new aptitude for poets and lovers to exploit.

The true inheritor of the best of earlier writers in this tradition is Waller, although it must be remembered that, while he died only a few months before Pope's birth, Waller, like Milton, was born in the first decade of the century, when Shakespeare was still in his prime. Waller is in fact a crucial link between the brilliant if erratic insights of the Elizabethan and Jacobean lyricists and the suave elegancies of the Augustans. His poem "Of Sylvia" deserves to be placed at the head of the tradition. Its apparent slightness and suave flow disguise a perfection of poise and awareness which demands that we recognize the devotion of writers like Dryden to Waller was not wholly misguided:

> Our sighs are heard; just Heaven declares
> The sense it has of lover's cares;
> She that so far the rest outshined,
> Sylvia the fair, while she was kind,
> As if her frowns impaired her brow,
> Seems only not unhandsome now.
> So when the sky makes us endure
> A storm, itself becomes obscure.
>
> Hence 'tis that I conceal my flame,
> Hiding from Flavia's self her name,
> Lest she, provoking Heaven, should prove
> How it rewards neglected love.
> Better a thousand such as I,
> Their grief untold, should pine and die,

Than her bright morning, overcast
With sullen clouds, should be defaced.[55]

The poem is perfectly balanced on the watershed between
Donne and Pope (which is in any case a less decisive one than
might be imagined). The poem has a conversational cadence
which, if it lacks the vehemence of Donne, sustains his spon-
taneity and briskness. But behind the pointed yet urbane style
lurks a bizarre assertion, implied by previous poems in this
vein, that kindness is a prerequisite of beauty. This is erected
by Waller's poem into a principle surpassing any local or merely
subjective factors. Waller's first stanza veils his personal
emotions so that the unkind beauty does not abruptly become ugly but merely "not unhandsome." This subdued
assertion is much more telling and convincing than the
brusqueness of the other poets. We are irresistibly convinced
by Waller's claim, while we were only curious about the
triumphs of Beedome, Cotton, and Stanley. The impartiality
is something that Horace alone could occasionally rival, but
without the intellectual sophistication Waller has inherited.
However, the Stuart poem is not simply a genteel triumph.
Though it is entitled "Of Sylvia," the real subject is the
woman concealed by the name "Flavia." Waller's assertions
about the fate of unsympathetic women are cynically extended to her also; but he is kind enough to act on the
knowledge that to invite Flavia's love might, by provoking
her hostility, reduce her to the same mediocrity as Sylvia.
His silence is at once gallant and critical. Hence this little
poem is not a quaintly cynical statement about women's
coldness but a polite warning, antedating even the possibility of the refusal of his advances. The increase in consider-
ateness and urbanity in comparison with classical admonitions to cold-hearted women is equal to the intellectual

[55] Thorn Drury, I, 97.

sophistication of the argument. How much more effective it is to say that one will not seek to make love to a woman because the harshness involved in any refusal will damage her beauty than petulantly to menace a hostile mistress with future regrets when finally she loses her charms. Waller unmistakably triumphs here, as he did in real life over the most appalling political tangles. From these he extricated himself with an equal, if less respectable, diplomacy.

[vi]

Clearly the poems discussed in detail in this chapter form a highly selective group in which the most interesting characteristics can be neatly and effectively isolated. However, these characteristics are present in all but the most incompetent Stuart lyricists, and it is worth attempting to formulate them in terms of more general purport than the subjective evasion of sexual defeat.

In the course of these studies we have seen the unmistakable pre-eminence of a sense of sequence as the source of inspiration for the seventeenth-century author. This sense was not merely, as it was to be for Wordsworth or Shelley, the finding of a fertilizing reference casually uncovered and given its final and never-repeated form as a poem. To the Renaissance lyricists a poem was, if memorable, only a starting point, just as an ingenious axiom might be for a mathematician. Having established a well-defined preliminary model the lyricist would work around it from every conceivable angle, as we have seen again and again in the reworking of successful lyrics.

The analogy with mathematics is not fortuitous. A fashionable figure in the culture of the high Renaissance bridges the gap between love and arithmetic—the figure of Plato. Plato is as unmistakably the presiding genius of the late

Renaissance as Aristotle was supposed to be of the Middle Ages. In fact, of course, their roles should temperamentally have been the reverse, for Plato was the mystic and Aristotle the scientist. But Plato was brought into prominence only when statistical analysis became a necessary adjunct of the flourishing schools of experimental science, which antedated Bacon's self-glorifying propaganda by fifty years in the writings and practical experiments of scientists like Robert Recorde and Dr. Dee. These men found the mathematics they needed for their scientific research honored not in Aristotle but in the mystical theories of the Pythagoreans inherited by Plato. At the same time, the increasing prominence given in a prosperous society to the sophistication of manners, demanded some pattern for the refined discussion of sexual love. This also was missing both from Aristotle and Christian theology in its basic forms. Again, therefore, Plato became prominent as the most noted theorist on the subject; but in both cases he brought an overtone to the special skills that were borrowed from him. In science this mysticism was often little short of disastrous as shown in the desperately ambiguous career of a man like John Dee. But in sexual love the effect was very much more beneficial, because Platonic love gave to sexual relations an intellectual status which encouraged ratiocination and debate.

In the sixteenth century, love dialogues abounded in Italy, and English writers often needed only to condense these to possess the essential matters for their lyrics. But having formulated a pattern of reaction in harmony with Neo-Platonic precedent, the very pressure of logic so characteristic of Platonic tradition suggested the possibility of intellectual permutation. The natural tension between Platonic theory and social fact provided a social pressure to back up this intellectual incentive. Many of the works of the best-known poets of the high Renaissance—Ronsard, Tasso, and Donne—

come from the attempt to integrate Platonic modes with sensual conventions. The equivocal results such efforts produced naturally bred imitators and opponents freely. The use of the word "experimental" is in fact no less applicable to the lyricism of Stuart England than to the contemporary advance of the physical sciences. It is tempting to see in lyricism a miniature war of hypotheses analogous to the larger and frequently less urbane rivalries of scientists of the sixteenth and seventeenth centuries. When we find one poet writing:

> Wert thou yet fairer than thou art,
> Which lies not in the power of Art;
> Or hadst thou in thy eyes more darts
> Than ever Cupid shot at hearts:
> Yet if they were not thrown at me,
> I would not cast a thought on thee, . . .
>
> I love thee not because th' art fair,
> Softer than down, smoother than air; . . .
> Wouldst thou then know what it might be?
> 'Tis I love you, 'cause you love me.[56]

we are aware of a theory of sexual attraction being asserted, which may be tested, if one chooses, more effectively against the data of one's own sensations than many scientists were then able to test their theories (since Bacon rejected Copernicus' theory). The assertion is more clearly sensed when set against Stanley's "Answer," whose title in turn is reminiscent of the parallel to the lyric sequences in contemporary Protestant apologetics with their pamphlets and counter-pamphlets ("Animadversions on the late animadversions . . . "). Stanley wrote rather more slyly and skillfully than the "M.W.M." to whom the previous poem is attributed:

[56] Saintsbury, III, 145.

Wert thou by all affections sought,
And fairer than thou wouldst be thought;
Or had thine eyes so many darts
As thou believ'st they shoot at hearts;
Yet if thy love were paid to me,
I would not offer mine to thee. . . .

I love thee not because alone
Thou canst all beauty call thine own . . .
Then, fairest, if thou wouldst know why
I love thee, 'cause thou canst deny.[57]

The mathematical precision with which Stanley recapitulates and revises M.W.M.'s theory argues strongly for a conscious sense of psychological speculation far transcending the casual assertion of classical poets such as Martial and Ausonius on the same kind of topic. Here there is a genuine debate, and paradoxically the two poems are not mutually exclusive. Stanley's poem does not refute M.W.M.'s poem, but merely extends its implications. The views of the first are perfectly compatible with the statement "thou canst deny," since a woman loving Stanley's lover would show this by living up to his negative expectations.

My argument is thus that these poets have liberated themselves from the prosaic facts of pagan amatory convention, just as Renaissance theoretical scientists increasingly escaped from the confining observations of earlier astronomers. Copernicus was little less hypothetical than Donne in his theories, and both were substantiated as accurate observers of their diverse subjects only with time. It is easiest to show how consciously exploratory the love poets were by comparing poems by the same author. Shakespeare's songs at the end of *Love's Labour's Lost* show that an author could echo and

[57] *Ibid.*, p. 146.

debate with himself. Marlowe's self-parody of the "Passionate Shepherd" in the *Jew of Malta* has been mentioned. But by the time we come to poets such as Milton and Marvell such contradictions may regularly become so absolute as to be mutually exclusive in theory if not in practice. Milton's "L'Allegro" and "Il Penseroso" were perhaps preliminary hypotheses which proved essentially in harmony, but Marvell's three poems "To his Coy Mistress," "The Definition of Love," and "The Garden" are equally experimental but basically incompatible approaches to sexuality, one favoring consummation, another reconciled to the lack of it despite a spiritual conjunction, and the third repudiating all relations with the opposite sex. While each poem is perfectly coherent within its own perspective, each is written by the same poet presumably at about the same time and under approximately the same conditions. They even represent, on closer analysis, three reactions to the same situation—a probably hypothetical love affair whose fulfillment proves impossible.

Marvell's role in my hypothesis is not so much particular and historical as exemplary and typical. In his poems is an exploration of possible attitudes to an easily visualized situation, ending perhaps in a commitment, sustained in his long poem "Appleton House," to one of the more sophisticated of these. This is an epitome of the effect of Stuart lyricism. After decades of almost endless experiment the whirling brilliance of Donne, the autobiographical intensity of Shakespeare and the lucid dignity of Jonson have fused into the resilient, crystal transparency of Suckling and Waller, whose best verse stands as the measure for generations of love poets just as Marvell's *Garden* seems to have done for his own poetic development.

Suckling and Waller have in common lucidity and precision, both devoted to the service of clarifying some specific issue with the minimum of stress and artificiality. It is typical of

their skill that Suckling should have condensed the theme
we have discussed in this chapter to forty words:

> Youth and beauty now are thine,
> O let pleasure, Celia, join:
> > Be divine.

> Shun the folly of disdain,
> Pride affords a short-lived reign
> > Full of pain.

> All the graces court the kind,
> Beauty by a tender mind
> > Is refined.[58]

The last stanza is a masterpiece of condensation—its elliptic
assertion is more effective than a fine-spun argument. One is
convinced by the confident note of self-evident logic that has
been distilled from decades of debate. And again the mathematical allusion holds good—what is first handled by massive
and cumbersome elaboration of formulas is refined by time,
as are here the complex patterns of Platonism, to some simple,
almost elusive statement that preserves the essential facts of
the pattern in a correct relationship.

There is more to be said of the analogy. Just as in mathematics pure experiment is almost always in the end applied
to some practical goal, one of the distinctive features of the
experiments of Stuart poets is the sense of purpose that governs many of their poems. Even their most conceited verses
usually have an intellectual direction that endows them inevitably with vitality and movement. Marvell sounds in his
triad as if he is seeking to vindicate the adequacy of each
version of the lover's reaction to an unresolved love. Suckling's slender lyric just quoted offers a resolution for a particular and classic tension. Thus one of the great virtues of

[58] Howarth, p. 242.

Stuart verse is that it is rarely the verse of simple or descriptive statement. Rarely does it merely establish a situation for the information or amusement of the reader, as is often the case in classical verse. The Stuart love poets are a restless group and their poetry nearly always applies a pressure for change of a kind which would liberate the mind from rigidity of judgment. Their most successful poems are devoted to the subversion of uncritically held dogmas about correct or judicious attitudes. But they are in no sense necessarily promiscuous or libertine in their intention. They are as willing to ridicule crudeness or cynicism, if it impedes the realization of a situation's fullest potential, as to satirize affectation or pomposity. This accounts for the curiously contradictory impressions derived from reading the works of any one poet. The writer seems to be running the whole gamut of attitudes in the course of a few love poems, and consistency will only be seen in the desire to vindicate the freedom of the human mind from the constraint of any single theory that will inhibit the most effective response to a given situation. Though one may be offended or bewildered by the attitudes taken, it will normally be found that the poet is true to the character of the situation he postulates.

Stuart poets are thus in unexpected harmony with the tendencies evident in contemporary religious and scientific thought. Puritan and scientist have much in common—a concern to focus theory on the conduct of practical affairs—and it will be found that the tendency of seventeenth-century poetry runs in this direction. Donne's complex speculations about love are focused but never repudiated in Marvell, Waller, and Suckling. The subjective disorders of Shakespeare's heroes are given exact ethical and personal meaning in the more explicit intentions of Milton. One has only to compare the ratios of Shakespeare to Prospero and Milton to Samson to see how much more crystallized and specific the relationship of the later poet is to his creations.

The elusiveness of Shakespeare is one of his fascinations, but the conscious self-mastery and dedication of Milton are more modern.

This search for method and control in the face of the complexities of experience marks Stuart literature at every level, not least the lyric one. In it the power and authority of the individual consciousness in the face of the most bizarre and challenging circumstances are consistently vindicated. The wounded sensibility that provokes the characteristically plaintive poetry of Wyatt has discovered weapons and resources in the complexity of Renaissance intellectual theories that arm that delicate sensibility against the challenges of any situation. Lament, the hallmark of lovers from earliest times, but more particularly since the era of the troubadours, becomes less and less characteristic of love poetry. Instead, we hear a new note of virile self-confidence, which was to characterize much of English literature for a century. The explanation lies in the fact that, just as the Middle Ages had given to the religious emotions a structure of logical concepts which allowed them the fullest and most effective development (until the intellectual machinery crushed the impulses it had once braced and assisted), so in the seventeenth century secular love had received the same invigorating injection of intellectual discipline, which liberated it from the elementary patterns of response afforded by most earlier models. The seventeenth century saw the advance in the intellectual awareness of love to be as significant as that in the revision of astronomy's picture of the universe. The revision did not arrive by a simple process, and before it can be fully defined its mode of evolution must be established. When we see by what tentative and ambiguous steps the new awareness came into being we shall sympathize with those who fail to detect a significant advance in human awareness, and be more alert to the methods by which the evolution of sensibility can be detected and investigated.

CHAPTER V

AN HISTORICAL PERSPECTIVE
(TO 1700)

[i]

T H E evolution of sensibility does not proceed consistently and explicitly but circuitously and tentatively. What distinguishes later from earlier periods of a literary tradition is not necessarily a change or rejection of particular values but a greater freedom of choice among possible topics, tones, attitudes, and figures. It is this condition of either limited or extensive choice that chiefly governs the character of the poetry produced. Where the resources of lyric poetry are finite and well defined the topics tend to be factual, the attitudes explicit, and the style brisk. Such is the case with much folk poetry, perhaps with Sappho, and to a lesser extent with Catullus and Wyatt. The two later poets reveal significant differences from Sappho since their perspective already extends, however fitfully, to other cultures contrasting with their own, while with Sappho this is not certainly the case. Thus the later poets' writing has a premeditation illustrated by some occasional echo or resonance of allusion that we cannot surely detect in Sappho's beautifully precise verse. On the other hand, Catullus and Wyatt retain a certain uniform clarity of values and purpose because they come at a relatively early stage in their national traditions at least—a clarity and consistency which we also find in Sappho.

Later in the development of a poetic tradition this poetry of comparatively plain statement becomes more complex because the increasing accumulation of topics, motifs, and methods permits the creative artist to manipulate inherited materials and to create new, synthetic forms of a more brilliant and more calculated texture. Such poets as Anacreon, Horace, Petrarch, Marot, and Sidney show this mastery of diversified technical resources. But as the culture in time ranges over the whole gamut of experience, from the heroic to the decadent, the lyric poet finds that he can extend the experiments earlier poets made with poetic skills to attitudes and values in general. This is the point at which each age seems to reach out toward the goals of some succeeding one and to anticipate later, more confident insights, sometimes with wavering and only half-intended effects. Typical lyric poets of such phases are Callimachus in Greece, Propertius in Rome, and Tasso, Ronsard, and Donne in later traditions. These hints of new perspectives may crystallize in a sufficient number of works to serve as the basis for a later age consciously to model itself on. Such a precedent was certainly afforded by the poets of *The Greek Anthology*, and in the writings of Martial, Ausonius, and other lesser poets of Rome's decadence. These resources were heavily drawn on by the later Renaissance, just as the "mannerist" poets themselves have been fashionable in the twentieth century. It is possible generally to explain the stimulating characteristics of the Stuart poetry that we have documented so far only in localized detail by carefully surveying these major movements of literary tradition. A study of the consecutive historical processes that gave Stuart verse its distinctive character will establish its own nature yet more coherently.

[ii]

The spirit of Sappho is almost wholly absent from Renaissance verse. Her unforced, melodious precision and intimate tone were beyond the reach of most poets aware of coming late in the literary tradition of western Europe. Even

the poems of Jonson, which often share her economical explicitness, have an artifice of manner and a premeditated quality
about their structure that contrast with the tender simplicity
of her most elegant verses. Typically the only echoes of her
verse, either from its imagery (as in Wotton's poem to the
Queen of Bohemia) or when she isolates a classic moment in
the physical relationship of lovers (the moment of entrancement in the beloved's presence), are, in both cases, when the
influence is likely to have come through intermediaries such
as Catullus. As a studied model she cannot have greatly in-
fluenced most Renaissance lyricists, chiefly because so little of
her poetry was directly accessible to them, but also because
they were much more self-conscious about inherited styles
than she seems to be.

On the other hand, the artifice and humor of the later
Greek epigrammatists were cherished consciously and lovingly by many poets to whom purity of feeling was less important than sophistication of texture. The poems of Anacreon and the *Anacreontea* recur endlessly and perhaps regrettably as models and sources for later love poets. I say
"regrettably" because, in comparison with Sappho's, most of
these poems are not love poems at all. In fact, it might be
argued that, apart from a conventional hedonism, most of
them are not "about" anything in particular. They are, like
Virgil's *Eclogues* or many Renaissance sonnet cycles, works
for the most part of pure artifice, where prettiness and
expertise outweigh meaning. Their popularity produced that
tinsel imagery and coy manner that is perhaps the vice of
Stuart verse. This aimless quaintness vitiates some of the
poems of Carew, much of Herrick, and most of the verse
of many of the lesser poets of the period. The emblem books
with their tedious ingenuity are typical products of this
limitation of artistic purpose. It is in some of the works of
George Herbert (such as "The Quip" or "Love") almost

alone that the apparatus acquires power and meaning, because there it is made an allegory for a deeply serious communication, whose seriousness is heightened by its contrast
with these mannered tones borrowed from Greek originals.

Only in the more intellectual Greek epigrammatists do
later poets find truly challenging models. Meleager, Callimachus, and some of the other poets included in *The Greek
Anthology* achieve their distinction not by the sugary designs of the *Anacreontea* but by triumphs of insight whose
originality appears in the paradoxes that, it is true, were
probably the poets' prime goal. Again and again such poets
seek to amuse or surprise, and end by illuminating the mind
of the lover—as does Callimachus when a friend refuses to
toast his boy friend. It is as if, in its latest phases, a tradition
has a choice between conventional and humorous affectations. Of these the latter are the more fertile choice, because
in them the poet identifies vividly and eagerly those apparently bizarre features of behavior in which lie the seeds of
new attitudes—what is ridiculous to one generation appears
common sense to the next. When the Greek epigrammatists
explore the margins of human experience for quaint configurations of mind and outlook they draw the attention of future
artists to the endless potentiality of human psychology. In
their blend of humor, precision, and curious observation,
these poets are among the most modern of classical writers.
They seek neither mere charm, like the Anacreontic poets',
nor purity of sentiment like Sappho's, nor yet eloquence like
Horace's—but discovery and reversal of expectation. The
other poets just mentioned all delight us, but the epigrammatists can do still more—startle us while they make us
smile; and the power to disconcert is not the least attribute
of great poetry. We have only to mention Donne for the
analogies between the Greek poets and the Stuart ones to
be clear in these terms, but Shakespeare's sonnets have often

the same quality. Every true lyric pearl has a sharp-edged grain of experience at its heart.

The earliest significant Latin lyricist is Catullus, and his poetry is of considerable importance to the Renaissance poets. In his verse the change of perspective from Sappho is already marked, despite his earliness in the Latin tradition, though his poetry has much of her unforced and serious feeling. There can be no more doubt of the actuality of Catullus' amatory experience than of Sappho's. At times the later verse of Catullus is wracked by the same blunt anguish as Keats' sonnet to Fanny, but, while Keats is reduced to exclamation in his sonnet, Catullus normally manages to transcribe his tensions with more humor and elegance. When he writes "odi et amo" ("I hate and love") (LXXXV), or:

> Lesbia mi dicit semper male nec tacet umquam
> de me; Lesbia me dispeream nisi amat. (XCII)

(Lesbia always speaks ill of me and is always talking about me. May I perish if Lesbia does not love me!)[1]

he shows a sense of ingenious paradox based on a subtle sensibility that was bound to serve as a model for later love poets. In fact, however, such paradoxes were too often formalized into the frigid antitheses of the Petrarchans. What later poets most effectively imitated was the more elaborate artifice of his kissing poems and the Anacreontic touches in poems such as his elegy on Lesbia's sparrow. The distinction of such poetry is that, in marked contrast to the *Anacreontea*, it shows how a gracious style may yet express authentic sentiment and even inner anxiety. Where Sappho sketches out topics that were to become the classic themes of love poetry, Catullus defines suitable stylistic motifs to heighten these occasions, which were to provide models for later love poets as

[1] Loeb edn., trans. F. W. Cornish, p. 166.

diverse as Skelton, Ronsard, Secundus, Donne, and Jonson, though revealingly only Skelton among these poets catches the unaffected eagerness of Catullus. Catullus is thus more important stylistically than in terms of sensibility in the debts that later poets owe him. A modern reader might be surprised by this indifference of poets to the character of Catullus, but the attitude of Horace is significant—as a master of style himself, he pays no avowed attention whatsoever to Catullus as a model and borrows from his verse sparingly. Apart from certain surface images and patterns that Horace chooses to overlook, Catullus, like Sappho, is endowed chiefly with an unreproducible graciousness of personality. Typically one of the most famous Renaissance recapitulations of Catullian effects is Jonson's "Come my Celia," which is put in the mouth of the sadistic and cynical Venetian grandee Volpone, when he tries to seduce the horrified and chaste wife of one of his victims. Anything less like a Catullian atmosphere could hardly be imagined.

With Horace it is otherwise. The style is indeed the man. He seems to have been much greater as a poet than as a personality. He is the perfect model for the poet wishing to master his craft, because in his odes perfection of expression is more nearly and consistently achieved than in the works of any other poet. He is the great craftsman, carpentering his works with a skill that later ages have admired and sought to reproduce. In him the control and redeployment of tradition are revealed in a way that Renaissance poets were consciously or unconsciously to follow closely. Horace's works are full of beautifully turned borrowings from the Greek poets. His ode to Chloe[2] is a gracious adaptation of a simile from Anacreon comparing a girl to a startled fawn. In another often-imitated warning[3] to a friend against forcing premature love on an

[2] *Odes*, i, xxiii.   [3] *Odes*, ii, v.

immature girl, Horace fuses a theme of Anacreon with the attitude of a Greek epigrammatist, Philodomenus. Horace's consummate mastery of such tactics of metaphor, allusion, and expression in general makes him perhaps the crucial stylistic model among the ancient poets for Renaissance poets such as Ronsard and Jonson who sought to acclimatize classical art to vernacular language. His work contained patterns for many styles of verbal distinction, and they plagiarized from his works endlessly. However, Horace is a poet to imitate, not to surpass. We may admire and copy his works but we would be foolish to try to improve on his unique stylistic achievements. On the other hand, he is not an investigator of novel or picturesque insights into the human mind. The Stuart poet no doubt admired the polished surface of Horace's odes, but their familiar themes hardly invited witty expansion.

Such possibilities were much more characteristic of the works of Ovid, Tibullus, and, above all, Propertius. Fine poets though these writers often are, their work is both narrower and more complicated than Horace's, because it is less flawlessly controlled. Yet they are more important sources than Horace from our point of view because he is a poet whose topics merely include love, while they are primarily, if not exclusively, concerned with the effective recapitulation of all the conventional material relevant to love available to the poets of the time. The very titles of Ovid's works, *Ars Amatoria* and *Remedia Amoris*, obviously imply an attempt to survey the material systematically, though in fact both works change only the format of the lush detail and eager or ironic tones of the *Amores* and the *Elegies* of Propertius. In these poems Renaissance lyricists found a host of patterns for love lyrics, verbal, metaphorical, and thematic, which stood out from the usually more elaborate context of the elegies and treatises. By the techniques examined in Chapter III, such motifs were given a form capable of existing independently of any larger frame of reference than their own contents. Partly because of their preoccupation with love, but also because of a difference in temperament, the Latin elegists provided subtler and more detailed insights into the psychology of lovers than did Horace. Horace concerns himself with the classic moments of lovers' experience—an eager appeal to the timid young Chloe, his ironic relief at his disillusionment in his ode to Pyrrha, urbane admonition to make the most of love to Ligurinus, savage triumph over the wreck of Lyce's beauty,[4] and so on. These expressions of the pivotal moments in a lover's outlook have never been surpassed in their own terms, but they do not communicate the whole gamut of a lover's sensibility. They ignore the wavering, ambiguous texture of a constantly evolving and sustained relationship such as that epitomized perhaps most authentically in Propertius' affair with Cynthia. The essence of Horace's art forbids the uneasy paradoxical tones and grotesque incidents found in more experienced love poets.

Catullus, too, shows many of these qualities. Unlike him, the elegists are primarily concerned with their experience as literary material, while for Catullus literature seems more important as a means of modifying his relations with Lesbia. Thus there is little possibility of later poets recapitulating Catullus' unique relationship. The bizarre, comic, or sophisticated exchanges of the elegists with their loves are governed primarily by the capacity of such scenes to sustain memorable literary patterns, no matter how artificial the means by which these are introduced. Ovid's "Esse deos, i crede"[5] is a triumph of virtuosity not of personality. His elegy on his mistress's loss of hair, or the one about his versatility as a lover,[6] are topics which neither Catullus nor Horace would care to discuss. This multiplicity and diversity remain, even if they are bought at

[4] *Odes*, i, xxiii; i, v; iv, x; iv, xii, respectively.
[5] *Amores*, iii, iii.
[6] *Amores*, i, xiv, and ii, iv.

the expense of good taste, the great virtue of the elegists as sources. For when European love poetry verged on the Renaissance rediscovery of the ancients, its own merit was a concern, like that of Sappho and Catullus, with love as a serious sentiment, but its defect was a deplorable lack of diversity and concreteness in the topics that it derived through Petrarch from the troubadours.

One growing point in the body of Renaissance verse corresponds with the awareness of the need to integrate the nominally incompatible worlds of the Petrarchan attitudes and of the Ovidian love themes. The challenge of this clash of possible modes gives the Renaissance poets their best inspiration to creative writing. Poems like Donne's "The Sun Rising" or "The Indifferent" start off on an Ovidian note of burlesque energy but modulate disconcertingly to a highly rarefied moral and spiritual level of argument, whether the essential point of the poem becomes serious or not. Less immediately juxtaposed effects are found even earlier in Ronsard, who can salute the rising sun as insolently as Donne with phrases such as "Va te cacher, vieil pastoureau champestre" ("Go and hide yourself, old shepherd of the fields")[7] yet turn a Petrarchan sentiment as frigidly as any poet. In a few of his poems one feels a significant tension between pagan and Petrarchan tastes:

> Las! pour vous trop aymer, je ne vous puis aymer;
> Car il faut en aymant avoir discretion;[8]

> (Alas! Because I love you too much, I cannot love you; for it is necessary in loving to have discretion.)

The complexity and energy of this sonnet apologizing for a lapse in self-control recalls in theme Ovid's apology for the severer fault of beating his mistress;[9] but the texture of thought, with its wholly un-Ovidian stress on the fact "que

[7] Cohen, I, 42.   [8] *Ibid.*, II, 825.   [9] *Amores*, I, vii.

la raison me faut" ("that I need to be rational") is Petrarchan. The same range of incident and attitude appears also in Shakespeare's sonnets, which show an Ovidian variety of subject matter and manner, with the marked distinction that there remains throughout the sonnets a moral dimension alien to Ovid and inherited almost involuntarily from the religious overtones of the Petrarchan traditions. The diverse mingling of these conflicting strains gives these sonnets, like Donne's poems, an extraordinarily varied and complex perspective, far superior to anything either tradition could accomplish in isolation. Earnestness is almost as rare in Ovid's treatises and elegies as humor or sensuality is in the conventional Petrarchan poets. Thus Horace's technical mastery of the art of fusing varied motifs into significant unities was successfully redeveloped in the later Renaissance and applied not so much to Horace's own works as to those of Ovidian elegists, and to the poems following the Petrarchan conventions.

There were other conflicting traditions that had to be assimilated. Among these must certainly be listed the epigrams of the later Latin poets, particularly Martial but also such writers as Seneca and Ausonius. The format of Martial's epigrams was particularly close to that of Renaissance lyricism. His poems are elegant and brief. They have often the syntactical poise and neat humor characteristic of Renaissance love poems. Many elegant Renaissance lyrics, such as Waller's "Go lovely rose," are based on classical traditions illustrated in Martial's verses, and a considerable proportion of Herrick's secular poetry is derived from Martial, including some of Herrick's somewhat rare adventures into ratiocination such as "The Lilly in Christal." A better-known poem, Jonson's "Still to be neat" (and also Herrick's well-known version of it, "Delight in Disorder"), may derive immediately from a contemporary Latin poet, but Martial's epigram to the too-perfumed Postumus[10] is the most obvious classical prototype for the English poem. More important than any single debt, however, is the diversity and intimacy of many of Martial's epigrams. Their texture and tone are more varied than those even of the Latin elegists, and the brevity of the poems also assures a consistency and focus that the longer poems lack.

On the other hand, despite many successful poems, Martial is not at all a consistent or flawless writer. In the rambling diversity of his works a clever poet can find many hints and tentative insights to redeploy and develop. These vary from the patterns of words and images such as that Jonson used in "Her Triumph," to the weird and decadent patterns of thought and attitude that earned Martial the title, from one Victorian classical scholar, of "a declared enemy to decency."[11] In an age conditioned by Freud to expect truth to take disconcerting forms we may be less cautious about examining a work that can "initiate the votaries of virtue in the mysteries of vice." Such a description illuminates perfectly the role Martial's epigrams played in relation to the chaste traditions of Neo-Petrarchan verse. Many of the Ovidian elegies of the Renaissance, such as some of Donne's, have more in common with the calculated obscenity of Martial than the exuberant frankness of Ovid. There is no doubt that many seventeenth-century poems, particularly by such poets as Henry Bold, Herrick, Lovelace, derived inspiration for their rather tedious obscenity from Martial. But it must also be remembered that Martial was among the first poets to document, even fragmentarily, those eccentricities of the individual temper that led to the surprising ingenuities examined in the previous chapter. We may say of the Latin poets that Catullus showed how literary motifs might be adjusted to serious love poetry; that Horace displayed the technical arts essential for a dra-

---

[10] *Epigrams*, ii, xii.
[11] J. Lempriere, *A Classical Dictionary* (London, 1840), p. 441.

matic sophistication of literary tradition; that Ovid and the elegists energetically accumulated the raw material for later love poets; and lastly that epigrammatists such as Martial gave this material the compact, calculated form of late Renaissance love poetry, while adding a few bizarre and provocative twists of their own.

[iii]

It is more difficult than might be expected to draw a line between the later poetry of Rome and that of the early Middle Ages. In *The Greek Anthology* pagan and Christian motifs are haphazardly confused. The secular love poem never really disappeared from European literature. Cultured clerics and wandering scholars alike ventured to write pagan-sounding verse, the former for diversion, the latter partly perhaps as a gesture of protest (like Villon later). But there is no doubt that ecclesiastical hostility and a decline in literacy outside the clergy diminished the volume of verse written in the classical tradition to the slenderest of streams. We can detect only faint traces of classical themes and motifs in the surviving love poems of the Middle Ages. When a literate secular society developed again around the twelfth century, the European literary culture was based, despite traces of an earthy folk tradition, on entirely different premises of attitude, subject and style. The more romantic tones of non-Roman cultures, such as the Arabic one represented by the figure of Ibn Hazm with his philosophic treatise on love, and the severe emotional discipline of Christianity, gave to the poetry of the troubadours a concern with sentiment that often reduced the interest in dramatic situation and frank sensuality to a minimum. It is possible to categorize the Provençal love poems with great simplicity because of their concentration on five or six basic situations. They are distinguished much better by their songlike quality. They are much more musical and operatic than any classical verses. The elaboration of stanzaic forms which finally produced the sonnet and the clear intention of a musical accompaniment make them much more flowing than classical verse and also reduce the verbal density and compactness of style. Techniques such as refrains and repetitions, which are essential to such verse forms as the rondeau, are much more common here than in Latin poetry, though Greek verse has more of these effects than does the Latin. It is the effect of the concern with music that makes these poems most important as a prelude to Renaissance love poetry. One cannot sing a complex and tortuous poem. Its shape must be simplified and reduced to decisive vocal inflections. This economy of resource is one way in which medieval lyricism anticipates many seventeenth-century poets. The long elegy is replaced by a small number of short-lined stanzas or short paragraphs of couplets as the standard format for a love poem. It is at this time of the troubadours and their followers that many of the stanza forms and attitudes we find in poets such as Wyatt begin to emerge.[12]

Perhaps the most important medieval achievement is the attempt, however narrow and equivocal its terms now seem, to codify the ritual of courtship. The value of this attempt transcends any practical virtue in the system's social attitudes. A system presupposes concepts, and concepts require analysis and application. Thus courtly love exacts the development of techniques of psychological debate that were unknown to classical authors. When singers were challenged with conventional topics for debate in singing contests they were faced with problems like these:

Who loves best, the lady who forbids her lover to fight in tournaments or the one who encourages hers to seek fame there?

[12] See P. Aubry, *Trouvères and Troubadours* (New York, 1914), Chapter III.

Should one wish to know all one's lady's secrets, or to have none from her?

Does a woman who offers to comb her lover's hair, or his beard love him better?[13]

One critic has described the discussion of these topics as "a waste of time."[14] This is to underestimate the importance of the skills such discussion presupposes—in particular the art of psychological analysis and also the power to reason in verse. No one has ever considered the debate[15] on the same kind of choice at the end of the Wife of Bath's tale "absurd." The dialogue that includes this challenge shows a capacity for ingenious discussion unmistakably indebted to the various forms of amatory debate popular among the troubadours. The appeal to public discussion and analysis explains the tone of almost forensic argument in such poems as Wyatt's "They flee from me." When Wyatt demands

> But syns that I so kyndely ame serued
> I would fain knowe what she hath deserued?[16]

he is appealing for the verdict of that loosely defined courtly audience whose opinions had succeeded the sanctions of the medieval courts of love. The same public concern appears in his poem "Blame not my lute":

> The faute so grett, the case so strainge,
> Of right it must abrode be blown:[17]

This sense of love as a *code* of behavior, liable to public discussion and objective analysis, distinguishes all English love poetry of the Renaissance and is completely absent from classical poetry, though present in Platonic and Neo-Platonic

[13] *Ibid.*, pp. 87-88.   [14] *Ibid.*, p. 88.
[15] G. Chaucer, *Works*, ed. F. N. Robinson (Boston, 1957), p. 88.
[16] Muir, p. 28.
[17] *Ibid.*, p. 122.

philosophy. Poets such as Donne, Carew, and Suckling are full of sophisticated debates about the nature of love and the nature of becoming conduct for lovers under various trying situations. The first precedents for these poets, though by no means the only or most significant ones, appear in the "jeux partis" of the troubadours.

The poetry of Dante and Petrarch is of greater significance as a direct source for the English lyric tradition, but their poems are a direct projection from the attitudes and themes of the troubadours, although with crucial modifications. Both poets find more importance in their own reactions to their loves than in the objective nature of the women themselves. In the true troubadour tradition, both Beatrice and Laura are married to other men, and neither shows much passion for her lover; but the poets manage to compensate for the lack of intimacy and responsiveness by endowing the women with symbolic qualities. Both women represent for their admirers an expression of those moral ideas with which the poets are increasingly concerned at the expense of personal and sexual matters. There are obvious analogies here to Plato's theory of love, by which cruder sexual relationships form only a pre-liminary incentive to more spiritual and ultimately purely intellectual ones. Christian theology at this time needed, in the absence of a distinctive pattern of conduct for love, a graft from Neo-Platonism, which thus flourished exceedingly in the next few centuries.

In Dante's case the initial sexual attraction is wholly transcended by this means, as we see in the apotheosis of Beatrice in the *Divine Comedy*, where her metaphysical attributes are clearly primary, giving her an allegorical rather than historical character. The intellectual analysis of her character is thus conducted properly on a highly abstract plane in the major poem; but this tendency is markedly, though more metaphorically, present in the poet's madrigals and sonnets. If there is such a thing as "metaphysical" love poetry, Dante is its most conspicuous and conscious master.

With Petrarch the balance is less strongly in favor of allegory and a purely intellectual or symbolic view of the lady. While Dante stresses the moral and intellectual potentialities of love, Petrarch stresses the amatory repercussions of intellectual love. Petrarch is closer to the varied and equivocal texture of an historical love relationship but is also fired by a less intense passion, at least on the moral level, than Dante. His importance as a literary influence on the love lyric tradition is thus greater and more diversified than Dante's. Here the importance of a diversified and mannered style of writing as the inspiration of later poets is very obvious. Though the remote, reverential posture of the lover in relation to his mistress was the most obvious feature of the Petrarchan tradition as it appears in such poets as Desportes, Marino, and Sidney, Petrarch's most fertile influence was actually in terms of the impressive diversity of motifs by means of which he illustrates his relationship with Laura. Despite the somewhat frigid nature of this relationship, Petrarch is the first poet writing in the tradition of medieval reverence for his mistress, who consciously and conspicuously integrates this attitude with the varied stylistic and thematic resources of the Latin love poets. Insofar as Petrarch consistently maintains, like Dante, a wholly "spiritual" attitude to love and gives no credit to a pagan or sensual one, he does not resemble many of his imitators, since both Ronsard and Sidney do recognize the practical difficulties of Neo-Platonic love. But as the earliest effective integrator of classical and medieval resources, Petrarch is clearly the prototype of lyricists like Shakespeare and Donne, in whom the assimilation of the pagan and Christian world has proceeded to a much deeper and more disturbing level. They seek to carry further a synchronization of inherited attitudes in a new synthesis such as Spenser sought between the sentiments of courtly love and puritan reverence for the institution of marriage. While Shakespeare and Donne approach this problem on a subjective level in their love poetry, it was left to Milton deliberately to attempt this at the fullest range of levels, from the emotional and ethical to the intellectual and aesthetic.

[iv]

The verse of the immediate European predecessors of the Stuart love poets is of more direct importance than these earlier sources, though in fact it often merely transmits the earlier influences to the English lyricists without enhancement. This is certainly the somewhat passive role of many poets whom we no longer consider imposing—figures such as Bembo and Desportes. It is equally certain that the European contemporaries and immediate predecessors of the Tudor and Stuart poets made the achievements of the latter possible by a distinctive contribution of their own to the European tradition. Pride of place among the earliest of these creative contemporaries must certainly go to Clement Marot, whose character and career as courtier and Protestant provide a prototype for those of many English lyricists in the following century. Marot inherited the somewhat emasculated and highly artificial tradition handed on by the *rhetoriqueurs* of fifteenth-century Burgundy, whose art had something of the elaborate refinement and inner weakness that gives to English Gothic of the decorated style its detailed beauty and structural defects. The *rhetoriqueurs* developed effects such as internal rhyme and perfected the arts of ambiguity and verbal resemblance to the point that one eight-line poem by Meschinot is supposed by a modern critic to have two hundred and fifty-five alternative meanings.[18]

[18] M. Bishop, *Ronsard Prince of Poets* (Ann Arbor, 1959), p. 72.

The religious tensions of the time demanded less playful media, and in Marot's pastoral elegies, such as his "Sermon of the Good and Bad Shepherds" and "Lament of the Christian Shepherd," we find serious and lucid models for such English poems as Spenser's fifth eclogue, "May," and Milton's "Lycidas." By contrast, Marot's love poetry is both elegant and witty, affording precedents for many deft compliments by Tudor and Stuart courtiers. He also brings this vivacity to the everyday situations of love that were later stressed by the English lyricists. Marot writes poems with titles like "To a Lady about a False Report," "To Anne on St. Anne's Day," "To a Learned Miss," and so on.[19] He also conducts dialogues with other poets in which contested points are debated in a series of matching poems, each attempting to cap the earlier ones, such as the series in which he censures a "Norman Lady" who says she feels that she ought to love him. The debate, in three poems, looks forward to Stuart lyricists' relentless recapitulations of arguments for and against debatable assertions and to Wyatt's precedents for these in his brief dialogue with an ambiguous lady.[20]

At his most playful Marot developed a genre of love poem that emulates the virtuosity of the *rhetoriqueurs*—an elaborate argument based on some single aspect of female beauty. Shakespeare's mockery of the lover's sonnet to his mistress' eyebrow in Jaques' "seven ages of man" speech probably refers to one of the most famous poems on just so specific a subject, written by an imitator of Marot's verses on a more intimate point of female anatomy.[21] These poems are important as among the first sixteenth-century ones to muster an elaborate dialectic in praise of some theme other than the rarefied speculations of courtly love. Marot's poems handled

[19] Jannet, III, 56-57.
[20] Muir, p. 25.
[21] See my note, " 'To His Mistress' Eyebrow,' " *PQ*, XL (1961), 157-158.

topics as sensual as anything by Ovid or Martial, with something of the finesse of the courtly debates. Shakespeare's reference in *As You Like It*, his own sonnets praising the brunette complexion of his Dark Lady, and poems such as Donne's "Autumnall," vindicating aged beauty, or Strode's "On a Good Leg," arguing that a girl's beauty is governed by the perfection of her legs, all show that the fashion was known in England.

It was in Italy, in the *capitoli* of Berni, Aretino, Tasso, and others, that this kind of elaborate disquisition became fully formalized into a virtuoso debate. The art of the *capitoli* lay in part in the adjustment of such virtuosity as that of the *rhetoriqueurs* and of Marot to certain sensual or grotesque subjects incompatible hitherto with the themes and attitudes of courtly love. Many of the *capitoli* were of course not of an amatory nature, arguing in favor of such propositions as "It is better to be sick than healthy" or "It is better to have no friends." Donne's phrase, "Those are my best days when I quake with fear," and Milton's "L'Allegro" and "Il Penseroso" all echo the Italian love of paradoxical argument. There were also poems on topics of love—Aretino's precedent for Shakespeare's "Sonnet 130" appears in a collection of *capitoli*. The most famous example is probably Tasso's "Sopra la Bellezza,"[22] which explains why an ugly woman is the best to love (because she is grateful and chaste, and there is little chance of rivals). It must be admitted that to a modern taste the *capitoli* are arbitrary in their topics and more ingenious than plausible in their arguments. Tasso's poem for example is not in the least serious in tone and lacks even that acid truth that vindicates Martial's assertion that any woman is attractive if she has money. All that one can say of the *capitoli* is that they give further intensity of focus to that virtuosity of argument

[22] Solerti, III, 190.

we first glimpsed in Marot, and that they often direct it to amatory topics. In this they were closely studied and imitated by English poets, but the translation of the motif involved increasingly a modulation of key. Some of the early versions such as Donne's elegy "The Comparison" owe much to Italian virtuoso and satirical poetry, but a foreign imitator usually seeks for meaning in his sources and may invest them with intentions not consciously present in the originals. Donne's "Anagram" is much more ingenious and equivocal than his Italian originals. What was affectation in Tasso often seems more willful than ironic in Donne. Thus when Donne writes:

> All love is wonder; if wee justly doe
> Account her wonderfull, why not lovely too?
> Love built on beauty, soone as beauty, dies,[23]

the context assures us that he is ironic, but the argument of itself is less certainly so. Indeed, when King, a generation or so later, writes:

> Say she were foul and blacker than
> The Night, or sunburnt African,
> If lik'd by me, 'tis I alone
> Can make a beauty where was none;
> For rated in my fancy, she
> Is so as she appears to me.[24]

it is no longer possible to question the poet's seriousness, though the elements of the poem are analogous to those in Donne and Tasso.

Further, if we examine the three lines quoted from Donne's elegy, it is easy to detect another important type of analogy. In "The Undertaking" Donne assumes approximately the posture of the Petrarchan, Neo-Platonic lover in writing:

[23] Grierson, p. 73.
[24] Saintsbury, III, 187.

But he who lovelinesse within
   Hath found, all outward loathes,
For he who colour loves, and skinne,
   Loves but their oldest clothes.[25]

Yet there is a surprising resemblance of argument between this ecstatic poem and the last line quoted from the sarcastic elegy. It could be argued that a sense of paradox is the growing point of the human mind, of which metaphor is the literary symptom.

Certainly the burlesque imaginings of Aretino, Berni, and Tasso again and again correspond exactly (and perhaps deliberately) in everything but tone to the central paradoxes of Christianity, many of whose sayings have the ring of *capitoli* topics—"he who seeks to keep his life shall surely lose it," "blessed are ye when men shall revile and persecute you," and so on. Donne's religious sonnet rejoicing in his fear shows the final conjunction of literary manner with theological assertion. The same avowed conjunction occurs in the Renaissance, on the level of secular love, between the only approximately Christian idealism of the Neo-Platonic view of love and the paradoxes of the *capitoli* and their imitations. Both *capitoli* writers and Platonists present challenges to the acceptance of apparent truth that are based on the masterly deployment of intellect. The only difference between them is one of tone and intention—the *capitoli* are humorous and satirical, often as a challenge to the Platonists' earnest yet artificial style. The decline of the Petrarchan tradition into a frequently satirized convention and the transposition thereafter of both Italian styles into English produces, only a little unexpectedly, an almost indistinguishable confusion of the two. Henry King's "Paradox. That Fruition destroys Love" is

25 Grierson, p. 10.

by title and dexterity of argument in the *capitoli* tradition, but in intention and texture it is Platonic:

> Fruition therefore is the bane t' undo
> Both our affection and the subject too.
> 'Tis Love into worse language to translate,
> And make it into Lust degenerate:
> 'Tis to dethrone, and thrust it from the heart,
> To seat it grossly in the sensual part.[26]

On the other hand Suckling's "Against Fruition" is ostensibly "Platonic" and even Christian, as its opening hints:

> Stay here fond youth and ask no more; be wise:
> Knowing too much long since lost paradise.
> The virtuous joys thou hast, thou wouldst should still
> Last in their pride;[27]

but the mode of argument and its flippant manner in later stanzas is clearly derived from the *capitoli*:

> Women enjoy'd (whate'er before th' have been)
> Are like romances read, or sights once seen; . . .
> 'Tis expectation makes a blessing dear,
> Heaven were not heaven, if we knew what it were.

In such subtle poems as these the latent attraction between Platonic attitudes and *capitoli* themes is made explicit by a mutual assimilation. While in Donne it is still sometimes possible to disentangle purely Neo-Platonic poems from satirically "Petrarchan" ones, and both from burlesque arguments (like "The Flea" perhaps) derived from the *capitoli*, by the time of King and Suckling the traditions have fused so that willfulness in love steals serious arguments from religion and philosophy to justify itself, and serious exposition of idealism becomes humorous and down to earth in tone.

[26] Saintsbury, III, 207.   [27] Howarth, p. 194.

This process was fostered by other sources popular with English poets, who may have found models not only in such Continental lyricists as Lorenzo de' Medici and Ronsard but also in the Neo-Platonic philosophers of the fifteenth and sixteenth centuries, particularly those of Italy. The earlier ones, like Ficino, expounded the views of Plato, Plotinus, Proclus, and others without major qualification; but in some of the later writers such as Equicola, Leone Ebreo, and Bembo one senses a distinct evolution from classical idealism, resulting perhaps from the pressure, under the mounting prosperity of the Renaissance, to recognize the claims of the material world. Ebreo is a most interesting illustration of the precedents for an assimilation of purely pagan and Platonic attitudes.[28] His *Dialoghi d'Amore*, written in 1501, was published in Rome in 1535 and diffused by such translators as Pontus de Tyard, after running through five editions in the twenty years following its first publication in Italian. The work was known by Castiglione, Montaigne, and Burton. The temper of Ebreo's philosophy can be gauged by a few typical illustrations. In the dialogues Philo attempts to modify the rigid intellectuality of Sophia—the names are clearly symbolic. Philo theorizes elaborately about the psychology of love, describing its preliminaries thus:

> . . . imaginary love may be felt for any object of desire, inasmuch as it exists in our imagination. Our imagining begets a certain love, whose object is not the real thing itself which we desire, that having as yet no proper being in reality, but only the idea thereof, derived from its general being.[29]

One senses at once the similarity of concerns here with Ronsard's curious madrigal discussed in the second chapter

[28] See the introduction to L. Ebreo, *The Philosophy of Love* (London, 1937).
[29] *Ibid.*, p. 10.

and with Donne's "Negative Love" or his "Aire and Angels."[30] All three authors are on the verge of effective description of undirected sexual desire. More important than such interesting details is the general argument of Philo for a love not narrowly abstract in character but ranging over the lovers' whole range of resources of communication, though not necessarily sensual in practice, as he explains:

> I do not admit that this is the end of perfect love; but I have been telling you that this act, far from dissolving perfect love, rather confirms and integrates it through the bodily activities of love, which are desired insofar as they give indication of such reciprocal love in both lovers. Furthermore, when two spirits are united in spiritual love, their bodies desire to enjoy such union as possible so that no distinction may persist, but the union be in all ways perfect; the more so as a corresponding physical union increases and perfects the spiritual love, even as prudence is perfected by the correspondence of prudent actions.[31]

Later Philo argues for the "soul" as an intermediate bridge between the world of intellect and that of sense where it "discerns those objects of perception which are necessary to life and thought."[32] Ebreo's dialogues lack dramatic tension for the most part, as the names of the disputants illustrate by their frank admission of allegorical intention, but the argumentative tone of Philo is significant. Again and again he verges on the argumentative pattern of the *capitoli*, and the discussion of the role of "fruition" or sexual consummation is clearly a preliminary to those by King and Suckling on the same topic. Ebreo is a good but not exceptional illustration of the tendencies of Neo-Platonic thought in the sixteenth century. Such

[30] See pp. 30 ff.
[31] *The Philosophy of Love*, p. 55.
[32] *Ibid.*, p. 206.

writers clear the way for later poets such as Donne, Carew, and Stanley to adjust many of the more sensual, worldly topics of the pagan love poets to the modified frame of reference of late Neo-Platonism. Milton's refusal, in *Comus* and *Paradise Lost*,[33] to break the continuity between mind and body is part of the same general process, which enhances the status of the physical aspects of even idealistic love. And in Marvell's "A Dialogue between the Soul and the Body" not only is the dialogue motif maintained but something like an equilibrium is preserved between the two components of human nature. There thus develops a literary pressure to integrate pagan and intellectual love motifs which results from the renewed popularity of the classical poets in the face of a sustained if conventional Neo-Platonic-Petrarchan tradition; and there is increasingly a philosophical justification for such integration in the tendency of Neo-Platonic thinkers to vindicate a reasonable admission of temporal and physical concerns into their schemes of perfect love. Their discussions, coupled with the more colloquial, humorous dialectic of the *capitoli*, sufficiently explain the tendency to analytic debate in late Renaissance love poetry, in which the academic exchanges of the theorists are transposed to the practical level of pagan love.

[v]

So far we have surveyed the European context of English Renaissance lyricism in order to vindicate historically the tendencies detected in previous chapters dealing with particular motifs. It is also necessary to examine the English intellectual climate and literary context if the primacy of English seventeenth-century lyricism in the European lyric verse of the time is to be asserted. This claim is not based on an arbitrary segment of English lyricism called "metaphysical

[33] *Comus*, ll. 453-475; *Paradise Lost*, v, 404-443.

poetry," but on an intention and accomplishment shared by most Stuart versifiers from Herrick to Cleveland—the systematic investigation of psychological states through the dramatic exchanges that naturally provide the themes of love lyrics. This concern with subjective states is a characteristic of all English love poetry of the time, not just metaphysical verse; but inevitably it is also the characteristic of its audience— educated English society during the century following 1550. In this period we find an increasing number of psychological treatises attempting to handle the complexities of human nature in more practical terms than those of Ficino and Ebreo. Works such as Sir Thomas Elyot's *The Castle of Health* (he also wrote Platonic dialogues), Timothy Bright's *A Treatise of Melancholy*, not to mention Jonson's theory of humors, all show how literary men, not necessarily qualified medical practitioners, were striving to define the nature and operation of the human mind. Of course the prime example of such works bearing on our topic is Burton's *Anatomy of Melancholy*. Despite its mathematical construction Burton's work turns on a principle analogous to the investigation of contemporary English lyricists—the accumulation of vivid and illustrative sources, illustrations, and anecdotes. His section on "love melancholy" covers exactly the same topics and sources discussed here in earlier chapters. Thus in their exhaustive scrutiny of the psychological attitudes of lovers the Stuart lyricists are in harmony with an interest of their fellow English intellectuals. It is hardly part of my intention here to explain fully how this general interest in psychology developed, but it was probably in part a reflection of the confident curiosity about the everyday world which is one of the characteristics of the era we call the Renaissance. The impact of the Reformation and the Protestant doctrine of grace, particularly prominent in Calvin's theology, also helped to turn men's minds to a study of their own operation, in pursuit of reassuring proofs of "election" by divine grace to a hope of heaven. We have already seen how these attitudes are present in such poems as Weaver's "To Jean of Chipping Norton." Donne and the so-called "metaphysical" poets are as much a mere reflection of this spread of interest in theology under the impact of Protestantism as they are an independent source of the positive displacement of theology to "secular" matters.

More immediately important than this religious context of the Stuart lyricists was the lyric tradition they inherited from their English predecessors of the Middle Ages and early Renaissance. From these eras sprang a lyricism by no means identical to that of southern Europe. Despite the prolonged efforts of English poets from Chaucer to Wyatt to acclimatize Continental motifs and style, the lyricism that flourished at the court of Henry VIII probably owed no greater debts to the elegantly aureate sonnets of Petrarch than those it owed to such poems as this:

> Fowelès in the frith,
>   The fisses in the flod.
>   And I mon waxè wod;
> Mulch sorwe I walkè with
>   For best of bon and blod.[34]

This medieval English poem is written in a style analogous to that of the famous early Tudor lyric, "O western wind," with the same simplicity, force, and succinctness. These qualities are probably the best and most characteristic features of English lyricism as a distinct tradition; certainly they profoundly modify the Italian influences to which the Tudor court poets were exposed. In explaining the character of Tudor lyricism, C. S. Lewis has written: "the stanzas used by this poetry are mainly derived from those of rhyming Latin. The rhyme schemes are never very complex. . . . Short lines or lines with

[34] *Early English Lyrics*, p. 5.

internal rhymes are favorites. The language is very plain. There is little aureation, few metaphors, no stylized syntax, and none of the sensuous imagery loved by the Elizabethans."[35] Mr. Lewis christens this style "drab," rather regrettably to some tastes since the style has excellencies of clarity and realism unrecognized in the epithet. It is also worth noting that though the Tudor analogies to the Latin verse of the medieval Goliardic poets are marked, the tradition had established deep roots in English long before Wyatt. However, C. F. Tucker Brooke observes justly that "Wyatt was perhaps the first English poet to adopt consciously the principle previously illustrated only by the anonymous writers of the popular song; namely, that the expression of personal feeling in the simplest and briefest form is itself the highest poetry and needs no narrative or allegorical support . . . in these respects Wyatt was following native influences."[36] With these anonymous precedents in mind it is salutary to compare a sonnet of Wyatt with a related one of Petrarch. The contrast will serve to explain in part the distinctive excellence of Stuart versions of Italian and French themes.

Though there are other possible sources and analogues for Wyatt's "Who so list to hount," and scholars have even suggested that the poem is essentially autobiographical, there is no doubt that the sonnet is similar enough in theme and imagery to Petrarch's "Una candida cerva" for them to be fairly compared and contrasted as samples of how these poets differ in detailed practice. Petrarch's sonnet is a typical example of his work:

> Una candida cerva sopra l'erba
> Verde m'apparve, con due corna d'oro,

[35] C. S. Lewis, *English Literature in the Sixteenth Century* (Oxford, 1954), p. 222.
[36] *A Literary History of England*, ed., A. C. Baugh (New York, 1948), p. 341.

Fra due riviere, a l'ombra d'un alloro,
Levando 'l sole, alla stagione acerba.
Era sua vista sí dolce superba,
  Ch' i' lasciai per seguirla ogni lavoro;
  Come l'avaro che 'n cercar tesoro
  Con diletto l'affano disacerba.
"Nessun mi tocchi," al bel collo d'intorno
  Scritto avea di diamanti e di topazi;
  "Libera farmi al mio Cesare parve."
Et era 'l sol già vòlto al mezzo giorno;
  Gli occhi miei stanchi di mirar, non sazi;
  Quand' io caddi ne l'acqua, et ella sparve.[37] (cxc)

(A white hind with two golden horns, appeared to me on
the green grass between two rivers, in the shade of a laurel
when the sun was rising in the season of sharp desire. Her
look was so sweetly proud that I left all I was doing to
follow her like a miser who blunts his hunger with delight
in hunting treasure. Round her lovely neck she had written
in diamonds and topazes: "Let no one touch me; leave me
free to go to my Caesar." And the sun had already moved
to the middle of the day; my tired eyes had still not seen
enough, when I fell into the water and she vanished.)

The poem is a subtle blend of medieval heraldic emblems
and oblique Christian and Platonic allusions. The white hind
on the green turf, with its golden horns and collar of allegorical diamonds (firmness) and topazes (chastity), reminds us
of the bold designs and colors of medieval tapestries or armo-
rial bearings. The spring setting is no less familiar, and the
characteristically veiled phrase "Et era 'l sol già vòlto al mezzo
giorno" seems to resemble an allusion in the first line of
Dante's *Inferno* and to suggest Laura's age (then about thirty-
three).[38] The adjectives are in general suave if not familiar:

[37] Carducci, p. 275.   [38] *Ibid.*, see notes.

"sua vista sí dolce superba," "alla stagione acerba." Periphrasis like that in the latter phrase is almost a reflex action of Petrarch's style—thus "io caddi ne l'acqua" is presumably a witty phrase for "began to weep for the death of Laura." The Platonic hint of "all'ombra d'un alloro," suggesting the "shade" which is Laura's mere body, and the Christian intent of "mio Cesare," are no less deft and deliberate overtones.

When we turn from this elegant and subtle performance to Wyatt's poem, our first sensation may well be one of loss:

> Who so list to hount, I knowe where is an hynde,
>   But as for me, helas, I may no more:
>   The vayne travaill hath weried me so sore.
>   I ame of theim that farthest commeth behinde;
> Yet may I by no meanes my weried mynde
>   Drawe from the Diere: but as she fleeth afore,
>   Faynting I folowe. I leve of therefore,
>   Sins in a nett I seke to hold the wynde.
> Who list her hount, I put him owte of dowbte,
>   As well as I may spend his tyme in vain:
>   And, graven with Diamonds, in letters plain
> There is written her faier neck rounde abowte:
>   *Noli me tangere*, for Cesars I ame;
>   And wylde for to hold, though I seme tame.[39]

The picturesque, medieval color and detail are completely absent. The deer has no physical attributes at all in the opening movement; the conventional spring setting has disappeared, like the topazes, while the diamonds are without allegorical point, merely matching the now literal sense of "Caesar," if the autobiographical allusion to Anne Boleyn is accepted. But while the style is stripped of all aureate images, its force and intensity have been much heightened by a wide variety of rhetorical emphases. The use of alliteration is very marked in

[39] Muir, p. 7.

the first eight lines, climaxed by the massing of "as she fleeth afore, faynting I folowe." The rhetorical energy is also enforced by the repetition of most of the first line in the ninth; by the exclamation "helas" in the second line; and by the marked caesurae and near enjambment of lines six and seven. The whole passage has a sustained continuity of thought and feeling that is much less visible in Petrarch. Thus Petrarch's image of the miser is rather more intrusive than Wyatt's slighter metaphor of "netting the wind"; and while Petrarch alludes to himself in personal pronouns only four times, Wyatt uses first person pronouns comparably twelve times, with a consequent intensification of involvement and emotion. Wyatt also uses more emotionally consistent, charged, and accumulated vocabulary—the sonnet is packed with words revealing weariness and defeat literally, not symbolically as in Petrarch. The image of the chase serves not chiefly to ornament the poem's intention as with Petrarch but to reinforce the sense of physical and mental fatigue resulting from Wyatt's love affair. And Wyatt's concern with this affair is literal and actual, without philosophic or religious overtones such as we find in the Italian tradition. Petrarch seems full of quaint artifice and detachment in comparison with the colloquial, committed manner of Wyatt.

That such analogies (with all their implications) could be made more widely between Wyatt and Petrarch is beyond question. That they could often be made between important English lyricists and their Continental counterparts is scarcely less certain, though Dr. Lewis is surely justified in suggesting that many of the sonnets of Spenser, Sidney, and Shakespeare have more in common with Petrarch than has Wyatt. Nevertheless, some of their most memorable poems derive much of their force and impact from Wyatt's method of plain, unmannered, frankly personal expression. Such poems as Sidney's "Because I breathe not love to every one" or Shakespeare's

"When my love swears that she is made of truth" triumph because the authenticity of the "drab" style holds the attention
better than that of their more facile, pretty, and elegant verses.
Spenser is even more characteristically Petrarchan than these
poets often are, but in a few of his most memorable sonnets
he also tends to use a less elaborate style, as in the justly pre-
ferred "One day I wrote her name upon the strand." As for
Donne, it is generally recognized that he shares both Wyatt's
general distaste for "poeticisms" and his concern for what
Hopkins called "the naked stress and screw of the English
language." Too often writers in the Continental tradition and
even its more slavish imitators in English sacrifice this immediacy and energy of their poetry for the sake of a kind of
ritualistic tribute to the muses. It remains the virtue of many
English poets that they resisted the wholesale acceptance of
the conventions of Mediterranean lyricism, much as Angli-
canism tempered Roman Catholic ritual to something distinctively English in the Anglican order of service. The total effect
on English lyricism of a tradition that instinctively reverted to
a vehement, plain, and colloquial style was to assist the Stuart
poets in giving immediacy and energy to the complex materials
they inherited from the Continental poets. Under the weight
of such artificial and intellectualized resources as the Petrarchan style and other mannerisms of French and Italian
lyricism, a less energetic tradition than the English one would
have collapsed into the dreary frigidity and stilted tones of a
Desportes or a Marino. Only an artist like Chiabrera, by limit-
ing himself to meters of airy brevity, gave the Italian tradition
any lightness. In France even poets like Marot and Ronsard
escaped the dead weight of tradition only occasionally. In
England, by contrast, many poets were able to carry off complex topics with a brusque or eager energy, which sweeps the
reader swiftly through what may well be an idea once pain-

fully explored by philosophers and theologians or customarily encrusted with traditional tropes.

This excellence has been apparent in innumerable poems discussed in earlier chapters, beginning with Shakespeare's Sonnet 130 and its evident superiority to its Aretino analogue. However, there are some distinct shifts of balance and resources between Tudor and Stuart lyrics, and it is worth illustrating both the continuity of the English tradition and its modification by a Stuart analogy to the relationship between Petrarch and Wyatt. Stuart poets are less easy to categorize as "drab" or "golden" than were their predecessors, and this represents both a virtue and a danger. It is possible to see an instance of the happy yet narrow escape of some Stuart poets from the triviality and flatness of their Italian prototypes, in the contrasting methods of an Italian poet like Giovanni della Casa and a typically competent yet minor English poet such as John Hall. Both poets admire Horace enough to borrow from him (as he did from Anacreon) an image analogous to that used by Petrarch and Wyatt; and both later poets share an alertness to the art of exploiting such a classical motif as an opening flourish for their own, differing lyrics. Thus della Casa begins one of his poems as follows:

> Come fuggir per selva ombrosa e folta
> Nova cervetta sòle,
> Se mover l'aura tra le frondi sente
> O mormorar fra l'erbe onda corrente;
> Così la fera mia me non ascolta;
> Ma fugge immanente
> Al primo suon talor de le parole
> Ch' io d'amor movo; . . .[40]

(As a lonely young hind flees through the shady and trackless woods, if she hears the air moving in the leaves

[40] *Le Rime*, ed. A. Seroni (Firenze, 1944), p. 140.

or a stream's flow murmuring through the grass, so does my wild one not listen to me but flees at once at the first sound of the words of love that I speak; . . .)

The parallel to Horace's ode to Chloe (i, xxiii) is close, and one feels the weight of the respectful awareness of tradition in della Casa's modest care to reproduce the substance and mode of his model, for Horace too had lingered lovingly over his simile. There is thus a small increase of realism over Petrarch's aureate landscape—we have progressed from the essentially symbolic tapestries of medieval landscape to the slightly more plausible countryside of classical Arcadia, with its pleasantly moderate climate.

When we turn to Hall's comparable opening for "The Call," the differences are interesting:

> Romira, stay,
> And run not thus like a young roe away;
> No enemy
> Pursues thee (foolish girl!), 'tis only I:
> I'll keep off harms,
> If thou'll be pleas'd to garrison mine arms;
> What, dost thou fear
> I'll turn a traitor? may these roses here
> To paleness shred,
> And lilies stand disguisèd in new red,
> If that I lay
> A snare, wherein thou would'st not gladly stay. . . .[41]

One sees at once the difference between an inherited tradition lovingly reproduced by della Casa and one glanced at for an instant by the more energetic and comprehensive English poet. All of Horace's elegant simile is summarized in the brief phrase "like a young Roe." The charming elaboration of

[41] Saintsbury, ii, 193.

background detail, so incompatible with the lover's urgent need to quell his mistress's apprehension in Hall's poem, has been lost, together with its epithets and Arcadian atmosphere. Instead of della Casa's "emotion recollected in tranquillity," there is the drama of re-enactment, plus the personal, urgent note of Wyatt. There is also the marked informality of "foolish girl," to which perhaps even Wyatt would scarcely condescend, as well as the constant flow of imperatives, interjections, and inquiries, skillfully suggesting the alert, positive presence of an actual love. There is perhaps a faint exploitation of the traditional English emphases in the repeated "r"s of the first two lines, "Romira," "run," "Roe," and in the important phrase "turn a Traitor." One's ear also admires the dexterous exploitation of the differing movement of the alternating short and long lines—the short ones emphatically detaining and self-vindicatory, the longer ones subtler and more fascinating. The poem oscillates comparably between diverse metaphors: "garrison" is military, "snare" reverts to the image of the hunt. It is true that Hall cannot wholly avoid also the piquant rhetoric of an Anacreontic style such as that favored by the Elizabethans and perhaps too often indulged in by Herrick. The somewhat coy oath might weaken the opening of the poem if it did not match the relaxed and playful atmosphere the lover needs to establish. The humor of the paradox in the last line quoted is part of the technique of reassurance— here is no violent amorist, but an elegantly witty courtier. Hall is thus more immediate, colloquial, and discreetly energetic than della Casa.

Yet even while he is less evidently literary, Hall synthesizes a wider range of resources than the Italian poet did in his lines, simply because he takes tradition in his rhetorical stride. Horace and the Anacreontics are used, not for purposes like their own, but to meet the needs of the moment (in a way characteristic of the Stuarts), then forgotten. Hall's verve and dramatic colloquialism are here essentially true to the English lyric tradition in general, not just to the Stuart vein. And what is so readily shown to be true of one minor Stuart poet may be shown no less readily to characterize his more distinguished contemporaries. It is from some of the English models that lie behind Hall that a major poet like Dryden inherited what Mr. Geoffrey Grigson calls "a rippling steel of English, a fierceness of metal";[42] and it is significant that Professor V. de Sola Pinto feels that both Dryden and a more lyric poet like Rochester "share qualities of masculinity and vigour, a tremendous simplicity and directness of observation and statement."[43] They, like the earlier Stuart lyric poets, depend upon many of the best resources of the sixteenth-century "drab" style, whose origins and character are typically English.

[vi]

One other important historical factor affecting the Stuart poets remains to be discussed. It is questionable whether any literature directly brings about an evolution of sensibility in the society that produces it, and probably at best art defines and fosters processes already latent in a social group. For art to flourish and advance we must therefore presuppose the existence of a responsive audience. There is no doubt that the courts of both the Tudors and Stuarts provided such groups of alert readers for every kind of artist—particularly those intellectual aristocrats who surrounded Henry VIII, Elizabeth, and Charles I. The distinction of the courts of the two earlier rulers is well known, but, while Charles' political failures are notorious, the much happier cultural climate of his court is rarely recognized. There is no doubt that at this court was laid down the pattern of the cultural society that was to be-

[42] J. Dryden, *Selected Poems*, ed. G. Grigson (London, 1950), p. 15.
[43] V. de Sola Pinto, "Rochester and Dryden," *RMS*, v (1961), 46.

come the ideal of eighteenth-century England. To some extent this was the product of Charles' own character, dignified and precise, tending to elegant magnificence. The great popularity of the masque is characteristic. It was under Charles that architects like Inigo Jones (typically also concerned with the staging of court masques throughout his career) began to develop the first native English style of architecture, which, from such a successful prototype as the Queen's House at Greenwich, was to evolve into the Georgian patterns of eighteenth-century Bath. It was at the court of Charles also that painting was first systematically cultivated by an English king, Charles' own Whitehall collection laying the foundations of those later ones that have dignified London's reputation. The successful importation of Van Dyck, a model for later English portraitists in his impeccable transcription of the ideals and self-expectations of his sitters, is another illustration of the character of the court. Even the concern with elegant formality that distinguished and destroyed Archbishop Laud must be closely linked to the tastes and influence of Charles and his associates.

In the sphere of literature in general and love poetry in particular, there is no doubt that Charles' queen, Henrietta Maria, was a major influence. This Frenchwoman proved, whatever the virtue or defects of her contribution to English politics and religion, to be a woman of considerable personal distinction and literary sensibility. She brought with her from the French court a highly sophisticated sense of the value and role of fashionable literature, which she imposed on a responsive English court that included such figures as Carew, Edward Herbert, and Waller. The influence of the queen was reflected, for example, in the enduring popularity of "Platonic" love at the English court, particularly in the early thirties. The immediate French prototypes for some of Henrietta's ideas may possibly be found at the private court of Henry IV's legendary first queen, Marguerite de Valois, in Usson, about the turn of the century. The nature of this erratic lady's so-called "Platonic" version of love is suggested by Howell's commentary: "She had a high and harmonious soul, much addicted to music and the sweets of love, and oftentimes in a Platonic way; she would have this motto often in her mouth: 'Voulez-vous cesser d'aimer? possedez la chose aimée' ['Would you cease to love? possess what you love'] . . . . She had strains of humors and transcendencies beyond the vulgar, and delighted to be called Venus Urania."[44] Links with various elements in the love lyrics of Ronsard and Desportes may be detected here, and Henrietta, while herself rigorously avoiding the license of her father's first, divorced, and childless wife, may well have sought to recreate the intellectual yet fanciful atmosphere of the earlier little court at Usson (not to mention the tradition of literary sophistication at the French court itself), so that the resources of Ronsard and later French poets were naturally recapitulated by their English successors. Henrietta's tastes may be traced in much of the poetry discussed earlier. No narrow prude, she delighted in wit and gallantry, and her distinctive strain of idealism helped to give focus, even in reaction, to the various elements of literary tradition coalescing in the lyrics of the time. Though she took care that there was little opportunity for her to become personally involved in the lyric verses of her poet courtiers, the influence of her ladies, who reflected her tastes in their freer relationships, is visible in many of the fashionable compositions of the time. And what the court favored, the local aristocracy readily disseminated throughout the country. Thus, while Donne addressed the Countess of Bedford, Wotton the Queen of Bohemia, and innumerable poets flattered the court's glittering epitome, Lady Carlisle—Milton, though no courtier, was soon to be writing similar Platonic flatteries in *Arcades* to the Countess Dowager of Derby. Even after the death of Charles and Hen-

---

[44] *Platonism in English Poetry*, pp. 156-157.

rietta Maria's flight back to France, this influence persisted. Marvell compliments the young Maria in the same gallant yet frank manner, the same idealistic yet humorous tones that Henrietta Maria and her ladies fostered.

The artificial distinction between "cavalier" and "metaphysical" poets is in fact impossible to substantiate, since the poets of the period of the Stuarts form a remarkably homogeneous group in audience, tastes, and tone. Urbane virtuosity is the hallmark of all the secular lyricism of the time, only the elements of this manner fluctuate. The pyrotechnics of Donne's early verse are less repudiated than sophisticated and tempered by the Stuart poets. Jonson's influence is not so much antithetical to Donne's as a necessary complement to it. Equally, Jonson's primary concern with classical poise in his lyrics does something to circumscribe his importance as a model for the up-to-date fashionable styles of the court which further required the greater diversity of Donne's verse. The court's gradual repudiation of Jonson after Charles' accession to the throne in 1625 is a demonstration of the taste for the more contemporary and cosmopolitan resources of poets such as Carew and Waller. Their clear minds, clever yet lucid manner, and stylish topics tactfully blended Jonson's elegant formality and Donne's eccentricity into the harmonious subtlety for which we have praised the Stuart poets. This conscious poise, transcending that of either poet, permits these later writers to formalize consciously and permanently the features in the earlier lyricists which suggest tentatively the superiority of the human mind and its emotions to the demands of fortuitous experience.

This emancipation of the human will from the vulgar demands of environment is the unique triumph of the Stuart period, and it is no surprise that this is reflected not only in the attitudes of Sir Thomas Browne (whose prose is distinguished by this elusive and tolerant self-assurance much more than by his merely quaint style) but also in the work of scientists such as Newton, who simultaneously submitted nature to the chains of human intellect, which they called scientific laws, just as Marvell did in "Appleton House." In every sphere of English life we see the human mind exceeding any previous culture's authority over its environment, both mental and physical, an achievement manifest in the greater power of objective perception and subjective independence among the intellectual leaders of society. Most previous societies had regulated their environment, but seventeenth-century Englishmen were prepared not merely to modify but to overpower its challenges even at the price of destroying conventional social structure. The rebellious spirit of the reformist Puritans is the perfect illustration of this contemporary confidence. How closely this evolution is linked to the first half of the seventeenth century is seen in the evolution from Shakespeare to Milton. Shakespeare lives in the Renaissance world of a visibly collapsing medievalism, and he dramatically illustrates the hesitant acceptance of its challenges and despairs. Milton meets more appalling confusions more confidently and braces the same resources as the early Renaissance drew upon, in the service of a new, essentially subjectively conceived order. Shakespeare is the last great poet to begin with a medieval frame of reference, Milton the first consciously to accept a modern one.

[v i i]

In such a larger scale of reference the significant place of the Stuart lyricists might well be questioned. In practice their influence was in some ways possibly greater than either Shakespeare's or Milton's, if only because it was more immediate and sustained. There was only one Shakespeare and, at this time, no conspicuous Miltonic sensibility to savor. On the other hand there were literally hundreds of lyricists, and their compositions must have been almost as inescapable as the popular songs that sweep our modern channels of communication with overpowering regularity (and which often succeed by drawing on the same techniques and themes as the Stuart lyrics). As a catalyst of social sensibility the Stuart lyric poets were therefore more important than figures who seem more imposing to us. It is hard to exaggerate the uniformity of their influence throughout the upper classes. If we turn to more allusive forms of writing such as drama or prose fiction, once the turbulence of the Commonwealth has been succeeded by the culturally more fertile Restoration we see the wide admiration for the lyricists of the generation before. Suckling, whom we have distinguished as one of the definitive exponents of the Stuart view of lovers' sensibilities, was enormously popular even at the end of the century, when we find Millamant, in Congreve's *Way of the World,* quoting him approvingly four times and then exclaiming "Natural, easy Suckling."[45] Mirabell later exchanges quotations from lyrics with her.[46] These tastes match those of characters in Etherege's *The Man of Mode,* for young Bellair praises Dorimant to Harriet in the same terms: "Lord, Madam! all he does and says is so easy and so natural."[47] The source of Dorimant's poise is made very clear when a few lines later he quotes Waller at a crucial point and in the same scene quotes a famous poem of Suckling. The popularity of light verse is confirmed in the same play by Sir Fopling, who observes, "Writing, Madam, 's a mechanic part of wit. A gentleman should never go beyond a song or a *billet.*"[48] The analogous character of Sparkish in Wycherley's *Country Wife* expresses identical sentiments:

[45] iv, i; Congreve, *Complete Plays,* ed., A. C. Ewald (New York, 1956), p. 343.
[46] *Ibid.,* p. 344.
[47] iii, iii; *Restoration Plays,* ed. B. Harris (New York, 1953), p. 197.
[48] iv, i; *ibid.,* p. 212.

"Yes; I'd have you to know I scorn writing: but women, women, that make men do all foolish things, make 'em write songs too. Everybody does it. 'Tis as common with lovers as playing with fans; and you can no more help rhyming to your Phyllis, than drinking to your Phyllis."[49] The upper classes of the Restoration thus appear fashionably committed to the writing and reception of verse modeled on the love poetry of the more famous Caroline lyricists.

If this fashion was a mere affectation the importance of the names of poets like Waller and Suckling might well be disregarded, but the influence of earlier lyricism is deeply embedded in the distinctive texture of Restoration drama. This confirms the impression derived from the three plays already quoted that the Caroline love poets were felt to be an important influence. We find Dryden writing in *Aurung Zebe*:

> O Indamora, hide these fatal eyes!
> Too deep they wound whom they too soon surprise;
> My virtue, prudence, honour, interest, all
> Before this universal monarch fall.
> Beauty, like ice, our footing does betray;
> Who can tread sure on the smooth slippery way?
> Pleased with the passage, we slide swiftly on;
> And see the dangers which we cannot shun.[50]

Here it is probable that he is thinking of Shakespeare's song in *Measure for Measure* as developed by Beaumont and Fletcher and later poets. When he writes in the same play "Had we but lasting youth, and time to spare"[51] he may be thinking of Marvell's "Had we but world enough and time," which he may have seen in manuscript, like "The Definition of Love," which seems to have given him the clue for a despair-

---

[49] III, i; *ibid.*, p. 94.
[50] II, i; J. Dryden, *Three Plays*, ed. G. Saintsbury (New York, 1957?), p. 290.
[51] III, i; *ibid.*, p. 308.

ing lover's speech in the play also.[52] The same play also reflects the virtuoso vindication of fickleness so popular in earlier witty songs:

Nor think that action you upbraid, so ill;
I am not changed, I love my husband still;
But love him as he was, when youthful grace,
And the first down began to shade his face:
That image does my virgin-flames renew,
And all your father shines more bright in you.[53]

This ingenious argument Dryden learned from the lyric poets' defenses of inconstancy alone. While one of the earliest Restoration dramatists thus draws freely on the lyric poets, one of the last of the series, Congreve, still has not forgotten their favorite themes and modes. Rather quaintly he makes the unprepossessing Lady Wishfort in *The Way of the World* exclaim to the vixenish Mrs. Marwood: "Well friend, you are enough to reconcile me to the bad world, or else I would retire to deserts and solitudes; and feed harmless sheep by groves and purling streams. Dear Marwood, let us leave the world, and retire by ourselves and be shepherdesses."[54] Thus Congreve picks up the century-old tradition of Marlowe's "Come live with me and be my love," so tenderly cherished by Stuart lyricists, in the satirical spirit with which Marlowe himself treated it in *The Jew of Malta*.

Such casual debts are to be found everywhere in Restoration literature, but the point is that often these effects are not casual but definitive. Often when a Restoration comedy makes a decisive effect it does so by deploying a device derived from some earlier love lyric of the Tudor or Stuart era. In Vanbrugh's *The Relapse* we find a passage that reminds us of the

[52] II, i; *ibid.*, p. 291.
[53] IV, i; *ibid.*, p. 323.
[54] V, ii; Ewald, p. 359.

lovers' symptoms outlined by Spenser and Sidney (following Sappho and Catullus):

> Now hear my symptoms,
> And give me your advice. The first were these: . . .
> My heart began to pant, my limbs to tremble,
> My blood grew thin, my pulse beat quick,
> My eyes grew hot and dim, and all the frame of nature
> Shook with apprehension.[55]

More explicitly indebted to recent lyricists is Wycherley's dexterous theft from Suckling's famous poem "Against Fruition," which is one of the more picturesque passages in *The Country Wife*:

> Harcourt: No, mistresses are like books. If you pore upon them too much, they doze you, and make you unfit for company; but if used discreetly, you are the fitter for conversation by 'em.
> Dorilant: A mistress should be like a little country retreat near the town; not to dwell in constantly, but only for a night and away, to taste the town the better when a man returns.[56]

The technique of ingenious allusion, and the repeated logical pattern of the imagery, are transpositions of the resources characteristic of Caroline lyricism. Even the imagery, which has been called "metaphysical," is visibly transposed in ways similar to those affecting these basic patterns. In *The Country Wife*, Horner's agile imagination is indebted for the style of many of his strokes of wit to the more virtuoso poets of the early part of the century. We might compare the following "persuasive" argument Horner offers to Lady Fidget, with analogies in Donne's *The Dreame*: "If you talk a word more

[55] III, ii; *Restoration Plays*, p. 456.
[56] I; *ibid.*, p. 66.

of your honour, you'll make me incapable to wrong it. To talk of honour in the mysteries of love, is like talking of Heaven or the Deity in an operation of witchcraft just when you are employing the devil: it makes the charm impotent."[57] Of course, there are significant modifications of Donne's effects in the imagery used here, but it is clearly intimately related to the "metaphysical" style. If a yet more conspicuous debt to the most extreme effects of Renaissance lyricism is required we might leave the theater and illustrate the range of the poets' influence by looking at that very lyrical work, Swift's *A Tale of a Tub*. Of the two hostile brothers in that book Swift writes: "Yet after all this, it was their perpetual Fortune to meet. The Reason of which is easy enough to apprehend: For the Phrenzy and Spleen of both, having the same Foundation, we may look upon them as two Pair of Compasses, equally extended, and the fixed Foot of each remaining in the same Center; which, tho' moving contrary Ways at first, will be sure to encounter somewhere of each other in the Circumference."[58] If Donne's compass image in "The Valediction: forbidding mourning" is taken, as it normally is, as the touchstone of the "metaphysical" style, then Swift is writing in this tradition. It is significant that after a display of stylistic virtuosity illustrating many of the techniques discussed in Chapter III, Swift concludes this passage in *A Tale of a Tub* with a sardonic comment on "all these *Metaphysical* conjectures."[59] It is thus fair to assert that much that is most striking in late seventeenth-century English literature draws directly on the resources of the lyric poets of the earlier part of the century. Many of their literary skills are inherited by later writers whose works are of much wider range. Though there

[57] IV, iii; *ibid.*, pp. 118-119.
[58] J. Swift, *Gulliver's Travels and Other Writings*, ed. R. Quintana (New York, 1958), p. 358.
[59] *Ibid.*, p. 334.

were certainly many other influences at work, neatness, epi-grammatic fantasy, logical mastery, and control of style were all fostered in literature at large by the writers of lyric poetry of the late English Renaissance.

More important than mere style, however, is the survival of those new subtleties of perception and psychological finesse that are the major distinction of the lyricists. These did not fade away as Eliot implies in his pessimistic summation of the evolution of seventeenth-century literary history. The lively insight into human behavior that fills the comedy of the Resto-ration with wit and humor of a more than transitory interest depends directly on the training in perception afforded by the study of contemporary lyricism. Once again close analogies and direct debts are the best illustration and proof of how the lyric sensibility spread and evolved. Congreve's *Double Dealer* is a useful source of those revealing lyric passages so typical of the prose of the time. Maskwell approaches Cyn-thia's affections with these sinuous arguments: "Cynthia, let thy beauty gild my crimes; and whatsoever I commit of treachery or deceit, shall be imputed to me as a merit.— Treachery! what treachery? love cancels all the bonds of friendship, and sets men right upon their first foundations.— Duty to kings, piety to parents, gratitude to benefactors, and fidelity to friends, are different and particular ties: but the name of rival cuts 'em all asunder, and is a general acquit-tance. Rival is equal, and love, like death, a universal leveller of all mankind."[60] The passage verges on becoming a lyric poem, complete in itself. The very veiled alliteration and ele-gantly sustained pattern of argument correspond exactly to the manner of the Caroline poets. The "metaphysical" strain ap-pears in the theological character of the argument, "whatso-ever I commit of treachery or deceit, shall be imputed to me as merit." But the conclusion is something more than arbitrary

[60] II, i; Ewald, p. 141.

fancy. "Love, like death, a universal leveller of all mankind" is a striking if not unfamiliar generalization about the pressure of human instinct, to which no earlier age could have so swiftly risen from an immediate dramatic context such as Maskwell's appeal to Cynthia. It is a further step toward that power for effective generalization about human psychology that we detected in the love poems.

More subtly and effectively analytic on a local plane is Cynthia's argument against Maskwell in the same play: " . . . it will never come to be a match. . . . My mind gives me it won't—because we are both willing; we each of us strive to reach the goal and hinder one another in the race; I swear it never does well when the parties are so agreed.—For when people walk hand in hand, there's neither overtaking nor meeting: we hunt in couples where we both pursue the same game, but forget one another; and 'tis because we are so near that we don't think of coming together."[61] There is an attempt to define the nature of love's psychology closely resembling that in Waller's "Fable of Phoebus and Daphne Applied" or Suckling's poem "Against Fruition," beginning "Fie upon hearts that burn with mutual fire." This passage clearly participates in that debate, so popular in the seventeenth century, whether lovers should seek that mutual affection favored in Donne's "The Good-morrow," or the faintly perverse tension favored both by Petronius Arbiter and, more subtly, by Suckling and other English poets. However, in addition to the way the passage prolongs the ancient debate, one must also notice how well the girl's apprehension of the failure of this potential marriage of lovers is communicated by the use of the pessimistic argument. The theme is not only skillfully handled but excellently integrated into the texture of the play.

A more ingenious analysis of the rhythm of each individual's psychological development appears in *The Man of Mode*.

[61] IV, i; *ibid.*, p. 157.

Bellinda finally comes to lament the betrayal she herself has prepared unawares: "I knew him false and helped to make him so. Was not her ruin enough to fright me from danger? It should have been, but love can take no warning."[62] The tight sequence of the psychological repercussions of her behavior, which Bellinda describes, resembles closely the perceptions shown in Donne's "Loves Deitie," which ends:

> Rebell and Atheist too, why murmure I,
>> As though I felt the worst that love could doe?
> Love might make me leave loving, or might trie
> A deeper plague, to make her love me too,
> Which, since she loves before, I'am loath to see;
> Falshood is worse then hate; and that must bee,
>> If shee whom I love, should love mee.[63]

In his play Etherege differs from Donne's analysis in the same way that many of the Caroline poets would—he clarifies and condenses his ideas much more. He also sets them effectively within the frame of the dramatic situation to which they apply —a control of insight which is the distinction of the later seventeenth-century writers. They manage to organize the disparate insights of the earlier writers into new and larger units, of which, of course, *Paradise Lost* is the epitome.

The subjectivity of the whole pattern of human relationships coming under the heading of "love," is fully recognized by the Restoration dramatists. *The Relapse* in fact opens briskly with the sentiment of the "Tell me where is beauty bred?" poems. Loveless exclaims:

> How true is that philosophy which says
> Our heaven is seated in our minds![64]

[62] v, ii; *Restoration Plays,* p. 231.
[63] Grierson, p. 49.
[64] I, i; *Restoration Plays,* p. 419.

But there is a more elaborate tracing of the path of the lyricists' discoveries in Mirabell's fierce reproach to Millamant, from *The Way of the World:*

> Ay, ay, suffer your cruelty to ruin the object of your power, to destroy your lover—and then how vain, how lost a thing you'll be! Nay, 'tis true: you are no longer handsome when you've lost your lover; your beauty dies upon the instant; for beauty is the lover's gift; 'tis he bestows your charms—your glass is all a cheat. The ugly and the old, whom the looking-glass mortifies, yet after commendation can be flattered by it, and discover beauties in it; for that reflects our praises, rather than your face.[65]

The argument, though less literary, is similar to that of Carew's poem "Ingrateful Beauty Threatened" and of the other fascinating poems that explore its theme. In fact, it can be argued that the brilliantly portrayed and glitteringly various relationship of Millamant and Mirabell is the consummation of the analysis of love accomplished by the Caroline poets. The immediacy and precision of their mutual analysis depend exclusively on the new insights of the seventeenth-century lyricists. If we compare this pair with their analogues in Shakespeare, Beatrice and Benedick of *Much Ado About Nothing*, we can see how much society's fuller awareness of lovers' natures has remodeled conventional behavior. Beatrice and Benedick are witty and antagonistic, while basically attracted just like the later lovers, but their wit is fortuitous and casual for the most part, never as intently and creatively focused on their own relationship as that of Mirabell in the passage just quoted. And, despite the fact that she "loves him violently," Millamant consciously maneuvers her lover and herself into the exact pattern of mutual respect and tension which she divines to be the expression of the cen-

[65] II, ii; Ewald, p. 319.

tury's ideal love relationship. On the other hand, Benedick and Beatrice are merely unwittingly betrayed by their friends into the fulfillment of their relationship. In such a decisive assumption of effective control and responsibility for the expression of their affections as we see in Millamant and Mirabell lies the conclusion of the Caroline tradition of love lyricism.

However, the repercussions of this self-consciousness were not always happy, though they were always stimulating. It is in Swift's writings that the challenge of self-awareness shows its threat to mental stability. To some extent Swift was indoctrinated by contemporary lyricism with his characteristic, intoxicating sense of relativity, of rapidly fluctuating values, and of the arbitrary persona available for the subtle human mind to assume. This may be illustrated by a passage from Rochester's "A Letter Fancied from Artemise," a poem recalling the subjective tradition that we have discussed. The supposed female writer of the poem observes:

> They little guess (who at our arts are grieved)
> The perfect joy of being well deceived:
> Inquisitive as jealous cuckolds grow,
> Rather than not be knowing, they will know
> What being known, creates their certain woe.
> Women should these of all mankind avoid,
> For wonder by clear knowledge is destroyed;
> Woman, who is an errant bird of night,
> Bold in the dusk before a fool's dull sight,
> Must fly when reason brings the glaring light.[66]

Here the tone is ironic, cynical and self-confident—an attack on female wiles by a man who knows the deceptions of love, but keeps his balance.

[66] J. Wilmot, Earl of Rochester, *Selected Lyrics and Satires*, ed. R. Duncan (London, 1945), p. 110.

Set this passage, however, against the following one from *A Tale of a Tub:* "Those Entertainments and Pleasures we most value in Life, are such as *Dupe* and play the Wag with the Senses. For, if we take an Examination of what is generally understood by *Happiness,* as it has Respect either to the Understanding or the Senses, we shall find all its Properties and Adjuncts will herd under this short Definition: That, *it is a perpetual Possession of being well Deceived.*"[67] Irony and satire there may be in the context of this quotation, but no one can read it without uneasily feeling that the author does not necessarily limit his meaning to the more trivial and conventional human sentiments. In this passage confidence in the objectivity of even basic human values is slipping under pressures analogous to those applied to love poetry. In his development of the idea, we can detect the risk of a total collapse of objective standards which is threatening Swift:

In the Proportion that Credulity is a more peaceful Possession of the Mind, than Curiosity, so far preferable is that Wisdom, which converses about the Surface, to that pretended Philosophy which enters into the Depth of Things, and then comes gravely back with Informations and Discoveries, that in the inside they are good for nothing. The two Senses, to which all Objects first address themselves, are the Sight and the Touch; these never examine farther than the Colour, the Shape, the Size, and whatever other Qualities dwell or are drawn by Art on the Outward of Bodies; and then comes Reason officiously, with Tools for cutting, and opening, and mangling, and piercing, offering to demonstrate that they are not of the same consistence quite thro'. . . . Last Week I saw a Woman *flay'd,* and you will hardly believe how much it altered her Person for the

[67] *Gulliver's Travels and Other Writings,* p. 342.

worse. Yesterday I ordered the Carcass of a *Beau* to be stript in my Presence; when we were all amazed to find so many unsuspected Faults under one Suit of Clothes. Then I laid open his *Brain,* his *Heart,* and his *Spleen;* But, I plainly perceived at every operation that the farther we proceeded, we found the Defects increase upon us in Number and Bulk: from all which I justly formed this Conclusion to myself: That whatever Philosopher or Projector can find out an Art to sodder and patch up the Flaws and Imperfections of Nature will deserve much better of Mankind, and teach us a more useful Science, than that so much in present Esteem, . . . He that can with *Epicurus* content his Ideas with the *Films* and *Images* that fly off upon his Senses from the *Superficies* of Things, Such a man is truly wise. . . . This is the sublime and refined Point of Felicity, called, the Possession of being well deceived; The Serene Peaceful State of being a Fool among Knaves.[68]

This is a curious terminus for the witty ironies of Ovid and Lucretius at the lover's expense. Just as the seventeenth century extended scholastic analysis to cover other activities of the human mind than the religious ones, so here the relativity of values first noted in a lover's "false" appreciations of his beloved are beginning to invade other types of mental activity. And it seems possible, from the allusions in the passage to women and beaux, that it is partly from love poetry that this contamination occurred. This passage deserves full quotation and close study because it marks a parting of the ways fertile both in new possibilities and in new threats to human nature. Swift divorces subjective perception and value from quantitative scientific mensuration and, by unwisely opposing the categories, he risks doing both a disservice. Each category of thought has achieved wonders

[68] *Ibid.,* pp. 342-343.

on its own in recent centuries, but today the two worlds are less dissimilar than appeared likely in the eighteenth and nineteenth centuries. The very author whose skepticism provoked this study, the scientist Sullivan, writes: "Nature, it appears, knows nothing of the distinction we make between space and time. The distinction we make is, ultimately, a psychological peculiarity of ours."[69] He goes on to say that certain curious facts, "throw a strange light on the scientific picture of the universe. We see that picture is much more of a mental creation than we had supposed."[70] And he sums up his conclusions by saying: "Enough has been said to show how different the scientific world has become from the plain, straightforward, objective universe with which we started. At the present day the scientific universe is more mysterious than it has ever been before in the history of thought."[71]

However, when Sullivan observes that "we cannot observe the course of nature without disturbing it,"[72] he is really only generalizing principles known to the love poets of at least three centuries ago—that the results of perception are governed primarily by the nature and perspective of the observer. When Sullivan calls earlier scientists who trusted quantitative analysis "naïve," he is unaware that their contemporaries could find in Caroline poetry a corrective to a naïve faith in the objectivity of perceived qualities. Art thus in some sense anticipated science by three hundred years. When Sullivan claims that science has advanced far beyond art he is premature; science has recently started, far too late for its own good, to pursue analogies in its own terms to the discoveries of artists. Let us put it this way: modern scientists say that the processes required to study the behavior of the electron change the behavior of that electron. Caroline poets observe that if an apparently ugly woman is recog-

[69] *Limitations of Science*, p. 55.
[70] *Ibid.*, p. 56.   [71] *Ibid.*, p. 69.   [72] *Ibid.*, p. 70.

nized as lovable by a man, the processes involved in that perception may change her character and she may well thereafter prove to be no longer ugly at all. That beauty lies in the eye of the beholder and that electrons behave in ways modified by how they are studied are probably manifestations differing in circumstances only of the same general truth—that the mode and conditions of perception largely govern what is seen.

A CRITICAL PERSPECTIVE (1700 TO THE PRESENT)

[i]

T H E value of the critical techniques used in the last few chapters should not be underestimated because the historic debates between critics and orthodox scholars over method have lost the intensity they displayed in the interwar period. It is true that it has been recently suggested that a truce, if not a stalemate, has concluded the internecine conflict in English studies between traditional scholarship and the more radical literary critics, particularly the New Critics.[1] The battle may well, however, have been decided in favor of traditional scholarship since it resulted in the extinction of *Scrutiny* some years ago in England, and the New Critics in the United States have lost the initiative in their crusade for a primarily critical rather than a historical basis for English studies. It may be that the battle should never have been fought, since it represents a conflict, not between opposed disciplines of literary appreciation, but between complementary functions of the same process. English studies fulfill two immediate functions—what we might call expository criticism and evaluative criticism. The first is concerned primarily with historical meaning, the second with modern value. Clearly these functions overlap: historical exegesis of a particular text presupposes its interest to the scholar's contemporaries; a judgment of the value of a text to a modern society is suspect if it involves appreciation of the text in

---

[1] See J. H. Raleigh, "The New Criticism as an Historical Phenomenon," *CL*, xi (1959), 21-28.

ways incompatible with its historical character. The editor and researcher are thus no less dependent on the critic than he is on them, and, while the New Critics may have been justified in demanding a re-examination of the relationship between critic and scholar, the possibility of the unqualified supremacy of either must be repudiated by responsible students of literature.

As we have seen in earlier chapters the implications of a reconciliation between the two functions of the literary mind make considerable demands on the resources of the student of literature. But at very least the quarrel between critic and scholar demonstrates the need for an attempt to establish a new relationship between documentation and evaluation. It is of course easy to demand a general synthesis of the two processes, but it is less easy to demonstrate the nature of such a syncretic criticism in action on a larger scale than the present study. However, it is clear that the existence of complex historical patterns in literary tradition does not of itself enhance that tradition. A failure to see this was probably the trouble with late nineteenth-century Miltonic scholarship. Enthusiastic appreciation of the contemporary value of certain writing from an earlier culture is also no guarantee of that accurate understanding which must precede effective assimilation. This has been the failure of the New Criticism in relation to the so-called "metaphysical" poets, as parts of our analysis have implied. Milton's historical status, not his modern importance, was once overstressed; and Donne's importance, but not his historical character, has more recently been equally overemphasized. Milton is more valuable to us than the New Critics were willing to admit; Donne is historically not quite the same writer that modern critics found inspiration in identifying with their own values. Milton's power of synthesis has been neglected as of no modern value despite his relevance to our fragmentary culture, while Waller's place in the same tradition that includes Donne has also been denied, despite all the historical evidence to the contrary.

The problem remains whether the present study has avoided this split between research techniques and principles of value that threatens the enthusiastic scholar and critic alike. For it is no use forcing the two modes into arbitrary conjunction. Fortunately the problem has proved to be related to one more central to the whole process of literary appreciation. Literary evaluation has tended to be retrospective inevitably. "This is important," we say, "because we need today to study works with these qualities." If we do not normally say how these interesting qualities come to be expressed in such works we fail in the fullest and most rewarding knowledge of them. We risk false attributions, saying "Milton does this," "Milton seeks to do that," when in fact it is the literary tradition that is moving in these directions and Milton's own contribution is different, more refined and finite, even perhaps contrary to the apparent trend. The whole pattern of interrelations between literature and the other arts and functions of society has scarcely been hinted at even in the earlier chapters. But only by such attempts at tracing the dynamic relation between individual, traditional, and social values in literary works can we hope to come to that awareness of the interpenetration of their value and their origins that will allow us to relate them significantly both to their own time and ours. Our "syncretic criticism" must thus always be historical criticism, not the study of sources and parallels but the use of sources and parallels as a preliminary to definition of the significant character of any one work. And this significant character has been defined in our detailed examinations not by the similarity of one work with another, nor by the differences between works, but by the differences at the points of maximum resemblance. When editors record sources and analogies they leave the conclusions to the reader when in fact, of themselves, the parallels signify very little. It is not that Wyatt drew on Petrarch for "Whoso list to hount I know where is an hind" that is important, nor simply that this is one of his few really popular sonnets with the modern reader. It is what Wyatt did to the Petrarch imagery that make his sonnet unique and memorable and Petrarch's scarcely distinguishable from its frigid companions. The study of contemporary taste which I. A. Richards initiated in *Practical Criticism* is equally irrelevant unless it is closely correlated with the exact historical nature of literary performance. A poet fashionably derided today, such as Waller or Cleveland, may well have made possible certain potentialities, such as brisk but lucid intellectuality, which we do treasure today. And what these poets were may also reflect seriously on certain limitations in their models and masters such as Donne and Jonson.

The discipline proposed here and illustrated tentatively in the preceding chapters is therefore one of study of the significance of departures from shared norms of topic and execution in literary tradition. In a sense it is only a sophistication of Arnold's "touchstone" theory, which represented some attempt to correlate tradition with evaluation, but on a dangerously arbitrary basis. Arnold is right in seeking to integrate critical and historical values in his essay "The Study of Poetry," but to compare Homer directly with the *Chanson de Roland* or *The Canterbury Tales* with the *Divine Comedy* is futile. It is not simply that the works belong to different cultures with different needs and values, but that they afford little practical basis for proper correlation. On the other hand, to compare Dante with Virgil, or Chaucer with Guillaume de Lorris and Jean de Meung is a proper way to approach the definition of each, because the correlations are functionally related to the authors' creativity and methods.

Arnold's "touchstone" theory must be doubly modified under the pressure of a greater historical sense and more critical awareness. Works should only be compared where there is a proper basis for intimate correlation of content or context, and there should be no attempt to enforce a rigid singleness of excellence. Only a rewarding departure from earlier models should deserve critical enthusiasm, not a mere reversion to the terms of previous classic performance.

Clearly the prerequisites of such demands are extreme. They imply that it is difficult for anyone to define the character, meaning, and value of a given poet's work without at least an approximation to that poet's cultural awareness. To write of Renaissance English literature without an effective awareness of the classical Latin and the contemporary French and Italian cultures would seem to be temerarious. Unless one knows approximately what Propertius and Martial had done, and what Berni and Tasso, Marot and Ronsard did later, it is difficult to define and evaluate what Sidney, Spenser, Shakespeare, Donne, and later lyricists achieved. On the other hand, the student must be prepared to say, not simply that Shakespeare's Sonnet 130 is like Aretino's "madrigal," but that it is better and more important to us for certain precise reasons of critical principle and taste, though this in turn does not mean that Aretino may not demand our respect in ways defined by other comparisons. It is curious to find that roughly this over-all critical perspective is sought by Pound, perhaps prematurely and with inadequate resources. Pound's attempt to integrate the world's cultures in the *Cantos* makes an artistic analogy to Toynbee's historical exegesis in *A Study of History*. Neither attempt at full correlation of terrestrial cultures is certainly a success, and perhaps the best we can seek in the West is a sense of European society as an integrated and compactly evolving unit. The critical methods sketched out here can only be fully achieved by the auto-

CRITICAL PERSPECTIVE

matic assumption of a European awareness, by the critic and his audience, such as has always existed for the major artist. The differences between so-called European cultures are really much more "dialectal" differences within the same culture. This is the first bridge we have had to cross. Shakespeare and Donne are at least as much European writers as English ones, or perhaps even, like Milton, more European than English. Their individual distinctions can only be defined accurately in this perspective.

[ii]

It might be argued that the framework for elaborate cross references and valuations in literary tradition exists in genre criticism; but as Croce has suggested in his *Aesthetic* this concentration upon such formal entities as tragedy, the novel, the lyric probably demands the support of other resources if it is to be authoritative. Within a single society, where the prescriptions and requirements are constant, the genre method is particularly useful—say in analyzing Jacobean tragedy, or the Russian novel. But if one seeks directly to compare Aeschylus, Shakespeare, Racine, Chekhov, and Ibsen the result will tend to be a comparison ultimately of whole societies, even if formally only one of individual philosophies. Even on the level of lyricism we find it difficult to correlate the impact of Ovid's *Ars Amatoria* and Shakespeare's sonnets, though they are closely related in theme. Genre criticism thus functions best in a narrow field of survey and tends to eliminate some useful perspectives even there. Influence often runs at right angles to genres as we see in the sources for Shakespeare's comedies in Italian *novelle* and the debts of Donne's lyrics to scholastic theology.

The only alternative to literary form as a basis for comparative criticism appears to be the content of the works to

· 283 ·

be compared. Within the area we have discussed—lyric love
poetry—this content has been defined in terms of three
things: the relationship of the lovers presupposed by any love
poem, the mode of communicating this relationship, and the
poet's attitude to these factors. These terms allow for complete interchange of material between all kinds of genres and
societies, provided only that basic constants are present.
Although there is no necessary direct connection between the
albae of the troubadours and the parting of Romeo and
Juliet after their marriage night, the situation, "dramatic"
mode of speech, and tender earnestness of the poet's manner
make a comparison perfectly plausible. The crucial divergence
in this case, Shakespeare's faultless weaving of his dawn
song into the texture of a larger more complex unit—a
tragedy—is exactly that "difference in similarity" that we
have praised as the key pattern for a critic to seek. It shows
how far the highly localized unities of early medieval lyricists have been surpassed and intensified without loss of
local precision by the evolution of the most complex and
integrated form of writing that we know. Identity of situation
is thus a primary basis for a literary critic on which to found
his judgments in comparative analysis. The method has this
advantage, that often it will function as a means of linking
disconnected traditions—say that of the antique Orient with
Occidental cultures. There is no denying that what is involved
trespasses on sociology and anthropology, but in practice
their disciplines can rarely be separated from the study of
aesthetic expression. The interplay of social experience and
artistic expression is so complex as to defy the categorization
of each into a distinct entity. Works such as biography and
history clearly occupy a middle ground available to both
sociologists and critics, and few major literary works can be
disentangled from their historical content and context.
Aeschylus' *The Persians*, Shakespeare's histories, and even

those of so enigmatic an artist as Strindberg, are all deeply rooted in essentially social and historical circumstances. The list could be extended endlessly in terms of less explicit historical features, such as the correlation of the situation of the university wits with malcontent figures in Jacobean drama, of which Hamlet is the most complex in Renaissance literature. And anthropology does no disservice to *King Lear* by showing how Lear's behavior to his triad of daughters is deeply rooted in various folk patterns of which Cinderella is the most popular heroine.

Doubtless it will be urged that none of these considerations tells us anything about the specifically artistic distinction of the works involved; but it remains questionable whether fully articulate expression of any kind can effectively be distinguished from that in the so-called "aesthetic" modes. It is hard to believe that the perceptions which constitute distinction in religion, philosophy, social performance, and so on, are not assets to literature and the other arts. The sociological importance of Ebreo or Castiglione is closely related to that of Donne, as we saw in the evolution of such poets as Suckling and Waller, whose works integrate literary tradition with social performance. It remains true, however, that literary composition is not simply an unqualified reflection of social concerns and fashion. In many ways it is just that, but there remain principles of selection and distortion governed partly by the individuality of the author and partly by the processes of premeditated composition, which govern most expression, but whose intensification is perhaps the only hallmark of literature. Within the range of possible situations or relationships on which literature may be founded, apparently fortuitous selections, like that of the Cyclops theme by Philoxenus, lead to an elaborate and consecutive tradition parallel to, rather than directly expressing, social concerns. The isolation and definition of such themes are valuable activities for the scholar

seeking to make critical judgments about authors who interest
him. By avoiding the large social scale of reference hitherto
surveyed, these essentially literary motifs provide a satisfac-
torily finite substitute by means of which to evaluate the
capacities and performance of individual writers. At this level,
however, the problems which to some extent invalidate genre
criticism are yet more challenging.

Literary sequences not only evade continuity within a genre,
they also escape from any necessary contextual frame whatsoever. A sustained sequence may be founded on a variety of
patterns, varying from a major thematic issue such as Milton's
concern with the magical power of chastity through very specific situations such as Polyphemus' courtship of Galatea,[2] or
the use of subordinate motifs like the hot summer day used as
an atmospheric background to some pastoral dialogues, down
to the merest stylistic device such as the juxtaposition of op-
posites—"hard-soft," "freezing-burning." Some of these effects
may tend to recur in certain standard kinds of composition,
but there is no guarantee of their consistent use. Mr. Chambers has suggested that the history of the "inverted tree" topos
for example takes us from its earliest known source in Plato's
Timaeus through most varieties of writing to at least "Appleton House" and Swift's famous *Meditation upon a Broom-
stick*.[3] Co-ordination of such diversified sequences to achieve
a critical as well as a scholarly perspective has clearly been a
thorny challenge to researchers. Granted this hazard of potential anarchy, which it is hard for the conscientious researcher
to avoid, it remains true that tactful correlation of such patterns is the best guide to evaluating literary talent. The absence of these patterns, which is extremely unlikely, is one of
the ways in which an author invites literary death at the hands

[2] See my "Polyphemus in England," *CL*, xii (1960), 229-242.
[3] See the discussion of this theme in A. B. Chambers, "'I Was But
an Inverted Tree': Notes Toward the History of an Idea," *S. Ren.*,
viii (1961), 291-299.

of critics. It is very significant that originality is not characteristic of major artists, but that a synthesizing power over such traditions is. This may be confirmed from highly diversified sources. While considering changes in Chou decorative motifs of the twelfth century before Christ, William Willets writes, "stylistic innovations seem to coincide with a marked deterioration in artistic and technical quality."[4] Writing of evolution in word meanings in English after the Renaissance, Josephine Miles observes, "we may note the clear fact that innovation in the materials of poetry comes strongly from minor poets, even from those derided in their time, like Blackmore, and that therefore at least this simple sort of poetic invention is not unlike other forms of invention, in which new details come gradually from minor sources and are brought into synthesis by larger spirits."[5] Hence it follows that, despite the potentially erratic sequence pursued by literary themes and motifs, it may be confidently asserted that the more important the writer in question, the more likely that his work will show considerable assimilation of classic material suitable for the development of comparative analysis.

[iii]

There is a kind of rhythm in the evolution of popular motifs that illustrates the development of literary tradition. In the first instance we find poets such as Sappho, Catullus, and the troubadours, whose work has a marked freshness, even originality, but who as far as can be judged concern themselves mainly with a memorable composition, founded on some such distinctive pattern or patterns as we have studied. Their works are successful and important as economical statements of themes and issues that will inevitably be called to the atten-

---

[4] W. Willets, *Chinese Art* (London, 1958), I, 168.

[5] J. Miles, *Renaissance, Eighteenth-Century, and Modern Language in English Poetry* (Berkeley, 1960), p. 50.

tion of later poets. By comparing the numerous sequences noted earlier, it will be seen that certain ratios regularly, though not invariably, recur in the relationship between these early writers who are in practice, if not necessarily in historical truth, the prototypes for later lyricists. In fact such ratios almost invariably recur between any important earlier and later writers, no matter at what point in a tradition this chronological relationship exists. The various characteristics of a later work can be summed up under two headings—condensation and integration. Both are the results of greater control and confidence resulting from the experiments and practice inherited from discussion of suitable material by earlier masters.

One notes at first a tendency to brevity. The earliest and the latest productions of a culture tend for antithetical reasons to extremely economical statement. At the start of a tradition there is little accumulation of material; symbolism and abstraction are much more characteristic of the earliest aesthetic expressions of a culture than somewhat later ones. Simple conceptual patterns better serve the needs of a compact, dynamic society that has only recently left the more primitive levels of culture. Techniques of discursive examination, exhaustive accumulation and systematic analysis usually characterize a fully developed, stable, and self-confident culture, though these processes may seem disturbing to individuals of that time. Such were perhaps the conditions of the Athens of Pericles, of Rome under Augustus, and of the England of Elizabeth and James. Once some sense of general perspective has been achieved, a surprising reverse movement often sets in, of contraction, selection, and condensation, whose results superficially imply a condition analogous to primitive art. Pre-Raphaelitism, and modern interest in African and tribal art in general are typical artistic manifestations in recent times; but in the eighteenth century the popularity of the ballad shown in such collections as Bishop Percy's *Reliques* and the whole

Wordsworthian mystique with its prefigurations in Burns and Blake illustrate the same tendencies. The reason for such work may be escapism, but it seems more likely that rather than simply seeking to revert to more elementary patterns of existence and expression, such art actually illustrates a new mastery of ideas and media which permits the whole range of complex analysis and speculation of intervening eras to be condensed into a brief but dynamic statement as capable of focusing a larger cultural consciousness as the more primitive artist was of giving definition to his limited one. Even while Blake and Wordsworth appear to be rejecting the past and present they are really simply giving a more satisfactory synthesis of contemporary intellectual and emotional resources. Neither is really a "primitive," and "Gauguin figures" cannot escape a European context, merely give it clearer and more dynamic outlines.

The latest writers of a tradition often successfully accomplish by deliberation what earlier ones did primarily by instinct or intuition. This, of course, is reflected in the texture of their works despite their apparent resemblance to simpler compositions. Possessing greater, even if repudiated, self-awareness, and technical *expertise*, such later artists show greater conceptual power and focused intention. In many primitive art forms, distinctive patterns are not handled with a sense of their individual integrity. They are juxtaposed or interwoven arbitrarily and sometimes grotesquely, giving an impression, very characteristic of primitive art, of vivid and overpowering confusion and exoticism. This may well persist in later stages of a culture, but in its ultimate phases there is invariably visible a marked tendency to separate the exotic from an ambiguous context and expose it in challenging isolation. This tendency is particularly visible in modern museum layout. Earlier Occidental displays tended to splendidly haphazard accumulations, such as are still visible in the Vatican collections. Now individual focus or chronological and systematic sequence is expected to be the invariable basis of display, otherwise critics become indignant or distressed. All these tendencies appear in literature, both on the largest scale and within very finite limits.

Point, focus, and clarity are progressively more important in English lyricism from 1600 to 1660. The fusion of disparate and apparently incompatible effects throughout the period illustrates the syncretic tendencies of a mature society, but the increasing preference for clarity of purpose and economy of outline is an essential component of the attitude of such an age. Jonson is no less syncretistic than Donne, as we see in the processes involved in distilling the lyric "Drink to me only with thine eyes" from its quaintly disparate sources.[6] Donne is no less conscious of the need for coherence and consistent movement than Jonson, as the structures of "A Valediction: forbidding mourning" or of "Goe, and catche a falling starre" clearly show. The differences between Donne and Jonson are thus more superficial than radical—differences of content and sources rather than of discipline and technique. Donne is more often concerned with contemporary Continental lyric verse than is Jonson, who depends usually on classical resources; but both bring fresh materials within the orbit of English lyricism and give to these firm patterns intelligible to their successors. These syncretic and integrating tendencies are apparent throughout the seventeenth century and give rise to that century's most imposing creations. Among these must be included such works as Milton's *Paradise Lost* and *Paradise Regain'd*, which attempt to give unity and focus on the largest scale to the accumulation of human experience, wisdom, and artifacts from the earliest times to Milton's own age. However, the process also functions outside the strict boundaries of art. Hobbes's *Leviathan*, with its attempt to formulate an absolute

[6] See *Ben Jonson*, xi, 39.

yet comprehensive summary of man's role as a political animal, is closely analogous to Milton's major works. *Leviathan* shows a similar consolidating power and intellectual control, with a consequent lucidity. The philosophies of Spinoza, Descartes, and Leibnitz are all products of similar aspirations to a synthesis of man's experience based on intellectual co-ordination. Such authors stand in the same relation to earlier less absolute and comprehensive writers as Montaigne, Machiavelli, Hooker, Raleigh, Burton, and others, as Suckling and Waller do to the early Jacobean lyricists. Suckling and Waller are not repudiators of "metaphysical," or Elizabethan lyricism, but consolidators of it.

They accomplish something else which is characteristic of a highly evolved tradition, namely, naturalness of tone and colloquialism of diction or style. Again primitive and sophisticate often seem to resemble each other, one by lack of alternatives to actual usage, the other by his capacity to assimilate all patterns to the texture of conventional communication. Mannered or highly artificial expression is essentially an intermediary form of style attempting to outdistance uncouth simplicity, but as yet unaware of suave elegance as an ideal. The evolution of the pastoral, an essentially sophisticated mode, is a typical illustration of the link between later and earlier styles. But plain style and colloquial tone are more than an affectation of rusticity. The manner involves the conscious cultivation of dramatic modes of expression for the twofold reasons of vividness and the fullest integration of intellectual values with socially viable and effective behavior. One is tempted to wonder whether all art forms do not tend in their most memorable examples toward dramatic modes of expression as a tradition develops. The manifestation of such a highly dynamic moment, enacted rather than described or analyzed, is one of the reasons why da Vinci's *Last Supper* has been so highly regarded. And many of the statues of

Michelangelo have been identified as communication of highly charged moments in the lives of their subjects, as Freud's discussion of the Moses illustrates.

In lyricism the lack of polarity between early and late style may come from the fact that the unconscious drama of subjective expression in the earlier writers is recaptured deliberately in the dramatizations of later poets. One might compare, for example, the artful dramatic monologues of Browning with the comparatively artless confessions whose customary existence they presuppose (historically extant in the sources for such cases as "A Death in the Desert" and *The Ring and the Book*, at least). It is this quality of self-dramatization that makes Catullus almost involuntarily memorable, and Horace much more self-consciously so. The more picturesque writings of Ovid and Propertius are enlivened by their apparently autobiographical nature and the speaker's affectation of actual participation in dramatic exchanges by means of their poetry.

This quality is not so evident in postclassical writing, until the sixteenth century. Retrospective soliloquy is normally the nearest approach to dramatic expression in the lyrics of Dante, Petrarch, Villon, Chaucer, and other poets of their era, though the form is sometimes masked as apostrophe. The same is true of Wyatt, whose tone is characteristically retrospective; but he nevertheless has an avowed intimacy of involvement which creates dramatic tension more convincingly than the aloof style of most earlier poets of the postclassical eras. It is most evident that Ronsard's verse is the first after classical times in which a fully dramatic expression of the author's sentiment is a normal and effective mode of communication. Though many of Ronsard's love poems conform to a somewhat mechanical Petrarchan pattern, all his best and most memorable ones involve a dramatic mode of presentation that often corresponds closely to the poet's historical relationships, as his biographers have demonstrated. Ronsard's frequent indebtedness to such models as the Latin elegists and Horace in such poems makes it clear that this technique is not instinctive but assiduously cultivated. It is this characteristic of Ronsard that earns him prominence as a source and influence on the lyricists of the late English Renaissance.

Though Shakespeare's sonnets show astounding originality and a personality more intensely and elaborately communicated than that revealed by any other group of English lyrics of the era, Donne's more ingeniously composite poems, with their calculated melodrama, are more characteristic of the Stuart lyricism which we have chiefly studied. Donne is the first poet to accomplish a convincing dramatization of the discoveries made in the most complex analyses of human sexuality. No one could be convinced readily that the subtleties of Ficino or Ebreo might be effectively translated into a norm of human behavior, but Donne's verse sometimes does make them seem feasible. The lover who starts off with "For God-sake hold your tongue and let me love" is dramatically convincing, yet he concludes with assertions which exceed even the excesses of Neo-Platonic subtlety.

We must, of course, be careful here to distinguish between the idea of the coexistence of passion and intelligence in the author and its apparent presence in the behavior of the characters in the poems. What we have is not necessarily an expression of Donne's own "witty passion" but the presentation by the author of reasonably convincing dramatizations of a hypothetical love that is both energetic and intellectually alert. It is one thing to say that Donne's dramatic monologues (since this is what most of his lyrics are) present lovers in whom passion and intelligence coexist, and another to say that these coexist in any historical individual. In fact, when we do begin to get full-scale dramatizations of lovers who correspond at all closely to the traits hinted at in Donne's sketches, we find that reason and feeling are still not fully articulated, but merely coexist under tension, as in the characters of Mirabell and Millamant.[7] The major virtue of Stuart lyricism is not so much that lovers actually behaved with the ingenious passion the poems affect, but that society was interested in considering such a possible mode as feasible. Henry James' own behavior and that of Edwardian society might as mistakenly be confused with what happens in James' novels as Stuart love lyrics with the sentiments of actual lovers. James' novels and the Stuart love poems are attempts to define human potentiality in harmony with the best intuitions of the time. The Stuart poets have this marked superiority to James, that their work often sounds more authentic and actual than do his novels, barring those few highly dramatic earlier ones, such as *The Bostonians* and *The Awkward Age* (a *tour de force* which significantly consists primarily of dialogue). The Stuart poets perhaps thus do more to encourage the emulation of their lyrical lovers by real lovers than does James to inspire the readers of his novels to copy his presentations.

The dramatic characteristics of Stuart lyricism are an important element in its effectiveness as a catalyst of social evolution, though there is no sure proof as yet that this evolution was actually accomplished. However, by discussing sexuality as an immediate and evolving human concern these poets have changed our perspective, or at least can change it, decisively. It is not for nothing that the earliest use of "sex" in our modern sense is found in Donne's "The Primrose." He uses it apparently not in the contemporary sense of the physical organs of sex, nor as a category equivalent to "men" or "women," but to cover the complex patterns of human relations governed by these attributes and distinctions. This conceptual originality gives the key to much later Stuart love poetry. It dissects the character and potentialities of this aspect of human

[7] For a thorough critique of Eliot's assertions see L. Unger, *The Man in the Name* (Minneapolis, 1956).

nature through the medium of dramatic lyric statement. The subject has rarely been subjected to such exhaustive review— we must turn to the impact of Freud on modern awareness to find some analogy. However, this analogy will also illustrate the limits of literary or intellectual influence on society as a whole. We are all aware of Freud's expansion of the potentiality of human nature, and artists such as Strindberg, Kafka, Lawrence, and Tennessee Williams have helped to give this potentiality a vividness comparable to that of Stuart love poetry. But, while our views and even our behavior may be slightly deflected by this pressure, very few people are wholly committed to Freud's general outlook, and even fewer (and this group may even exclude Freud himself) have lived in harmony with his ideals. Thus Stuart love poetry maps an avenue in the human imagination, a hypothetical mode of behavior, which might be partly realized in practice. But to a large extent it probably remains a hypothesis. That Donne, or Jonson, or Suckling actually behaved or felt in the ways they portray lovers as doing is very dubious. "Felt thought" and "thought feeling" exist only in the world of art, where feeling is often as skillfully synthesized by intention as is intellectual control. These poets should be praised for their power of dramatic presentation of ideas, not for communication of an historical norm of conduct. Congreve gives us a better knowledge of the actual practice of Donne's suggestions, and this proves somewhat different from the lyric poet's conceptions. However, the dramatic manner, which for historical reasons perhaps flourished best in England as we have shown, is a key to the successful realization of these ideals in practice.

[iv]

It is worth clarifying the exact relationship between the arts and those less explicit, nonliterary pressures as a result of which human nature is both sustained and even modified, and whose earlier appearance in our study of lyric verse now permits some generalizations. Despite the modern repudiation of the idea of theology as the queen of the sciences, a moral scale of reference remains the primary basis for aesthetic creation. This does not imply either a conventional moral pattern in the artist, or an explicit series of dogmatic principles; but it does imply a definite awareness of, and concern with, value. Some kinds of experience and shades of feeling are more important and worthy than others to all important artists. Their distinction as artists lies in their unique capacity to give such awareness a tangible and vivid expression—an "objective correlative." In the case of Stuart lyricism the moral principles which govern the views of love are derived from Christianity in its dual forms of scholastic dialectic, and the subjective enthusiasm of the Reformation. J. B. Leishman has rightly declared the importance of Rudolf Kassner's assertion that "Christianity gave a new depth-dimension to human consciousness." Despite the apparent licentiousness and libertinism of at least half of the Stuart love lyrics, their distinction lies in an extension of sexual feeling by means of the apparatus afforded by contemporary religion. Religious feeling had acquired a magnificent conceptual mechanism for the analysis of religious sentiment, and this remained part of the framework of religious orthodoxy in seventeenth-century England, as can be seen in the prose works of Hooker, Donne and others. Many of the most distinguished seventeenth-century English lyricists were, in fact, Anglican clerics. Despite the nominal divergence from Christian norms of the sentiments of poems such as "The Flea" or "To his Coy Mistress," both poems lay stress on the need for effective argument about, and analysis of, feeling; and, since the only analogous pattern was that of Christian (or Christian-Platonic) metaphysics, the consequence of such analytic discussion was in general apparently to reconcile sexuality with religious formulas. Even the licentious verse of the time has an earnestness of self-appreciation quite lacking in classical love poetry. And the sensualist is "anti-Platonic" or decries "conscience" with a fervor not unlike that of the Lutheran censure of papism, or belief in "works." Thus a sense of moral purpose gives an essential color to the Stuart lyric, a color lacking in most earlier lyric verse, which had escaped direct subjection to Christian orthodoxy. Stuart lyricism is at least partly a by-product of the conjunction of Renaissance rediscovery of classical authors with Reformation concern about the individual's moral psychology.

This lyricism was also directly dependent on the manners of the courtly society which flourished under the Stuarts. The ideal of gentlemanly literacy advocated by authors like Castiglione, Elyot, and Ascham, and epitomized by Sidney, was crucial to the emergence of such a large body of writing, and its intimate connection with the everyday life of the court. Though few of the authors whom we have discussed would have considered their poetry a primary, or even important part of their lives (Congreve's later betrayal of literature is a good illustration of courtly attitudes throughout the century), literature could not but gain by the fashionable delight in versification. Lyricism was the natural mode for the expression of such a marginal concern with literature, as we see also with "public" figures such as Abelard, Wyatt, or, in our own day, Stevens and St. John Perse. However, the court was indeed a happy environment in which lyricism could flourish. Wittiness, briskness, conversational ease—these attributes of courtly life all enhance lyric expression. In such societies sophisticated, artificial, and even somewhat unrealistic views of human nature can be expected to develop more freely than in classes concerned with full-time professional activities, such as the middle class, or those governed by rigid traditional values, such as the lower strata of a non-industrial society. The Stuart aristocracy thus represents one of those interesting extremes of human activity that have always fostered the development of art forms of enduring interest. The society of Pericles, the courts of Augustus Caesar, Frederick II of Sicily, Louis XIV, and Napoleon III, all illustrate this link between artistic development and the existence of a prosperous, cultured, and leisurely aristocracy. Thorstein Veblen's theory of "conspicuous consumption" is only a satirical view of this recurring situation favoring marked cultural florescence. Our ultimate generalization on the social context of Stuart lyricism may well be to note that if we specify as the two most fortunate attributes of a Stuart lyricist that he be a courtier, or attracted to the aristocracy, and deeply involved in religious matters, ideally in holy orders, we cover most of the major lyric poets of the time, and explain the character of their compositions. No critical evaluation of their work can avoid an awareness of the impact of these moral and social pressures on the processes of lyric composition. This verse is the product not only of a literary tradition but of a highly specialized and unique society in which metaphysical awareness, social elegance, and classical scholarship were for a time coexistent, though synthesized alone perhaps in art.

[v]

The affectations of a recognizably extreme and precarious society, such as that led by the Stuarts, are in many ways antithetical to our modern cultural patterns and consciousness. Further, it is difficult to define the nature and practical value of such poised works as the Stuart love lyrics in modern terms without destroying their unique character. To vindicate their importance some such abstraction must be attempted. The quality which is most fascinating in these poems is surely their rich sense of human potentiality, particularly in expressing the nature of sexual love. Because of dual traditions, Christian and pagan, which clashed in the Renaissance, poets began to realize that the human mind was capable of a wider range of choice among patterns of conduct than either the classical or medieval eras alone were able to conceive. Love could be sensual or intellectual; desire could be fulfilled or delicately attenuated; passion could be hammered by intellect into the same kind of delicate yet psychologically sustaining arabesques and paradoxes as those of the scholastic philosophers who hypnotized their hearers in the halls of the Sorbonne. But these are not the things that we may hope to transpose fully to our own society. It remains for us simply to use these processes of subtle dialectic to justify our liberation from any arbitrary psychological constraints imposed by conventional self-analysis. If the *capitoli* could liberate their writers from the logical pressure of common sense, and if later writers showed that what an Aretino probably argued tongue-in-cheek, a real lover might properly come to feel (as in Shakespeare's Sonnet 130), then why should any elementary pressure, sexual or otherwise, to react in any predetermined way prove irresistible or, on the other hand, necessarily be repressed? We cannot but feel with a wretched poetaster of the seventeenth century called Stevenson, who, having praised a sickly young woman energetically, suddenly turned on her with these words:

> But stay my whiting, though I took thy part
> Twas not to show thy beauty but my art.
> My conscience tells me red and white best please,
> White not set off with red portends disease:
> But poets pro and con, salute and slight:
> Tell you the dove is black, and the crow white,

I could have writ as much, and given a grace
As ample, to the calf with a white face.
Thus have I made thee fair and foul; so truly
Starch be it ne'er so white, comes off but bluely.[8]

Stevenson's self-supposed virtuosity is in fact the inheritance of all of us, not just as poets, but as effective human beings. Only propriety as we choose to see it (what Stevenson calls "conscience") need exercise a restraint on what we do. Otherwise we can find a logic to vindicate almost any taste with some confidence that unlocalized desire will soon rally to back up our ingenuity. For example, those "beautés de langeur,"[9] as Baudelaire called them, which Stevenson finally repudiates in his poem, predictably had their day in due course. Victorian romance has many examples of which La Dame aux Camelias and the Mimi of La Bohème are the most popular; and Emily Brontë did her best to live up to the pattern in real life, like many other middle-class Victorian maidens.

Historically this idea of the freedom of human nature from any effective absolutes in its view of human beauty and of sexual attractions is a very useful concept. It enables us to set in line the utterly disproportionate characteristics of ideal female (and male) appearance throughout pictorial history, without a sense that one version alone from the whole sequence was truly the most beautiful. If we put together a Degas or Lautrec dancer, a Rembrandt study of a woman bathing, and add paintings of a Renaissance great lady and a medieval princess, we may at first glance find a horrid dissonance, yet in the end we shall see that they share a common logic—the power to "adjust" physical circumstance to the needs and tastes of a particular time. The same potentialities of human form apparently existed in all these

[8] M. Stevenson, Occasions Off-spring (London, 1645), p. 32.
[9] See "J'aime le souvenir de ces époques nues" in Spleen et Ideal.

periods. However, it was convenient for a multiplicity of reasons to see certain things and not others. And in the world of intangibles we find artistic perceptions to have been much freer still. It becomes almost impossible not to find an historical vindication for every possible phase of human love and sexual relationship.

Philosophically it may be argued that there is great danger in this freedom from any objective constraint which we first find fully realized, if usually only affected, in Stuart lyricism. Perhaps indeed we do see its consequences in the excesses of Restoration society. In practice, however, this freedom can also be a buttress of orthodoxy, as much as a destroyer of it. Potentially, sexual desire as defined and illustrated by the Stuart lyricists ceases to be a destructive force. Its vagaries may be anticipated, dexterously focused, or cunningly distracted. Ovid's study of the arts and remedies of love verged on this awareness, but flippantly and without the certainty derived from that scientific mechanism for detailing human emotion with which scholastic philosophy has endowed us. No one can read the poems of Shakespeare, Donne, Carew, and those others which have been particularly praised in this study, without some sense of illumination— not a mere sense of aesthetic euphoria, but a sense of extended understanding of the workings of the human mind and a consequent extension of power over himself and his environment.

More important than this tempering of the indiscriminate operation of sexual desire is the refocusing of relationships between the sexes. What is established as the key axis between lovers is decisively clarified by Stuart poets as not a physical, nor an intellectual attraction, but a mutual sympathy to which these other details are incidental and subordinate. It is this sense of the essential mutuality of love that permits these poets to surpass all earlier authors, even those like Ovid who show great wit and insight in describing the nature and functions of sexual love. Ovid detected the wavering subjectivity of lovers' evaluation of the facts of their experience, but he failed to realize that this potentially emancipated lovers from all the assaults and challenges of mechanical actuality. If a feeling for beauty and virtue is founded only on the sense of reciprocal affection, love becomes essentially a psychological relationship, and self-aware lovers become superior to all the mere accidents of time and space. This idea and its discussion are the primary foundations for all the major love poems of seventeenth-century England. Obviously the view governs much of Donne's most impressive love lyrics, but even as Jonsonian a poet as Marvell hints at the debasing effects of the absence of this mutuality in "To his Coy Mistress," where lack of harmony between the lovers apparently enslaves them to time and space, while its presence in "The Definition of Love" helps to secure the lovers against all threats to their mutual self-confidence. It is probable that this sense of reciprocated affection conditions the character of many later literary presentations of love.

[vi]

For it is wrong to assume that the themes and attitudes of this lyric tradition simply died in England by the end of the seventeenth century. Perhaps the best way to bring the tradition into focus with modern values is to see that at least some of the Stuart attitudes to love have survived and evolved through successive generations of poets, and are present, if in severely modified form, in much poetry which figures prominently in modern consciousness. Most of the mannerisms of Stuart lyricism are certainly current today. A poet, for example, who can write "Come gentle bombs and fall on Slough"[10] has much the same sense of shock values as one who begins "Batter my heart three personed God." However, mannerism is more conspicuous than attitude and the historical sequence connecting Stuart and twentieth-century lyricism better shows the shared interests than mere arbitrary conjunctions. Such pivotal figures as Pope, Shelley, Browning, and Hardy illustrate the survival of Stuart resources in certain forms.

It is true that many of the motifs discussed earlier reappear in lesser poets contemporary with Pope, such as Prior and Gay. However, the brutal immediacy of Swift's awareness of women as shown in his poems is a more important development, though his unwillingness to compromise the absoluteness of his standards of delicacy was clearly inimical to the establishment of fully effective relations with women. His letters to Stella do suggest a more complex intimacy than any earlier writings. Similarly it is in Pope's epistles to Martha Blount that he communicates most fully this deft assimilation of the arts of the poetry of the previous age to the facts of immediate social life. In his lines "To Miss Blount with the works of Voiture," Pope soon begins talking about life as if it were regulated by artistic principles, either as "a long, exact, and serious comedy" or "an innocent gay farce." He stresses the primacy of subjective fulfillment in love, even at the price of all the more glittering and substantial rewards. A woman fortunate in all but a responsive husband, whatever her state, "sighs and is no duchess at her heart." The climax comes when Pope summarizes effectively some of the basic premises of the most interesting Stuart verse, in admonishing the woman to whom he is deeply but diffidently attracted:

[10] J. Betjeman, *Collected Poems* (London, 1958), p. 21.

But, Madam, if the Fates withstand, and you
Are destin'd Hymen's willing victim too;
Trust not too much your now resistless charms,
Those, Age or Sickness soon or late disarms:
Good humour only teaches charms to last,
Still makes new conquests, and maintains the past:
Love, rais'd on Beauty, will like that decay,
Our hearts may bear its slender chain a day;
As flow'ry bands in wantonness are worn,
A morning's pleasure, and at evening torn;
This binds in ties more easy, yet more strong,
The willing heart, and only holds it long.[11]

Pope has studied and mastered the techniques and perceptions of such poets as Carew, whose "Ingrateful Beauty Threatened" has much this pattern, though lacking the avowed actuality of Pope's epistle. His other poem to Miss Blount, while she was away in the country, has many of the attributes of Stuart poems upon absence, but again it is fuller, more actual and personal than they are. Less distinguished as poetry, but closely linked in concept to the Voiture epistle, is Pope's poem "The Looking Glass." This makes Carew's point as stringently and explicitly as possible:

With scornful mien, and various toss of air,
Fantastic, vain, and insolently fair,
Grandeur intoxicates her giddy brain,
She looks ambition, and she moves disdain.
Far other carriage graced her virgin life,
But charming Gumley's lost in Pultney's wife.
Not greater arrogance in him we find,
And this conjunction swells at least her mind.

[11] A. Pope, *Complete Poetical Works*, ed. H. W. Boynton (New York, 1903), p. 81.

O could the sire, renown'd in glass, produce
One faithful mirror for his daughter's use!
Wherein she might her haughty errors trace,
And by reflection learn to mend her face:
The wonted sweetness to her form restore,
Be what she was, and charm mankind once more.[12]

The prosaic actuality of the situation is perhaps imperfectly assimilated to poetic poise and elegance, but the idea of Stuart poets that beauty lies only in responsiveness has clearly become axiomatic to Pope in writing of it.

In "Eloisa to Abelard" there take place perhaps the fullest digestion and resynthesis of elements of Stuart lyric love motifs, which were probably transmitted to Pope at least partly through the medium of the "heroic" plays of Dryden and others. It is not a poem that has fixed itself deeply in popular awareness, but artistically it is of great interest, and even importance. Without resorting to a vulgar biographical interpretation of the poem it is clear that here Pope attempts in lyric movement the kind of fusion of his own amatory experience with mythic statement that Milton more imposingly achieves in dramatic form with *Samson Agonistes*. As his attentions to Martha Blount reveal, Pope was emphatically responsive to female attraction, but his physique made him effectively impotent. Though the poem brings Pope's personal tragedy vividly into aesthetic focus, it does much more by harmonizing most of the resources of Stuart love lyricism with this pattern. Without artifice, the poem may be considered as a climax to the "metaphysical" style. Theology and sexual passion are deeply and tensely interwoven, but less bizarrely than in Donne because the tradition has matured and the varied connections between religious terminology and amatory experience have become

[12] *Ibid.*, p. 107.

actual and logical rather than metaphorical ones. However much more lucid Pope may be, there is no mistaking the antecedents of lines such as:

> O come! O teach me Nature to subdue,
> Renounce my love, my life, myself—and You.
> Fill my fond heart with God alone, for He
> Alone can rival, can succeed to thee.[13] (ll. 203-206)

There are hints of Donne's *Divine Sonnets*, like that beginning "Batter my heart. . . ." The awareness of metaphysical sanctions and pressures also deeply colors Eloisa's awareness —for historical rather than aesthetic reasons, another step toward normality and actuality. Though she speaks in a fainter manner, Eloisa might well be recapitulating the effect of Donne's *The Dreame* when she says:

> . . . truth's divine came mended from that tongue.
> From lips like those what precept fail'd to move?
> Too soon they taught me 'twas no sin to love:
> Back through the paths of pleasing sense I ran,
> Nor wished an angel whom I loved a man.
> Dim and remote the joys of saints I see;
> Nor envy them that Heav'n I lose for thee. (ll. 66-72)

This is not scholastic in tone, nor does it have Donne's jolting vividness, but it does presuppose the same conscious juxtaposition of two types of awareness, religious and secular, that governs his verse. No less rationalized but still somewhat extravagant are sentiments like these:

> Should at my feet the world's great master fall,
> Himself, his throne, his world, I'd scorn 'em all:
> Not Caesar's empress would I deign to prove;
> No, make me mistress to the man I love; . . .

[13] *Ibid.*, p. 113.

Oh, happy state! when souls each other draw,
When Love is liberty, and Nature law:
All then is full, possessing, and possess'd,
No craving void left aching in the breast:
Ev'n thought meets thought, ere from the lips it part,
And each warm wish springs mutual from the heart.
This sure is bliss (if bliss on earth there be)
And once the lot of Abelard and me. (ll. 85ff.)

This has more the style of the heroic drama we examined in
the previous chapter than of Donne, but it implies the absoluteness of his attitudes and of those in such plays by his
contemporaries as *Antony and Cleopatra*. It also follows the
vocabulary of their metaphors. All that has happened is that
the texture of this verse has become regularized and that
any hint of humor and affectation has disappeared. But as
with Pope's "versification" of Donne's satires, the substance
of his thought remains. And if the mannerisms of Donne
rarely appear in Pope, those of Stuart verse in general certainly do. Pope appears to be echoing specific patterns when
he makes Eloisa exclaim:

Take back that grace, those sorrows, and those tears,
Take back my fruitless penitence and prayers;
Snatch me, just mounting, from the blesst abode:
Assist the fiends and tear me from my God!

No, fly me, fly me, far as pole from pole;
Rise Alps between us! and whole oceans roll!
Ah, come not, write not, think not once of me,
Nor share one pang of all I felt for thee.
Thy oaths I quit, thy memory resign;
Forget, renounce me, hate whate'er was mine.
Fair eyes, and tempting looks, (which yet I view),
Long lov'd, ador'd ideas, all adieu!

This passage recapitulates most of the characteristic effects of the tradition whose epitome is Shakespeare's "Take, oh take those lips away."

Nearly one hundred years later the concern with material and attitudes analogous to those of Stuart verse is much diminished, but in such a poet as Shelley traces of Stuart resources may still be detected. An opening line like:

> I fear thy kisses, gentle maiden[14]

recalls immediately Waller's poem "To Flavia" with its observation, "Flavia! 'tis your love I fear." More impressively the virtuoso arguments of the poem to Harriet, beginning "Thy look of love has power," recall those of Carew and others. Shelley affects to ask for more coolness on her part, in his own interest. The following lines show that Shelley's apparent personality here is not unlike that affected by the earlier poets, for he reveals the same virtuosity of sentiment:

> Be thou, then, one among mankind
> > Whose heart is harder not for state,
> Thou only virtuous, gentle, kind,
> > Amid a world of hate;
> And by a slight endurance seal
> A fellow-being's lasting weal.[15]

We might recall Carew's "Mediocrity in Love Rejected" as a parallel to this passage—though Shelley's poem lacks those aureate allusions whose conventional ring sometimes impairs Stuart verse. Another, earlier, Shelley lyric needs little commentary to demonstrate its analogies to the Stuart tradition of subtle psychology blended with elegant precision:

> Yet look on me—take not thine eyes away,
> > Which feed upon the love within mine own,

[14] P. B. Shelley, *Complete Works*, ed. T. Hutchinson (Oxford, 1934), p. 610.
[15] *Ibid.*, p. 522.

Which is indeed but the reflected ray
  Of thine own beauty from my spirit thrown.
  Yet speak to me—thy voice is as the tone
Of my heart's echo, and I think I hear
  That thou yet lovest me; yet thou alone
Like one before a mirror, without care
Of aught but thine own features, imaged there; . . . [16]

The poem has the vivid subjectivity that distinguishes Shakespeare's sonnets even more than Donne's verse. Its eager and direct mode of address to the mistress and the restless energy of the syntax give the poem this quality. A closer scrutiny of the syntactical pattern will, however, demonstrate that there is a more precise reason that Shakespeare and the Stuart poets come to mind. The poem's movement somewhat resembles, like part of Pope's "Eloisa to Abelard," that of the song in *Measure for Measure,* "Take, oh take those lips away." More particularly it matches the form of that poem's second movement as developed in Donne's "The Message." The structural massing of the clauses introduced by "yet" follows Donne's technique. No less interesting is the juggling with concepts. The play with eyes recalls the visual exchanges of "The Extasie," while the elaborate attempt to define just what is what in terms of actual and perceived is a process Donne also undertook in "Aire and Angels." Though the actual meaning of both these poems approximates to Shelley's, it is surprising how little of Donne's scholastic apparatus is necessary to transmit Shelley's meaning and how seriously the Romantic poet takes his argument. Donne's ingenious and highly subjective view of love can by now be easily transmitted in conventional language without hyperbole, though the subtle counterpoint of thought survives unimpaired. Rather like Donne in his elegy, *The Dreame,*

[16] *Ibid.,* p. 523.

Shelley suggests very effectively that the nature of love is a kind of endless mutual refraction—something more even than the "mirroring" he suggests in passing at last. This poem is not only psychologically ingenious and suggestive but historically interesting because it shows neatly how well the type of perceptions achieved by Stuart sensibility may accommodate themselves to the styles of later ages. When the Romantic poets consciously revived an interest in extreme or eccentric psychology they necessarily found inspiration in Stuart lyricism.

Browning is an obvious choice to illustrate the relevance of such models to the goals of a nineteenth-century poet. The very title of one group of his poems, *Dramatic Lyrics,* at once puts him in touch with Stuart tastes in lyricism, and this series actually begins with three "Cavalier Tunes," while his "Garden Fancies" in the same group is clearly in the tradition of the quainter poems of Herrick and Marvell. As a love poet Browning also shows some psychological as well as stylistic affinities with the resources of the Stuart poets. Not only does he, like them, find in Pierre de Ronsard a useful guide to the intricacies of love ("The Glove") but many of his poems are devoted to the analytic scrutiny of human nature in love. Both "Porphyria's Lover" and "Andrea del Sarto" investigate the conduct of lovers in a way that echoes the subtle tensions and mutual dependencies that distinguish the love poetry of Ronsard, Donne, and their imitators. Nevertheless, it is in the *Dramatic Lyrics* that Browning demonstrates with arresting vividness that a practicing artist had almost necessarily anticipated by more than seventy years the fashionable twentieth-century interest in the so-called "metaphysical" poets and their contemporaries. The evolving "Stuart" tones of Drayton's famous sonnet "Since there's no help come let's kiss and part" is caught in more modern circumstances by Browning's "The Lost Mistress":

> All's over, then: does truth sound bitter
> As one at first believes? . . .
>
> Tomorrow we meet the same then, dearest?
> May I take your hand in mine?
> Mere friends are we,—well, friends the merest
> Keep much that I resign: . . .
>
> Yet I will but say what mere friends say,
> Or only a thought stronger;
> I will hold your hand but as long as all may,
> Or so very little longer![17]

Browning reveals the desire to define an exact amatory situation that was in Drayton the prelude to the subtler investigations of the Stuart poets. The more exotic note of Stuart style is visible in this Browning song:

> Nay but you, who do not love her,
> Is she not pure gold, my mistress?
> Holds earth aught—speak truth—above her?
> Aught like this tress, see, and this tress,
> And this last fairest tress of all,
> So fair, see, ere I let it fall?
>
> Because, you spend your lives in praising;
> To praise, you search the wide world over:
> Then why not witness, calmly gazing,
> If earth holds aught—speak truth—above her?
> Above this tress, and this I touch
> But cannot praise, I love so much![18]

The poem stands heir to a whole tradition of English Renaissance poetry including sonnets by Spenser and Sidney, as

---

[17] R. Browning, *Poetical Works* (Oxford, 1940), p. 215.
[18] *Ibid.*

well as later lyrics such as Herbert's "Jordan" poems and many others. It has inherited their colloquialism, hyperbole, subjective self-hypnotism, with perhaps even a faintly sinister overtone in its absolutism, which is Browning's own contribution ("ere I let it fall" reminds us almost unconsciously of Porphyria's fate!).

More interestingly comparable to the Stuart amorists' analysis of particularized situations is "Cristina." A few fragments will illuminate the analogy:

> She should never have looked at me
>   If she meant I should not love her!
> There are plenty . . . men, you call such,
>   I suppose . . . she may discover
> All her soul to, if she pleases,
>   And yet leave much as she found them:
> But I'm not so, and she knew it
>   When she fixed me, glancing round them. . . .
>
> Doubt you if, in some such moment,
>   As she fixed me, she felt clearly,
> Ages past the soul existed,
>   Here an age 'tis resting merely,
> And hence fleets again for ages,
>   While the true end, sole and single,
> It stops here for is, this love-way,
>   With some other soul to mingle?
>
> Else it loses what it lived for,
>   And eternally must lose it; . . .
> This she felt as looking at me,
>   Mine and her souls rushed together.[19]

This resembles "metaphysical" love poetry in several details —use of a dramatic incident (the lover fails to maintain the

[19] *Ibid.*, p. 214.

instant of recognition), colloquial style, poised psychology, and serious metaphysical overtones. The major differences between this and seventeenth-century poetry lie in its greater seriousness of tone and in that Browning has elaborated the impact of the facile flow of modern society on subtle emotions in a way earlier poets, less aware of social pressures, rarely did. The same kind of war between metaphysical or psychological truth and social fact distinguishes the rather more sentimental "Any Wife to Any Husband" with its faint overtones of Bishop King's "Exequy." And sentiments like this:

> Because thou once hast loved me—wilt thou dare
> Say to thy soul and Who may list beside,
> "Therefore she is immortally my bride;
> Chance cannot change my love, nor time impair."[20]

share some of the idealism of such a poem as Donne's "The Good-morrow." However, it is interesting to see how Browning again uses in full earnest what Donne hints often that he thinks to be chiefly hyperbole.

The explicit impression of Stuart traditions on the verse of Tennyson has already been noted in one instance—the song toward the end of *The Princess*. But rather than multiply mid-Victorian illustrations of the recovery of Stuart resources and concerns let us turn to Thomas Hardy, whose complex impact on modern verse is so immediate that, despite tributes like that of Auden (who found him his own prime model),[21] it has not yet been fully analyzed. His poetry puts us at once into the range of twentieth-century verse with the analogies it affords to Robert Frost's rural poetry, to Eliot's vivid but gloomy dramatic monologues (whose resemblance to Browning may partly result from the inspiration of Hardy's bitter

[20] *Ibid.*, p. 236.
[21] In his inaugural lecture as Professor of Poetry at the University of Oxford.

episodic poems), and even to the urgent nostalgia of Betjeman. The appropriateness of choosing Hardy as our last vantage point is shown by the analogies in much of his work to the tradition we are studying. Anyone seeking an interesting series of analogies might compare "A Wasted Illness" with Donne's "Hymne to God my God, in my sicknesse," "A Drizzling Easter Morning" with "Goodfriday, 1613. Riding Westward," and "Channel Firing" with some of *The Holy Sonnets* (say VII, IX, XIII). More specific analogies to Donne, in this case his "Twicknam garden," appear in the haunted lovers cut off from the countrysides in which they find themselves in "The Rambler" and "Wessex Heights." Here the dynamism of subjective impressions is vividly communicated —the idea in the mind of the lovers proves more substantial than the objective reality around them. This is a theme that dominates much of Hardy's best verse. Poems like "The Haunter," "After a Journey," "The Glimpse" all clarify and illustrate just how superior to adverse circumstances and death a truly meaningful relationship can be.

These are perhaps the most moving of Hardy's developments of themes found in Stuart verse, but there are other revealing analogies with the earlier poets. One of the most arresting is "The Well-Beloved." The poem is too long to quote, but it shows decisively the dangerous risk of conflict between the subjective awareness of a lover and the facts of his external relationship. It dramatizes vividly the naïveté of views such as that taken by Crashaw in his "Wishes to his Supposed Mistress." Hardy crystallizes the lover's ideal into a presence that accosts him on the way to his betrothed and proves fatal to his love for her. In this poem Hardy manages to recall the nature of pagan divinities in a way not perhaps equaled since the plays of Euripides. In doing so he also shows that he grasps firmly the psychological perceptions governing Shakespeare's Sonnets 53 and 106 and Donne's opening to "Aire and Angels" and the lines in "The Good-morrow":

> If ever any beauty I did see,
> Which I desir'd, and got, 'twas but a dreame of thee.[22]

It is significant that Hardy sees this hallucinatory vividness of the lover's idealized desire as much more sinister and independent of reality than any seventeenth-century poet could have realized, though the nearest analogies to the blasting effect of the vision of Hardy's lover on his beloved's beauty is found in seventeenth-century poems defending fickleness in the pursuit of ideal beauty. Among poems by Edward Herbert, Lovelace, and Howard, one by Alexander Brome will make the resemblance explicit:

> The self same beauty that I've often sworn
>   Dwelt only in my dearest,
> I see by other Ladies worn,
> Whom the same Graces do adorn: . . .
> Thus out of all, Pygmalion like,
>   My fancy limns a woman;
> To her I freely sacrifice,
>   And rival'd am by no man.[23]

Where this Stuart poet is flippant, Hardy sees the dangers of imagination, just as did Donne in his elegy, *The Dreame*. Gaily and ironically Hardy also wrote "a fickle lover's song" full of idealistic praise beginning "I said and sang her excellence." The lover discovers an incarnation of his ideal *after* he has written praising its beauty. But Hardy implies that so carelessly imaginative a lover cannot be trusted, just as the seventeenth-century poets had shown in poems like Brome's quoted above.

[22] Grierson, p. 7.
[23] A. Brome, *Poems* (London, 1661), p. 13.

While Hardy was not simply the pessimist that he resented being considered, the closest analogies in his work to Stuart intuitions of lovers' psychology do come in verse of disillusionment. Where the intellectual assurance and sympathy of the lover weakens, Hardy shows how the supposed causes of love fade and the sentiment is extinguished. The failure of the beloved to behave sympathetically to others destroys her lover's attachment in "Outside the Window" for reasons better and more abstractly explained in "At Waking":

> With a sudden scare
> I seemed to behold
> My Love in bare
> Hard lines unfold.
>
> Yea, in a moment,
> An insight that would not die
> Killed her old endowment
> Of charm that had capped all nigh,
> Which vanished to none
> Like the gilt of a cloud,
> And showed her but one
> Of the common crowd.[24]

Less harsh but more pathetic is Hardy's awareness that beauty lies in an attitude of mind when he studies "mid-aged market dames" in "Former Beauties":

> They must forget, forget! They cannot know
> What once they were,
> Or memory would transfigure them, and show
> Them always fair.[25]

Lastly we might quote one of Hardy's first poems, which shows that he started on his career as a versifier well charged

[24] T. Hardy, *Collected Poems* (London, 1930), p. 208.
[25] *Ibid.*, p. 223.

with apprehension about the threats implied by the subtleties
of human psychology:

> Though I waste watches framing words to fetter
> Some unknown spirit to mine in clasp and kiss,
> Out of the night there looms a sense 'twere better
> To fail obtaining whom one fails to miss.
>
> For winning love we win the risk of losing,
> And losing love is as one's life were riven;
> It cuts like contumely and keen ill-using
> To cede what was superfluously given.
>
> Let me then never feel the fateful thrilling
> That devastates the love-worn wooer's frame,
> The hot ado of fevered hopes, the chilling
> That agonizes disappointed aim!
> So may I live no junctive law fulfilling,
> And my heart's table bear no woman's name.[26]

Once again one hears the tones of Euripides (in the chorus
from *Phaedra*), but, while Euripides helplessly anticipates the
threats of physical passion, Hardy approaches the whole
problem with a sense of the possibility of a personal choice,
in which high stakes are played for, indeed, but in which the
individual is largely autonomous. If he is ruined, it is not by
fate, but by his own misjudgment. Characteristic of our new
condition, Hardy's poem is not a prayer but a decision.

[vii]

To give this study its last hint of contemporaneity it is
worth considering an historical novel of the second half of
the twentieth century, which, while not lyric poetry, offers a
perfect vantage point from which to survey the evolution of

[26] *Ibid.*, p. 11.

that subjective perspective in value judgments that has increasingly characterized lyric love poetry. In his vivid fictional evocations of classical Rome, Rex Warner has sometimes sought to recreate the characters in his setting by methods of analysis which are essentially modern. Such a device does not necessarily do injustice to the motives of the unusual characters he has to display, such as the young Caesar, but it does give them a transparency that, however acceptable to modern eyes and necessary to the novelist, may well have been lacking for their historical contemporaries and even for themselves. This is the privilege of the novelist's art. One notes this unexpected transparency most appreciatively in Caesar's supposed account of his love life in *The Young Caesar*. Despite his numerous affairs Caesar claims that base motives have not governed him:

> It has been rather a question of curiosity, of a passion to understand and to be understood, and, almost most important of all, a devotion to humanity when this humanity is seen stripped of its affectations, so that, even through what is, as it were, incrusted, something generous and divine appears. I am naturally both enticed and in a sense, enthralled by adornment and by grace of manner; yet these, to me, are nothing in the end, unless they are the signs or else, perhaps, the disguises of something different—something firm and, if not predictable, at least honest. This respect for personality has prevented me from becoming very often the victim of illusion or fantasy; I have been spared the sufferings felt by, for example, the poet Catullus, since it would have been quite impossible for me to have seen the loose, grasping and lustful Clodia in the rôle of a goddess or heavenly creature; . . . Moreover my interest in human beings is such that I have been by no means re-

stricted in the objects of my affections by any particularities
of person, character or age.[27]

It is perhaps reasonable to assume that this soliloquy does
reflect the conduct of Caesar, or at least how Caesar would
have wished his conduct to have been interpreted, whether
truly or not. But the condescending reference to Catullus is
a challenge to our acceptance, because Catullus was in fact
far in advance of his age in meaningfulness of feeling and
precision of expression. Whether Caesar felt as Warner suggests or not, he could never actually have *expressed* himself
with such assured insight and finality, without Warner's literary hindsight. The best that the most distinguished classical
theorists about sexual love could actually produce was a sense
of the possibility of "illusion and fantasy" in love. The power
to use this awareness to undermine the absolute value of
objective criteria in love, such as "adornment and grace of
manner," so that affection was no longer governed by "any
particularities of person, character or age" but simply by
"something generous and divine"—all this no man was apparently able to think of in relation to women until the
Renaissance, despite all that Plato wrote of homosexual love.
Warner thus, in seeking to illuminate fully the conduct of
Caesar, shows us how far we have advanced since Caesar's
time in insight into the workings of human psychology. Whatever Caesar's behavior, his motivations must have remained
opaque at this level of understanding—the soliloquizing
Caesar Warner portrays has the mental aptitudes of modern
man alone. Or rather, he has the aptitudes which modern
man should normally possess. But the very doubts of the
evolution of sensibility, which were shared by Sullivan,

27 R. Warner, *The Young Caesar* (New York, 1958), p. 140. Reprinted by permission of the publisher, Little, Brown and Co.

Shelley, Arnold, and Eliot, and which provoked this systematic study of sexual attitudes, suggest that, unlike Warner, many of our best modern thinkers have not yet recognized that conscious sense of the power of the human mind in the face of apparently objective reality that it has been my purpose to illustrate.

···⌡⌐ BIBLIOGRAPHY ⌐⌡···

I N a study such as this, which must by nature be illustrative rather than definitive, the boundaries for sources are almost nonexistent. The following references are therefore not exhaustive, but display only those works that seem essential or directly relevant to the material specifically discussed. The list is divided into two main groups, primary and secondary sources. Primary sources are broken down into three sections: classical with later Latin; French and Italian; English. Secondary sources are separated into books and articles. *Anthologies* are in all cases listed at the end of the relevant section under editor or, if he is unknown, by title; otherwise all works are listed alphabetically by author's name. There is no duplication of sources, even where adequate alternatives exist.

I. PRIMARY SOURCES

A. *CLASSICAL WITH LATER LATIN*

Ausonius, Loeb edn., trans. H. G. Evelyn White, London, 1919.

Bonefonius, Johannes, *Carmina,* London, 1720.

Callimachus and Lycophron, Loeb edn., trans. A. W. Mair, London, 1921.

Catullus, Tibullus and *Pervigilium Veneris,* Loeb edn., trans. F. W. Cornish, J. P. Postgate, and J. W. Mackail, London, 1950.

Hesiod, *Hesiod and the Homeric Hymns,* Loeb edn., trans. H. G. Evelyn White, London, 1936.

Horace, *Odes and Epodes,* Loeb edn., trans. C. E. Bennett, London, 1947.

Juvenal and Persius, Loeb edn., trans. G. G. Ramsay, London, 1924.

Lucretius, *De Rerum Natura*, ed. and trans. C. H. Bailey, Oxford, 1947.

Martial, *Epigrams*, Loeb edn., trans. W. C. Ker, London, 1943.

Marullus, *Carmina*, ed. A. Perosa, Turici, 1951.

Ovid, *The Art of Love and Other Poems*, Loeb edn., trans. J. H. Mozley, London, 1929.

———, *Heroides and Amores*, Loeb edn., trans. G. Showerman, London, 1931.

———, *Metamorphoses*, Loeb edn., trans. F. J. Miller, London, 1928.

Propertius, Loeb edn., trans. H. E. Butler, London, 1912.

Secundus, *The Love Poems*, ed. F. A. Wright, London, 1930.

Theocritus, ed. and trans. A. S. F. Gow, Cambridge, U.K., 1952.

Tibullus, see under Catullus.

Virgil, Loeb edn., trans. H. R. Fairclough, London, 1935.

❂   ❂   ❂

Duff, J. W., *et al.*, ed. and trans., *Minor Latin Poets*, London, 1934.

Edmonds, J. M., ed. and trans., *Greek Elegy and Iambus*, London, 1931.

———, ed. and trans., *Lyra Graeca*, London, 1928.

Gherus, R., ed., *Delitiae cc. Italorum Poetarum*, Frankfurt, 1608.

———, ed., *Delitiae c. Poetarum Gallorum*, Frankfurt, 1609.

Greek Anthology, Loeb edn., trans. W. R. Paton, London, 1916.

Page, D., *Sappho and Alcaeus*, Oxford, 1955.

Waddell, H., ed., *Mediaeval Latin Lyrics*, London, 1933.

B. *FRENCH AND ITALIAN*

Aretino, P., *Piacevoli e Capricciosi Ragionamenti,* ed. A. P. Stella, Milan, 1944.

Baif, J. A. de, *Œuvres,* ed. C. Marty-Laveaux, Paris, 1881.

Bellay, J. Du, *Poësies,* ed. M. Hervier, Paris, 1954.

Bembo, P., *Le Rime,* ed. F. Sansovino, Venice, 1561.

Berni, F., *Opere,* ed. G. Daelli, Milan, 1864.

Boiardo, M. M., *Le Poesie Volgari e Latine,* ed. A. Solerti, Bologna, 1894.

Casa, G. della, *Le Rime,* ed. A. Seroni, Florence, 1944.

Chiabrera, G., *Canzonette, Rime Varie, Dialoghi,* ed. L. Negri, Turin, 1952.

Dante, Alighieri, *Tutte le Opere,* ed. E. Moore and P. Toynbee, Oxford, 1924.

Desportes, P., *Œuvres,* ed. A. Michiels, Paris, 1858.

Guarini, B., *Il Pastor Fido . . . Aggiontovi . . . Le Rime,* Venice, 1621.

Malherbe, F. de, *Les Poésies,* ed. J. Lavaud, Paris, 1936.

Marino, G., *Poesie Varie,* ed. B. Croce, Bari, 1913.

Marot, C., *Œuvres Complètes,* ed. P. Jannet, Paris.

Medici, L. de', *Opere,* ed. A. Simioni, Bari, 1939.

Petrarca, F., *Le Rime,* ed. G. Carducci, *et al.,* Florence, 1957.

Poliziano, *Poesie Italiane,* Milan, 1825.

Ronsard, P. de, *Œuvres Complètes,* ed. G. Cohen, Paris, 1950.

Tasso, T., *Aminta,* ed. P. Renucci, *et al.,* Paris, 1952.

——, *Le Rime,* ed. A. Solerti, Bologna, 1898-99.

Théophile, *Œuvres Complètes,* ed. M. Alleaume, Paris, 1861.

Tyard, P. de, *Les Œuvres Poétiques,* ed. C. Marty-Laveaux, Paris, 1875.

Warnke, F. J., *European Metaphysical Poetry*, New Haven, 1961.

C. *ENGLISH*

Beaumont, F., *Poems*, London, 1653.

—— and J. Fletcher, *Works*, ed. A. R. Waller and A. Glover, Cambridge, U.K., 1906.

Beedome, T., *Poems, Divine and Humane*, London, 1928.

Bold, H., *Poems*, London, 1664.

Brome, A., *Songs and Other Poems*, London, 1661.

Browning, R., *The Poetical Works*, Oxford, 1940.

Carew, T., *Poems*, ed. R. Dunlap, Oxford, 1949.

Cartwright, W., *Comedies, Tragi-Comedies, and Other Poems*, London, 1651.

Cavendish, W., Duke of Newcastle, *Phanseys*, ed. D. Grant, London, 1956.

Cotton, C., *Poems*, ed. J. Beresford, London, 1923.

Cowley, A., *Poems*, ed. A. R. Waller, Cambridge, 1905.

Crashaw, R., *Poems*, ed. L. C. Martin, Oxford, 1927.

Donne, J., *Poems*, ed. H. J. C. Grierson, Oxford, 1933.

Drayton, M., *Works*, ed. J. W. Hebel, Oxford, 1931.

Drummond, W., *Poetical Works*, ed. L. E. Kastner, Manchester, 1913.

Fletcher, G., and P. Fletcher, *Poetical Works*, ed. F. S. Boas, Cambridge, 1909.

Fletcher, J., see Beaumont.

Hall, J., *Poems*, London, 1646.

Hardy, T., *Collected Poems*, London, 1930.

Herbert, Lord Edward, *Poems*, ed. G. C. Moore Smith, Oxford, 1923.

Herbert, G., *Works*, ed. F. E. Hutchinson, Oxford, 1953.

Herbert, William, Earl of Pembroke (and B. Ruddier), *Poems*, London, 1660.

Herrick, R., *Poetical Works*, ed. L. C. Martin, Oxford, 1956.

Jonson, B., ed. C. H. Herford and P. Simpson, Oxford, 1925-52.

Jordan, T., *Poetical Varieties*, London, 1637.

Lovelace, R., *Poems*, ed. C. H. Wilkinson, Oxford, 1953.

Marvell, A., *Poems and Letters*, ed. H. M. Margoliouth, Oxford, 1927.

Milton, J., *Complete Poems and Major Prose*, ed. M. Y. Hughes, New York, 1957.

Pope, A., *Complete Poetical Works*, ed. H. W. Boynton, New York, 1903.

Prior, M., *Poems on Several Occasions*, ed. A. R. Waller, Cambridge, U.K., 1905.

Ralegh, Sir W., *Poems*, ed. A. M. C. Latham, London, 1951.

Randolph, T., *Poems*, ed. G. Thorn-Drury, London, 1929.

Rochester, see J. Wilmot.

Sedley, Sir C., *The Poetical and Dramatic Works*, ed. V. de Sola Pinto, London, 1928.

Shakespeare, W., *Complete Works*, ed. H. Craig, New York, 1951.

Shelley, P. B., *The Complete Poetical Works*, ed. T. Hutchinson, Oxford, 1934.

Sherburne, E., *Salmacis*, . . . *with Several Other Poems*, London, 1651.

Shirley, J., *Poems*, London, 1646.

Sidney, Sir P., *Complete Poems*, ed. A. B. Grossart, London, 1873.

Spenser, E., *Poetical Works*, ed. J. C. Smith and E. De Selincourt, Oxford, 1948.

Stevenson, M., *Occasions Off-spring*, London, 1645.

Strode, W., *Poetical Works*, ed. B. Dobell, London, 1907.

Suckling, Sir J., *Works*, ed. A. Hamilton Thompson, London, 1910.

Tennyson, Lord A., *Poems 1830-1870*, Oxford, 1912.

Townshend, A., *Poems and Masks*, ed. E. K. Chambers, Oxford, 1914.

Vaughan, H., *Works*, ed. L. C. Martin, Oxford, 1914.

Waller, E., *Poems*, ed. G. Thorn-Drury, London, 1905.

Weaver, T., *Songs and Poems of Love and Drollery*, London, 1654.

Wilmot, J., Earl of Rochester, *Selected Lyrics and Satires*, ed. R. Duncan, London, 1945.

Wither, G., *Poetry*, ed. F. Sidgwick, London, 1902.

Wyatt, Sir T., *Collected Poems*, ed. K. Muir, Cambridge, U.S.A., 1949.

❀   ❀   ❀

Academy of Compliments, The, London, 1650.

Ault, N., ed., *Seventeenth Century Lyrics*, New York, 1950.

——, ed., *Unfamiliar Lyrics*, London, 1938.

Bullen, A. H., *Speculum Amantis*, London, 1889.

Bullett, G., ed., *Silver Poets of the Sixteenth Century*, London, 1947.

Chalmers, A., ed., *The Works of the English Poets*, London, 1810.

Choyce Drollery, London, 1656.

C[otgrave], I., ed., *Wit's Interpreter*, London, 1655.

Cutts, J. P., *et al.*, *Seventeenth Century Songs*, Columbia, 1956.

Facetiae, London, 1817.

Fellowes, E. H., ed., *English Madrigal Verse*, Oxford, 1920.

Howarth, R. G., ed., *Minor Poets of the Seventeenth Century*, London, 1953.

Marrow of Compliments, The, London, 1655.

Muses' Recreation, London, 1655.

Parnassus Biceps, re-edited by G. Thorn-Drury, London, 1929.

Playford, J., *Select Musicall Ayres, and Dialogues*, London, 1652 and 1653.

Recreations for Ingenious Head-peeces, London, 1663.

Saintsbury, G., *Minor Poets of the Caroline Period*, Oxford, 1905.

Wilson, J., *Cheerfull Ayres*, London, 1660.

Wit Restor'd, London, 1658.

Wit's Interpreter, London, 1655.

Wit's Recreations, London, 1640.

II. SECONDARY SOURCES

A. BOOKS

Aiken, P., *The Influence of the Latin Elegists on English Lyric Poetry 1600-1650*, Orono (Maine), 1932.

Allen, D. C., *Image and Meaning*, Baltimore, 1960.

Allen, P. S., *Medieval Latin Lyrics*, Chicago, 1931.

Aubry, P., *Trouvères and Troubadours*, New York, 1914.

Auerbach, E., *Mimesis*, New York, 1957.

Bowra, C. M., *Greek Lyric Poetry from Alcman to Simonides*, Oxford, 1936.

Bush, D., *English Literature in the Earlier Seventeenth Century*, Oxford, 1945.

Chaytor, H. J., *The Troubadours and England*, Cambridge, U.K., 1923.

Cohen, H. L., *Lyric Forms from France*, New York, 1922.

Curtius, E. R., *European Literature and the Latin Middle Ages*, New York, 1953.

Denonain, J. J., *Thèmes et Formes de la Poèsie "Metaphysique,"* Paris, 1956.

Eliot, T. S., *Selected Essays*, London, 1932.

Ellrodt, R., *Les Poètes Métaphysiques Anglais*, Paris, 1960.

Erskine, J., *The Elizabethan Lyric*, New York, 1903.

Fletcher, J. B., *The Religion of Beauty in Women*, New York, 1911.

Foxwell, A. K., *A Study of Sir Thomas Wyatt's Poetry*, London, 1911.

Freeman, R., *English Emblem Books*, London, 1948.

Gibbon, J. M., *Melody and Lyric from Chaucer to the Cavaliers*, New York, 1930.

Goffin, R. C., *The Life and Poems of William Cartwright*, Cambridge, U.S.A., 1918.

Grierson, H. J. C., *Criticism and Creation*, London, 1949.

———, *Cross Currents in English Literature in the Seventeenth Century*, London, 1929.

Harrison, J. S., *Platonism in English Poetry*, New York, 1903.

Highet, G., *The Classical Tradition*, Oxford, 1949.

John, L. C., *Elizabethan Sonnet Sequences—Conventional Conceits*, New York, 1938.

Leishman, J. B., *The Monarch of Wit*, London, 1951.

———, *Themes and Variations in Shakespeare's Sonnets*, London, 1961.

Legouis, P., *André Marvell, poète, puritaine, patriote*, Paris, 1928.

———, *Donne the Craftsman*, Paris, 1929.

Levin, H., *The Overreacher*, Cambridge, U.S.A., 1952.

Luck, G., *The Latin Love Elegy*, London, 1960.

McEuen, K. A., *Classical Influence upon the Tribe of Ben*, Cedar Rapids, 1940.

Nelson, J. C., *Renaissance Theory of Love*, New York, 1958.

Nelson, L., *Baroque Lyric Poetry*, New Haven, 1961.

Nykl, A. R., *Hispano-Arabic Poetry*, Baltimore, 1946.

Pattison, B., *Music and Poetry of the English Renaissance*, London, 1948.

Pearson, L. E., *Elizabethan Love Conventions*, Berkeley, 1933.

Praz, A. M., *Seicentismo e Marinismo in Inghilterra*, Florence, 1925.

Rougemont, D. de, *Love in the Western World*, New York, 1940.

Scott, J. G., *Les Sonnets Elizabéthains, les Sources et l'Apport Personnel*, Paris, 1929.

Sharp, R. L., *From Donne to Dryden*, Chapel Hill, 1940.

Tuve, R., *Elizabethan and Metaphysical Imagery*, Chicago, 1947.

Unger, L., *The Man in the Name*, Minneapolis, 1956.

Upham, A. H., *The French Influence in English Literature from the Accession of Elizabeth to the Restoration*, New York, 1908.

Valency, M., *In Praise of Love*, New York, 1958.

Whicher, G. F., *The Goliard Poets*, Norfolk, 1949.

Whipple, T. K., *Martial and the English Epigram from Sir Thomas Wyatt to Ben Jonson*, Berkeley, 1925.

Wilkinson, L. P., *Ovid Recalled*, Cambridge, Eng., 1955.

Willey, B., *The Seventeenth Century Background*, London, 1938.

Williamson, G., *The Donne Tradition*, Cambridge, Mass., 1930.

✿   ✿   ✿

Bateson, F. W., ed., *Cambridge Bibliography of English Literature*, Cambridge U.K., 1940.

Seventeenth Century Studies Presented to Sir Herbert Grierson, Oxford, 1938.

Spencer, T., ed., *A Garland for John Donne*, Cambridge, Mass., 1931.

B. *ARTICLES, ETC.* (*PMLA* abbreviations are used; works of particular relevance are marked by asterisks)

Alden, R. M., "The Lyrical Conceit of the Elizabethans," *SP*, xiv (1917), 129-152.

———, "The Lyrical Conceits of the Metaphysical Poets," *SP*, xvii (1920), 183-198.

* Brown, H., "The Classical Tradition in English Literature: a Bibliography," *Harvard Studies and Notes in Philology and Literature*, xviii (1935), 7-46.

* Bruser, F., "Comus and the Rose Song," *SP*, xliv (1947), 625-644.

Cunningham, J. V., "Logic and Lyric," *MP*, li (1953-54), 33-41.

Davidson, D., "Marvell's 'Definition of Love,' " *RES*, vi (1955), 141-146.

Duhamel, P. A., "The Logic and Rhetoric of Peter Ramus," *MP*, xlvi (1948-49), 163-171.

Duncan, J. E., "The Revival of Metaphysical Poetry, 1872-1912," *PMLA*, lvi (1941), 307-336.

Forsythe, R. S., "*The Passionate Shepherd* and English Poetry," *PMLA*, xl (1925), 692-742.

* Françon, M., "Un Motif de la Poèsie Amoureuse au XVIe Siècle," *PMLA*, lvi (1941), 307-336.

* Gardner, H., "The Argument about 'The Extasie'," in *Elizabethan and Jacobean Studies* (Oxford, 1961), 279-306.

Garrod, H. W., "Cowley, Johnson and the Metaphysicals," in *The Profession of Poetry etc.* (Oxford, 1929), 110-130.

————, "Donne and Mrs. Herbert," *RES*, xxi (1945), 161-173.

* Hart, E. F., "Caroline Lyrics and Contemporary Song Books," *Library* (1953), 89-110.

* ————, "The Answer Poem of the Early Seventeenth Century," *RES*, vii (1956), 19-29.

Hughes, M. Y., "The Lineage of 'The Extasie'," *MLR*, xxvii (1932), 1-5.

* Kermode, F., "The Argument of Marvell's 'Garden'," *EIC*, ii (1952), 225-241.

Lea, K., "Conceits," *MLR*, xx (1925), 389-406.

Lederer, J., "John Donne and the Emblematic Practice," *RES*, xxii (1946), 182-200.

* Leishman, J. B., "*L'Allegro* and *Il Penseroso* in Their Relation to Seventeenth Century Poetry," *E&S* (1951), 1-36.

Mackerness, E. D., "The Transitional Nature of Wyatt's Poetry," *English*, vii (1948), 120-124.

Mazzeo, J. A., "A Critique of Some Modern Theories of Metaphysical Poetry," *MP*, l (1952-53), 88-101.

* Miller, H. K., "The Paradoxical Encomium with Special Reference to Its Vogue in England, 1600-1800," *MP*, liii (1956), 145-178.

Pinto, V. de S., "Rochester and Dryden," *RMS*, v (1961), 29-48.

Potter, G. R., "Donne's *Extasie*, contra Legouis," *PQ*, xv (1936), 247-253.

Praz, M., "Stanley, Sherburne and Ayres as Translators and Imitators of Italian, Spanish, and French Poets," *MLR*, xx (1925), 280-294.

Raleigh, J. H., "The New Criticism as an Historical Phenomenon," *CL*, xi (1959), 21-28.

* Richmond, H. M., "The Fate of Edmund Waller," *SAQ*, LX (1961), 230-238.

* ———, "The Intangible Mistress," *MP*, LVI (1959), 217-223.

* ———, "Polyphemus in England," *CL*, XII (1960), 229-242.

* ———, "The Syntax of Passion," *BUSE*, IV (1960), 214-222.

Rugoff, M. A., "Drummond's Debt to Donne," *PQ*, XVI (1937), 85-88.

Siegel, P. N., "The Petrarchan Sonneteers and Neo-Platonic Love," *SP*, XLII (1945), 164-182.

Smith, A. J., "Donne in His Time: a Reading of *The Extasie*," *RLMC*, X (1957), 260-275.

———, "An Examination of Some Claims for Ramism," *RES*, VII (1956), 348-359.

* ———, "The Metaphysic of Love," *RES*, IX (1958), 362-375.

Spitzer, L., "Marvell's 'Nymph Complaining for the Death of Her Faun': Sources versus Meaning," *MLQ*, XIX (1958), 231-243.

Stein, A., "Donne and the Couplet," *PMLA*, LVII (1942), 676-696.

Towne, F., "Logic, Lyric, and Drama," *MP*, LI (1953-54), 265-268.

Walton, G., "Abraham Cowley and the Decline of Metaphysical Poetry," *Scrutiny*, VI (1937), 176-194.

Warren, A., "Donne's *Extasie*," *SP*, LV (1958), 472-480.

Wiggins, E. L., "Logic in the Poetry of John Donne," *SP*, XLII (1945), 41-60.

* Williamson, G., "The Rhetorical Pattern of Neo-Classical Wit," *MP*, XXXIII (1935), 55-81.

———, "Three Thefts from Cleveland," *MLN*, XLIV (1929), 384-385.

* Winters, Y., "The Sixteenth Century Lyric," *Poetry*, LIII (1939), 258-272, and 320-335.

Wolf, E., " 'If shadows be a picture's excellence'," *PMLA*, LXIII (1948), 831-857.

The devices on the title page
and on the binding spine are adapted from
Richard Gething's *Calligraphotechnia*.
This manual on the Art of fair writing was
printed and sold in "Pope's head alley,
over against the roiall Exchange
in London," during the reign of the first
Stuart, King James I